MW00979814

Realignments in Russian Foreign Policy

Editor

Rick Fawn
University of St Andrews

FRANK CASS
LONDON • PORTLAND, OR

First published in 2003 in Great Britain by
FRANK CASS PUBLISHERS
Crown House, 47 Chase Side, London N14 5BP

and in the United States of America by
FRANK CASS PUBLISHERS
c/o International Specialized Book Services, Inc.
920 NE 58th Avenue, Suite 300
Portland, OR 97213-3786

Website www.frankcass.com

British Library Cataloguing in Publication Data

Realignments in Russian foreign policy
1. Russia (Federation) – Foreign relations
I. Fawn, Rick II. European security
327.4'7

ISBN 0 7146 5496 5 (cloth)
ISBN 0 7146 8396 5 (paper)

Library of Congress Cataloging-in-Publication Data

has been applied for

This group of studies first appeared in a Special Issue on 'Realignments of
Russian Foreign Policy' of *European Security* (ISSN 0966-2839) 11/4
(Winter 2002).

Printed in Great Britain by Antony Rowe Ltd., Chippenham, Wiltshire

Contents

Realignments in Russian Foreign Policy: An Introduction

RICK FAWN

Russia's foreign policy alignments have always held great sway over the European balance of power and, since the middle of the twentieth century, over the international balance of power as well. Russia's realignments after the Cold War offer historic opportunities for both Russia itself and the wider world. The Western hope, and that of many within Russia, was that the very tentative democratization undertaken by the Gorbachev leadership would become fully-fledged after the demise of communist rule, and that a Kantian pacific union of like-minded liberal, democratic polities, eschewing war among themselves, would confidently emerge across the whole of the northern hemisphere.

Such aspirations were buoyed by a Western-leaning post-communist Russian government that espoused, at least rhetorically, many aspects of liberal democratic and economic reform. Much opposition to a closer relationship with the West of course exists within Russian society, and debate rages about what Russia should adopt from the West, and how it is to preserve its own, arguably unique, culture, history and geopolitical role and destiny. Punctuating 300 years of Russian history, this dilemma has been framed as one between 'Slavophiles' and 'Westernizers'. Where the former have stressed the preservation of Russian values from foreign adulteration, the latter argued for at least a selective importation of technology to modernize Russia.[1]

This classic debate has been elaborated and expanded since the end of Soviet communism, taking on such terms as 'Eurasianists' and 'Euro-Atlanticists',[2] but was sharpened to three strands of foreign policy thinking, perhaps best defined and articulated by Margot Light. Those supporting Western-style reforms were identified as 'Liberal Westernizers', while others who expressed hostility to economic reform and demonstrated extreme nationalism were called 'Fundamental Nationalists'. With nationalism gaining significance across the political spectrum in 1992, the category 'Pragmatic Nationalists' was devised for those who advocated a more independent policy towards the West and greater integration in relation to former Soviet republics.[3]

Anyone outside a pro-Western viewpoint in Russian foreign policy potentially posed risks to the West. Even a Westernizer like Andrei Kozyrev, Russian foreign minister until January 1996, gave a taste of what international life would be with a nationalist government in Moscow. At the Conference on Security and Cooperation in Europe (CSCE) meeting in Stockholm in December 1992 he declared that CSCE principles were no longer relevant to the Soviet successor states, that the West should stay out of that region, and that Russia was offering all assistance to former Yugoslavia. He exited the forum, then re-entered it to proclaim his comments an exercise.[4]

A further taste of a radical Russian foreign policy was given by Vladimir Zhirinovsky. Despite several electoral successes, including nearly one-quarter of the parliamentary vote in December 1993, Zhirinovsky did not achieve power. But his policies could not have served Western interests. He advocated dumping nuclear waste in the Baltic and advancing Russia's border so far south that Russians could 'wash their boots in the warm waters of the Indian Ocean and forever change to summer uniforms'.[5] Perhaps only with hindsight have Western governments been able to appreciate the best-case scenario of the Western-leaning Russian governments that have been in power thus far.

Even so, Zbigniew Brzezinksi forcefully warned of Russian neo-imperialism in the Near Abroad, and its participation in a string of conflicts that coincided with the outer borders of the former Soviet Union.[6] Russia's partial solution of 'peacekeeping' gave further fears of realpolitik cloaked in the language and practice of the new interventionism.[7] The wars in Chechnya, which resulted in possibly tens of thousands of deaths and hundreds of thousands displaced, also gave concern, even if Western criticism was quiet in relation to the intensity of the Russian military response.[8] For even Russian commentators, the Chechen war was assuming the proportions of France's war in Algeria.[9] In this context, partnership with Russia was even more questionable. For wider geopolitical purposes, the course that Russia took meant that it could be at best isolationist, or even aggressive towards its neighbours.

Westernization involves money, and while Russia is resource-rich, its technological base remains limited and has faced the flight of both capital and human resources. With popular associations being made through post-communist Central and East Europe between democracy and economic wealth, the whole democratization project rested on palpable successes in socio-economic reform. Outside funds, whether private or public, were therefore essential; noting that five trillion dollars were spent on containing Soviet communism, Graham Allison and Robert Blackwill called, even before the end of the USSR, for economic assistance of 'Marshall Plan proportions' for Russia. Among their proposals were outright grants of $15–20 billion dollars a year for three years.[10]

The reconstruction of postwar Germany occurred under the direct management of Allied powers; that prospect was absent in the case of post-communist Russia. But Western promises of funds were relatively few, and what was offered was rarely provided in full, even if the Clinton administration also may have misunderstood and downplayed the extent of corruption in the Russian political and economic system.[11]

Russia arguably has had much to fear as well. President Boris Yeltsin initially claimed that everyone won with the end of the Cold War but subsequently charged in December 1994 that, with the prospect of NATO expansion, there was danger of 'plunging into a cold peace'.[12] The succeeding order appeared to vindicate Western ideology and allowed for the implementation of Western policies that threatened Russia. Foremost among these was the enlargement of NATO announced at the Madrid Summit in July 1997, despite vociferous Russian protest. Even Western-leaning, market-inclined reformers like Anatoly Chubais foresaw this decision as 'inevitably leading to a new dividing line across the whole of Europe' and 'the biggest mistake made in Western policy for 50 years'.[13] The most sensitive piece of real estate in the Russian mindset – Poland – would join an alliance that to many Russians served no conceivable purpose other than aggression.

The depth of anxiety about NATO was further illustrated by Grigory Yavlinsky, leader of the liberal Yabloko alliance and a known pro-Westerner, who said in 1998: 'Talk that this is a different NATO, a NATO that is no longer a military alliance, is ridiculous. It is like saying that the hulking thing advancing toward your garden is not a tank because it is painted pink, carries flowers, and plays cheerful music. It does not matter how you dress it up; a pink tank is still a tank.'[14] To strain relations further, enlargement physically advanced the alliance towards Russia in March 1999 just as NATO began the Kosovan war against Russia's fellow orthodox and Slavic Serbs.

NATO's previous diplomatic reassurances to Russia could hardly be satisfactory. NATO responded to Russian assertions of still being a great power with no concrete acknowledgement but with the multilateral Partnership for Peace that gave Russia participation in selected NATO activities on the same level as Armenia and Kyrgyzstan. When NATO sought to assuage Russia with the Founding Act of 1997, which apparently elevated its status in Europe, this coincided with the announcement of NATO enlargement. The alliance also signed a similar document with Ukraine, a demographically and geographically smaller state, and one that many Russian nationalists questioned its cultural or historical right to exist.

Russia's status therefore seemed unrecognized; some argued it was better at least to give Russia a place in Europe that was delayed rather than denied.[15]

This has been done belatedly and partially. The Group of 7 (G7) was refashioned in 1994 to include Russia, but only as a political member of a new G8 for political issues while G7 remained for economic matters; after all, the Russian economy in absolute terms was no larger than the Dutch. Full membership in the G8 was given at the Kananaskis Meeting in June 2002. While NATO introduced various initiatives with Russia to give it at least a voice in the alliance's activities, NATO Secretary-General Lord Robertson made clear in February 2002 that Russia was not, contrary to media reporting, being given full status within the North Atlantic Council and said that suggestions otherwise were 'completely inaccurate'.[16]

The undermining of Russian prestige and confidence by actions abroad may have been heightened by the demise of military and technological showcases at home. The sinking of the nuclear-powered submarine *Kursk* and Moscow's Ostankino television tower fire occurred within days of each other in August 2000. A Russian rear admiral even wrote, referring to the loss of three principal Russian submarines in 14 years, that Russian submarines sink and American ones do not.[17] Even so, economist Anders Åslund recently argued that: 'In fact, Russia has seen an extraordinary improvement in its infrastructure. Investment in fixed assets (i.e., buildings, equipment) increased by 18 percent last year—a healthy investment ratio of 20 percent of GDP (higher than the standard U.S. ratio of 16 percent)'.[18]

The prospect of a revived, and internationally viable arms industry is still forecast by some Western economists. As Steven Rosefield wrote in 2000, 'Russia possesses the resources, assets, cultural and doctrinal traditions to rebuild its armed forces to global competitive levels, and it has developed an "eastern" market that could make its military-industrial economy more efficient than under central planning.'[19] Even if Russia has such military-economic potential, former dissident Aleksandr Solzhensityn probably echoed widespread feelings that the decay of Russia's military capacity was due to privatization in the Yeltsin era.[20]

While popular support for a Western orientation in foreign policy has grounds to be limited, the terrorist attacks of 11 September 2001 have given the Russian government considerable scope for foreign policy realignment. Those attacks have been taken as the embodiment of Samuel P. Huntington's 'clash of civilizations'. Classifying Russia as one of seven or eight civilizations based on its orthodox religion, Huntington recommended that as part of a number of policies to safeguard Western interests, the West should grant Russia its sphere of influence and improve relations.[21]

As some of the contributions in this collection show, Russia may actually have lost sway in its immediate sphere of influence because of the American military presence in former Soviet states in the Caucasus and Central Asia. Nevertheless, the need for information-sharing and over-flight rights and access to military bases in Central Asia made Russia an important strategic partner in the 'war on terrorism'. In return, Putin could recast his war in Chechnya, one that had increasingly blighted relations with the West, as part of the same struggle against the international Islamic extremist menace.

It is in this geopolitical context that this collection examines changes in Russian foreign policy since 1991 through to, and beyond, the security challenges and opportunities presented by 11 September 2001. Authors analyze the evolution of Russian foreign policy and also assess whether 11 September is proving a watershed in Russia's attitudes and relations with the outside world. The general conclusion by the authors is that 11 September has not overwhelmingly changed Russian policy, but perhaps has served most to internationalize hitherto domestic problems, providing international legitimization to existing state action, particularly regarding Chechnya. To be sure, certain policy objectives have been gained, such as full membership in the G8. But as these contributions show, suspicion of the West remains in various circles of Russian society.

Of the contributors, historian Ludmilla Selezneva most deems 11 September to be a watershed. She argues that Russian foreign policy has become increasingly pragmatic which, in her view, is nothing short of revolutionary. This new-found pragmatism is characterized by: the replacement of geopolitics by geoeconomics; the prioritization of domestic over foreign policy and not the other way round; the emphasis of integration over isolationism; and multi-directionality in foreign policy. This, Selezneva describes, is tantamount to a depoliticization of foreign relations. In what Selezneva then argues is a changed foreign policy, President Putin has to struggle with deeply embedded anti-Western sentiments among the political establishment and population.

Mary Buckley continues by illustrating the scope and depth of the criticism of Westward-leaning Russian foreign policy. While developments after 11 September have allowed for improvements in US-Russian relations, easing some of the tensions created by the 1999 Kosovan war, she demonstrates the unlikelihood that the Bush administration will concede all that the Putin administration seeks. She points out that after the Moscow hostage crisis of October 2002, some Russian human rights activists also charge Putin with emulating Bush's anti-terrorism program to justify renewed military action in Chechnya.

Perceptions play an important part in Russia's relations with the West, and data presented by Ian McAllister and Stephen White underline the East's ongoing suspicion of the West. Attitudes to NATO are part of a wider debate about the future orientation of the post-communist countries:

towards integration with each other (a 'Slavic choice') or towards integration with the West (a 'Western choice'). The evidence of representative surveys conducted in Belarus, Moldova, Russia and Ukraine in 2000 and 2001 is that, though relatively few believe there is a serious and immediate threat to their security, of potential threats the US remains the most important, followed by Iran, Iraq and China. And the US continues to be perceived as the likely threat to European security. Almost half of Russian respondents in their study saw some threat to their security in further NATO enlargement. The public opinion findings by McAllister and White further indicate the difficulties the Russian government will face in seeking a pro-Western stand after 11 September.

Institutionalization of relations, with the hope that, in regime language, values become mutually embedded and the whole process of enlargement is better understood, is part of the reason why both Russia and the West have explored their relations through the existing institutions of NATO and the European Union (EU).

Martin A. Smith characterizes Russia's relations with NATO as six distinct phases since 1991: the honeymoon period, 1991–93; deterioration, 1994–95; upgrading of institutional links, 1996–97; the Kosovo crisis, 1998–99; phased restoration, 1999–2001; and post-11 September. Throughout, overall objectives have not been identified by either side, but an underlying stability has nevertheless become apparent in the relationship.

The pragmatism that Selezneva argues has been increasingly part of Russian foreign policy is seen in Smith's point that Kosovo led to only a 'limited disruption of relations' between Russia and the West. Russia did not sever relations because of its own sense of impotence, its fear of self-imposed isolation and its continued reliance on economic sponsorship from the West.

Unlike Selezneva, however, Smith contends that 11 September has not led to a fundamental change in Russia's relations with NATO. He argues that the two sides would have, in any case, come to the agreement of what became the May 2002 formation of the 'NATO-Russia Council' (NRC), which includes significant issue areas such as military crisis management, counter-terrorism, non-proliferation of weapons of mass destruction and theatre missile defence. The decision in June 2001 to proceed with a second round of eastern enlargement, he argues, set in motion more intense cooperation with Russia. Indeed, argues Smith, 'the NRC idea was not dramatically new. Rather, it seemed like an attempt to relaunch the NATO-Russia relationship on a basis not too dissimilar to what was, officially at least, set out in the 1997 Founding Act'.

Smith's conclusions dovetail with those of McAllister and White, who argue that 'there is little evidence, at the same time, that popular attitudes have shifted significantly in a Western direction...by the spring of 2002 there was more popular hostility towards the United States than there had been at any point in the first half of the 1990s'.

Incremental steps in Russia's relations with the West, with no clear destination, also characterize Russia's relations with the EU, argues Graham Timmins. Strategic partnership also underscores Russia's relations with the EU, as seen by both the EU *Common Strategy on Russia* and the *Russian Medium-Term Strategy for Development of Relations with the EU*, published in 1999. But, as with NATO, Russia and the EU do not share a common agenda or 'a shared normative basis'. Distinct differences exist in foreign policy goals. Russia's central concern remains that of gaining a place at the 'European table' and establishing its claim to being a regional power, while Europe seeks to encourage dialogue and to propagate shared norms and values. Timmins concludes in much the same way as Smith does for NATO: 'Although there remains considerable doubt regarding the extent to which the EU and Russia are able to interact in any meaningful way within a framework of strategic partnership, it remains the case that neither sees its interests as best served in marginalising the other.'

The events of 11 September have, superficially at least, made cooperation between Russia and the West more possible. John Russell argues that Russia has used the global war on terror to 'absolutize its conflict with the Chechens' as part of the 'coalition's overall struggle with Islamic insurgents, ranking in importance with that of Israel against the Palestinians and the West against the Taliban and al-Qaeda'. The timing of 11 September was furthermore useful to the Russian government, coming when public support for the second Chechen war was waning. The events of 11 September have therefore not fundamentally changed Russia's policy towards Chechnya; they have simply given it international legitimacy – even if the war against 'Islamic' terrorism has little in common with the Bush-led 'war' against global terrorism. This is because, notes Russell, the Russo-Chechen war might equally be perceived as 'an unresolved war of conquest against a more traditional way of life, as a war of liberation from colonialism, or indeed, as a war against anarchy, crime and lawlessness'.

A significant aspect of Russia's war with Chechnya has been about perceptions and Graeme Herd focuses on the information warfare aspects of the second Russo-Chechen campaign between 1999 and 11 September. Unlike during the first campaign, Russian authorities in the second campaign have been winning the information war by imposing an 'information blockade' and reorganizing the management of federal media. Russia's main media aims in the second war have been 'to isolate Chechnya from re-supplies of both practical aid – men and military materiel – and moral and ideological support from the West and the Islamic world, de-legitimize and divide internal Chechen opposition to the war (this was mirrored in the 'Chechenization' of the military conflict) and ensure that the Russian public gave strong support to the campaign conduct and objectives'. The issue of al-Qaeda has become dominant within information warfare battles.

The international legitimization outlined by Russell has prompted the Russian authorities to internationalize the conflict in their information war also, arguing that the objectives of the state and the conduct of its security services are given legitimacy by the wider threat posed by the links and collaboration between Chechen separatists, al-Qaeda fighters and the war.

The events of 11 September have added a new dynamic to Russia's policy towards the South Caucasus. As one of the conflicts that seemed to fit the pattern of Russian neo-imperialism, the Georgian–Abkhaz stand-off has resulted in the presence of Russian militarily involvement through its deployment of peacekeepers. The final contribution by Rick Fawn examines the impact of an American initiative to train specialist Georgian forces, that has been interpreted by some Abkhaz and Russians as American interference in the Russian sphere and the bolstering of a weak Georgian state. What gains Russia has made in aligning the West in the war against terrorism are arguably lost by having to concede to an unprecedented US presence, including a military presence, in the Near Abroad.

Many Russians doubtless are unsettled by this new American presence, and consider it as American imperialism and/or a means to undercut Russian influence in what was not only a sphere of influence but actually part of the Russian and Soviet inner empires. Ultimately, if Russia is forced to retreat from the Near Abroad it will cease to face the trade-off Brzezinski identified between democracy and empire.[22] Shedding imperial ambition would make Russia fit more comfortably with Europe and lessen tension with the US. Kozyrev said that a democratic Russia and the West were 'natural friends'.[23]

Few countries willingly or easily cede imperial desires; but European states today are surely more pacific for having shed overseas possessions that provoked conflict between colonizer and colonized and between colonizers. Recalling Brzezinski's statement that Russia cannot simultaneously be democratic and an empire, being forced to shed imperial temptations in the Near Abroad on account of events following 11 September may ultimately bring about a lasting realignment in Russian foreign policy.

NOTES

These articles grew from a conference at the University of St Andrews held in March 2002. The British Foreign and Commonwealth Office kindly provided funds, although no opinions that follow can be construed as representing any official British government view. Professor Paul D'Anieri deserves thanks for taking this proposal on board and assisting with it at every stage thereafter. The late Professor John Erickson, who informed and inspired countless others on Soviet and Russian affairs and who bequeaths a remarkable scholarly legacy, was invited to participate in the conference but was prevented from so doing by illness. It is to his memory that this collection is modestly dedicated.

1. See Nicholas V. Riasanovsky, *Russia and the West in the Teaching of the Slavophiles* (Cambridge: Harvard UP 1995) and Andrej Walicki, *The Slavophile Controversy* (Oxford: Clarendon Press 1975).
2. Yeltsin's foreign policy adviser Sergei Stankevich used the term 'Eurasianist' in March 1992 but was referring which was meant not so much as fundamentally anti-Western but an advocacy of a Russian foreign policy serving its own interests. See Neil Malcolm, 'The New Russian Foreign Policy', *The World Today*, Feb. 1994, p.29.
3. Margot Light, 'Foreign Policy Thinking', in Neil Malcolm, Alex Pravda, Roy Allison and Margot Light, *Internal Factors in Russian Foreign Policy* (Oxford: OUP 1996) esp. p.34.
4. The speech is contextualized in independent Russia's foreign policy in Hannes Adomeit, 'Russia As a "Great Power" in World Affairs: Images and Reality', *International Affairs* 71/1 (Jan. 1995) p.45.
5. Vladimir Zhirovsky, *Poslednii brosok na yug* (Moscow: LDP 1993), p.64, cited in Jacob W. Kipp, 'The Zhirinovsky Threat', *Foreign Affairs* 73/3 (May/June 1994) p.78.
6. Zbigniew Brzezinski, 'The Premature Partnership', *Foreign Affairs* 73/2 (March/April 1994) pp.72–3.
7. For the emergence of Russian peacekeeping, see Suzanne Crow, 'Russia Seeks Leadership in Regional Peacekeeping', and 'Processes and Policies', *RFE/RL Research Report*, 9 April and 14 May 1993, pp.23–34 and 47–52.
8. For an analysis of Western reactions to the first war, see Gail Lapidus, 'Contested Sovereignty: The Tragedy of Chechnya', *International Security* 23/1 (Summer 1998) pp.5–49.
9. Pavel Felgenhauer in *Moskovskie Novosti*, 24 April 2002. For analysis, see Jamestown Foundation Chechen Weekly, III/13 30 April 2002.
10. Graham T. Allison and Robert D. Blackwill, 'America's Stake in the Soviet Future', *Foreign Affairs* (Summer 1991) pp.95 and 97.
11. Strobe Talbott, *The Russia Hand* (NY: Random House 2002).
12. Cited in, e.g., Daniel Williams, 'Clinton and Yeltsin Clash Over Future Role of NATO', *Washington Post*, 6 Dec. 1994, p.2.
13. Cited in Larry Elliot, 'Ignore Moscow at your peril, warns Chubais', *The Guardian*, 4 Feb. 1997.
14. Grigory Yavlinsky, 'Russia's Phony Capitalism', *Foreign Affairs* 77/3 (May/June 1998).
15. Jonathan Haslam, 'Russia's Seat at the Table: a Place Denied or a Place Delayed', *International Affairs* 74/1 (Jan. 1998) p.130.
16. George Robertson, Secretary-General of NATO, 'Russia is not being invited to join North Atlantic Council', *Financial Times*, 28 Feb. 2002, p.20.
17. Admiral Valery Alexin, *Nezavisimaya Gazeta*, 16 Dec. 2000.
18. Anders Åslund, 'Think Again: Russia', *Foreign Policy* (July/August 2001) p.22.
19. Steven Rosefielde, 'Back to the Future? Prospects for Russia's Military Industrial Revival', *Orbis* 46/3 (Summer 2000) p.509.
20. Solzhenitsyn particularly noted the frequent crash of military helicopters. Associated Press, 31 May 2002.
21. Samuel P. Huntington, *The Clash of Civilizations and the Remaking of Order* (NY: Touchstone Books 1996) pp.163–86 and p.312.
22. Brezinski, 'Premature Partnership' (note 6) p.72.
23. Andrei Kozyrev, 'The Lagging Partnership', *Foreign Affairs* 73/3 (May/June 1994) p.59.

Post-Soviet Russian Foreign Policy: Between Doctrine and Pragmatism

LUDMILLA SELEZNEVA

For the purposes of this essay it is necessary to define the relationship between ideology and pragmatism. Ideology is a system of ideas or views describing attitudes to a reality, social issues and to the aspirations of classes, political parties and nations. Pragmatism is a way of making short-term decisions, grasping opportunities to achieve practical results, without considering the long-term consequences and, in some cases, even the morality of the decisions. The ideological approach and the pragmatic approach usually appear to be contradictory. An excessively doctrinal approach can be destructive of social and political stability. In fact, excessive ideology can destroy politics itself.

Ideologization of politics in the Soviet era reached an extreme level. Politics was completely dominated by the theory of 'Class Struggle' and 'World Revolution'. In these circumstances, liberalization of politics could have been presented as an alternative ideology, one giving more space for pragmatism. In this context we find it possible to differ more or less on 'pragmatic' ideology. For example, liberalism as an ideology is more pragmatic than the 'World Revolution' concept. After giving economic support to half of Asia and Africa, in an attempt to spread the tenets of communism throughout the world, and yet being unable to provide even basic living standards for its own people, the change to a pragmatic approach in foreign policy, especially in foreign economic policy, itself seems like a revolution. In 1991 the world witnessed the collapse of the Soviet empire and the birth of a new country, the Russian Federation. The reborn Russia began to formulate a completely new outlook on foreign policy.

SOVIET AND RUSSIAN FOREIGN POLICY: HOW THEY DIFFER

At least four main factors have to be taken into account to explain the difference between Soviet and Russian post-Soviet policy. The new Russia has no imperial status. Its population has decreased by 110 million people. Fifteen independent states have replaced the former Soviet republics, which used to have no real sovereignty, and came under heavy pressure to accept the centralized power of Moscow. The Baltic countries did not join the

Commonwealth of Independent States (CIS) at all and look very firmly towards Western Europe. The CIS has been more of a formal declaration of independence than a real Commonwealth of States.

There has been a considerable reduction in the size of the armed forces, from five million in 1991 to 1.2 million today, and the army has lost its position as the cornerstone of privilege in the Soviet political system. The highest rate of suicides in the 1990s was among army officers and retired military staff. Only 10–25 per cent of industrial output is now for military purposes. Currently Russia produces 40 helicopters and 21 military aircraft annually. Before 1992 the figures were 690 and 620 respectively.[1] There has been an economic decline, a collapse of traditional Soviet industry; previously 80 per cent of its output was for the military. The USSR had the second biggest GNP in the world, whilst modern Russia comes only 14th.[2] The current Russian GDP is only 30 per cent of what it was in 1990.[3]

All Soviet policy, including foreign policy, was based on ideology. It did not exclude some elements of pragmatism, which even dominated from time to time. The 1918 Treaty of Brest-Litovsk with Germany, the coalition of anti-fascists during World War II, and détente in the first half of the 1970s are examples of this. Sometimes elements of pragmatism were more obvious, as in the first half of the Khrushchev decade, when there was an attempt at peaceful coexistence with some Western countries. But these can be classed as small islands in an ocean of ideology, the ideology of two opposite and hostile systems: the ideology of class struggle and of the 'World Communist Revolution'. Several generations had a strong perception that a world communist revolution would have universal success sooner or later. The Soviet Union was regarded as the source of it.

Militarization of the economy, social relations and spiritual life; confrontation; expansion; and isolation as the main features of foreign policy, were the direct consequence of this theory. That ideology appeared, for example, in the famous Khrushchev speech to the UN, threatening the world during the Cuban Missile Crisis of 1962. The concept of 'Cold War' had also been a visible characteristic of world revolution ideology. The most dramatic change in the whole Soviet foreign policy was made by Gorbachev, who eliminated the 'World Revolution' approach, and started the era of real cooperation with Western countries. After 70 years, this confrontational foreign policy culminated in the break-up of the Soviet Union. Hence, the level of pragmatism increased considerably, but neither Gorbachev's rule nor the collapse of the Soviet empire could liberate either domestic or foreign policy from the cultural tradition of doctrine.

The doctrine in foreign policy itself has changed radically. It can be described as a mixture of neo-imperialism, liberalism and social-chauvinism. Sometimes during the post-Soviet era, liberal or chauvinistic approaches were more evident. However, neo-imperialism has been the dominant trait.

Initially this can be explained, in part, by the following three reasons. First, the Soviet empire and its status as the world's second superpower disappeared too quickly and unexpectedly even for the key participants in the meeting at Belarus on 8 December 1991. The new political elite of Russia consisted mostly of former communists who could not change their political philosophy and did not want to – the philosophy of confrontation with Western countries. The Soviet population was used to the idea of the Soviet Union being the strongest country, a social paradise whose historical mission it was to bring happiness to humanity.

Second, 'market reform' appeared as 'shock therapy'. It was followed by the decline of the whole economy and of living standards. In the middle of the 1990s, 70 per cent of the population was living below the poverty line. The equality of Soviet times was replaced by an enormous social gap between differing sections of society. The one million richest people had living standards a hundred times higher than the one million poorest. Surveys show a 20–25 times difference in living standards between the wealthiest seven per cent and the poorest 30 per cent. A difference of more than seven or eight times has long been regarded as the level that induces social frustration calling for some kind of consolation. Throughout Russia's history, ideology has been the main compensation, and it is an imperial ideology. The Russians want their country to stay great despite all its privations.

Third, some aspects of the policies of the Western countries, such as the extension of NATO, the discriminatory policies of the IMF and the bombing of Belgrade in 1999, stimulated suspicious feelings towards Western countries among the population, and among the political and military elite. It is important to realize that imperial ambitions have deep social and cultural roots in Russian traditions. Its main features are the lack of a developed democratic tradition; a long-established and strong agricultural community based on egalitarianism, domination by the state and autocratic governments; and the weakness of civil society. All these resulted in the relative weakness of individual self-consciousness, individual self-esteem and individual responsibility. On the contrary, the strong domination of a kind of 'group' or 'collective' psychology developed.[4] Russian people never write capital 'I'; their 'i' ('я') is always written small. A small 'i' needs to be part of something big. Imperial ambitions are the psychological compensation and the defence for weak individualism. This is the social and cultural background for the strength of the imperial legacy in the modern Russian psyche.

In sum, we can see a strong legacy of doctrine in post-Soviet foreign policy. Russia still remains an 'ideological' nation. Compared with the past, the new policy is sometimes the complete opposite of Soviet ideas. It is a mixture of the liberal ideology of those who wish to westernize, and the ideology of a Great Russian Statehood, but with a clear domination of the latter. At the same time, post-Soviet foreign policy is the most pragmatic it has been for the past century. I would say that the present ideologies are more pragmatic than the Soviet ideology of confrontation and isolation.

However, during the ten years 'after communism', the relative strengths of doctrinal and pragmatic tendencies have varied. I propose to divide the Russian foreign policy of 1991–2002 into four periods: 1991–96, 1996–99, 2000–11 September 2001 and 11 September 2001 to the present day. Russian policy towards the West and the other 14 successor states in the CIS has been changing considerably.

HONEYMOON RELATIONS WITH THE WEST, 1991–96

The first years following Soviet collapse can be described as domination by a liberal ideology, due to the mass anti-communist aspirations and the personality of the foreign minister, Andrey Kozyrev. He stood for a comprehensive partnership with Western countries and complete integration with them. That policy was rooted in what had been Gorbachev's similar ideology of 'universal human values'. Russian politicians in the infant democratic Russia tried to emphasize the differences from the previous political system and its foreign policy. In their opinion even Gorbachev's approach was still based on the concept of two opposite political systems, world capitalism and world socialism, and on a belief in the possibility of constructing a communist society. This might lead to confrontation sooner or later.

The first Russian democratic rulers wished to create, as soon as possible, a society based on the rule of law and a prosperous economy. The West was seen as an absolutely necessary strategic, political and even ideological ally. The first Russian president, Yeltsin, repeated many times that Russia and the US have 'common interests'. In his report to the UN Security Council meeting on 31 January 1992, he said that Russia 'considers the USA and other western countries not only as partners but also as allies. Moscow shares the main western values, which are the primacy of human rights, freedom, rule of law and high morality.'[5]

The democratic leaders of Russia at that time saw a strategic partnership as necessary to internal democratic reform, and recommended that the protection of national interests should not be promoted too aggressively. At the same time, in 1992 all branches of power agreed that the main objective for Russia's foreign policy was to get access to world markets for finance, goods and for Russians to be able to work abroad, and they linked their hopes to considerable Western economic and financial support. The democratic part of the Russian political establishment at that time openly wished to Westernize Russia, to make it a member of the 'Western prosperity zone'. Russia had to follow the Western pattern.

Moscow's relations with the independent states of the former Soviet republics were not regarded at that time as the main direction of Russian foreign policy. At the same time this new direction was not neglected, but Soviet political consciousness, or maybe even more sub-consciousness, did not accept the new reality and remained imperial in outlook. The Russian government and the political elite were strongly convinced of the need for good relations with CIS countries and close integration of current military and foreign policy. Radical liberals, like Gaydar, had a different approach. They foresaw almost complete disintegration as a natural and inevitable 'divorce', and were happy to accept that.

Disillusion soon followed. Post-Soviet countries diverged from each other as well as from Moscow. The common market and common foreign and defence policies did not happen at all. Divisions within the former Soviet empire exacerbated the economic crisis, and market reforms followed in Russia, bwith GDP declining by 40 per cent. The Soviet population as a whole suffered a myriad of problems – health care, welfare, education and unemployment – causing huge migrations. It is, however, impossible to regard Russian foreign policy as completely fruitless. The administration of the CIS was established. Despite the emptiness of all its formal declarations, the CIS has fulfilled some objectives. Even if the CIS has been far from a perfect model of devolution, devolution of the huge empire nevertheless took place largely peacefully.

The CIS remained a formality for two main reasons: first, the severe economic crisis did not give the Russian state the chance to be the centre of a new regional world organization which might have attracted other post-Soviet states; and second, the domination of the ideological approach was succeeded by an eclectic mixture of imperial ambitions and an ideology that was the exact opposite of Soviet international unity, the ideology of unlimited sovereignty.

The strong influence of Western ideology appeared in relations with former allies and Third World countries. Russia broke off relations with communist regimes, and, for example, the government officially repented for the events of 1956 in Hungary and 1968 in Czechoslovakia, and for the annexation of the Baltic countries.

In the first of our chosen periods of post-Soviet Russian foreign policy we can see that the level of pragmatism increased considerably compared to Soviet times. There could be nothing more pragmatic than the policy of openness with the West, and cooperation with Western countries. The Russian economy and Russian society had great need for these. However, it had a very strong ideological framework. The most pragmatic direction of policy was managed in the most ideological way. It represented the direct opposite in ideology, namely anti-communism. At least two main reasons account for this: first, there was too recent and too strong a legacy of the Soviet system and, after the political revolution of 1991, the people clamoured for the opposite ideology; and second, the 'culture of extremes' as the dominating tendency in Russian political culture, had developed throughout the history of Russia, up to the twentieth century. Even if the first half of the 1990s had been characterized by a high level of doctrine, the doctrine itself had become more pragmatic.

THE 'POLICY OF ALTERNATIVES', 1996–99

The second period was connected with the appointment of Evgeniy Primakov as foreign minister of the Russian Federation. In practice the change in the attitude of the Russian establishment happened earlier. The beginning of 1994 was marked by the victory of the Zhirinovsky's Liberal Democratic Party. Zhirinovsky's triumph was due to the popularity of his extreme nationalistic ideas, and brought about the resignation of Kozyrev. Zhirinovsky and the communist leaders called for an isolationist policy. This faction of the Russian political establishment considered Western countries, especially the US, as eternal enemies of Russia, and that political dogma was widespread among the rest of the political elite, though expressed more quietly. The Western-oriented part of the elite became a fairly small minority, and even this group had to refer to the West as 'partners' rather than as 'allies'. It is very important to note that anti-Western feeling did not reach the same degree as in Soviet times. Cooperation with the West was continued and was marked by several considerable steps. In 1997 the agreement between Russia and NATO was signed. Russia continued to seek loans from the IMF, and joined the G7 group of nations. However, according to opinion polls, only 13 per cent of the population had an open attitude towards the values of Western democracy, and more than 50 per cent openly declared themselves anti-Western.

Primakov's foreign policy can be called the 'policy of alternatives'. Instead of animosity towards the West, alternative steps to those of the West were offered. Contention with the West reached its peak in the spring of 1999, with the NATO bombing of Yugoslavia. In the two weeks after 24 March 1999 the number of people with anti-American feelings doubled, from 32 per cent to 64 per cent. The two main causes of stronger anti-Western feeling in the second half of the 1990s were twofold:

First, the continuation of a severe economic crisis, 'shock therapy', combined now with frustration at the lack of economic assistance from the

West. For various reasons, the 'Marshall plan' for Russia, more expected by the Russian government elite than promised by the West, did not happen. In addition, the comprehensive economic crisis, which began in 1992, was considerably exacerbated by the default on loans in August 1998, followed by devaluation of the ruble. Already low living standards decreased by a further 30 per cent.

Second, several steps by the West, such as plans for NATO extension and the NATO bombing of former Yugoslavia, increased support for the militant nationalists inside the Russian political establishment. To them these steps proved that the West was selfish and militant, and a 'natural enemy' of Russia. Particularly in the case of Kosovo, the West did not take Russia, or the UN, or international law, into consideration. Hence, relations between Russia and the West became much more antagonistic than they were immediately after the collapse of the Soviet Union.

The situation in 1999–2000 looked very much like a return to the Cold War, especially in Russian-US relations. The nationalistic ideology of 'Great Russia' rapidly strengthened and won over the great majority of the Russian political elite. Many of them were disappointed with the outcome of the 'multipolar world' idea, remarking that in practice it had turned into a unipolar one, with domination by one superpower. Nostalgia about Russia's 'superpower past', fashioned by the ideology of strong statehood, became the most widespread feeling among the political and academic elites.

The concept of an 'alternative' foreign policy used the theory of 'Eurasia' as its philosophical background. In accordance with the ideas of past Russian thinkers like Leonid Karsavin and Petr Savitskiy, Russia cannot be included in a European civilization. From a social and cultural point of view, 'Continent Eurasia' is a unique phenomenon. The key idea is that of strong state unity as the core of the Russian nation. Thus the whole of Russian history has been characterized by the dominance not of personality, or of society, but of the state. For this reason Russia appears different from Europe with its tradition of civil society and human rights.

The second period in post-Soviet foreign policy did not bring any great changes in the way in which the CIS functioned. Reintegration of the post-Soviet state was announced as a foreign policy priority. Its political purpose was formulated as a Eurasian confederation, which implied political sovereignty, independence, a common economy, common security system and the maintaining of 'humanitarian relations', as specifically defined for relations among post-Soviet states. In practice, it remained a formality. The steps towards a reunion with Belarus (the announcement of the union of the states of Russia and Belarus in 1997) were made for opportunistic political reasons. The default in 1998 made Russia much less attractive to post-

Soviet states and almost all of them felt greater security in developing their independence from Russia's foreign policy. Several of them appeared as active opponents to Russia: Ukraine with its strong Western leaning, Azerbaijan with its strong southern leaning, Uzbekistan with its southeastern leanings. They have been trying to dominate in their regions.

PUTIN'S 'GREAT RUSSIA', 2000–SEPTEMBER 2001

In early 2000, Vladimir Putin ran his presidential campaign under the slogan of 'Great Russia' and 'Strong Russian Statehood', but without any detailed program. This ideology could have evolved as a policy of 'an alternative to the West' or even as one of 'isolation'. Later, at the beginning of 2001, Putin put forward his criteria: a clear definition of national priorities, pragmatism and economic effectiveness.[6] Nevertheless, it could still have been interpreted in various ways. It sounded promising, but it did not shed enough light on the concept of his foreign policy.

However, it appeared as a dynamic development of relations with other countries. It was only in the autumn of 2001 that Putin himself declared the non-isolationist character of his foreign policy, but it has been non-isolationist from the very beginning. In 2000 alone, Russia participated in 260 international meetings at the highest official level.[7] The other features of Putin's foreign policy are: prioritization of European relations (not US, as in the first post-Soviet years), pragmatism and the dynamic development of economic relations with other countries.

Russian foreign policy from 2000 has been predominantly European-oriented. That is different from the US-oriented policy in the earlier post-Soviet period. Europe has been recognized as a natural partner. Putin and his government have started to develop bilateral relations with all West European countries. Germany has remained the main trade and economic partner since the fall of communism in Russia. However, there is an obvious emphasis on British-Russian relations. British Prime Minister Tony Blair was Putin's first international partner. In less than two years they had ten personal meetings.

At the beginning of 2000, Putin had already shocked public opinion at home by accepting the idea of Russian cooperation and even membership of NATO. Two years later the political establishment conceptualized cooperation as a 'Return to Europe'. If Russia follows democratic ways and market forces, its return to Europe will be inevitable. In early 2002 a group of experts, including Alexey Arbatov, Andrey Kokoshin and Sergey Rogov, presented the paper 'Between past and present: Russia in a transatlantic context'. Their main conclusion is that neither an extended EU nor Russia can in isolation to each other claim to be the world power centre. They have revived de Gaulle's idea of a united Europe as the only way to European self-identification, with this big change: the model of a united Europe includes Russia. The authors stress that Russian foreign policy should not be limited by controversial relations with the US and NATO. They say that the EU has some advantages as a partner in politics and security. Needless to say, these relations are very important in the economic sphere: Europe attracts 34–35 per cent of Russian foreign trade.[8]

This demonstration of priority in European relations is especially significant, considering that the identification of Russia with Europe is not recognized by an important part of the Russian political and academic establishment. Intellectually and politically, Russia is still looking for its national identity. Some authors describe this as a crisis of national identity. According to liberals and democrats (including the Union of Right Forces, Yabloko, United Social-Democrats and Gorbachev), Russia is a natural part of Europe as well as of world civilization, and must become integrated with the world and the European community.

The opposite approach has been developed by some communists and nationalists. They see Russia as a leader of the anti-Western world. It is hard not to agree with Vyacheslav Nikonov that 'anti-Westernism would bury Russia'.[9] The most popular view favours the Eurasia pattern, which essentially includes concentration on Russia's own development, the maintenance of foreign relations with only those countries which would like to be friendly towards Russia, modernization based only on the nation's natural resources, and the use of strong political power and mobilization.[10]

There are various interpretations of the Eurasia pattern. One meaning is taking a 'third path', presumably Asian and so non-European. Dmitri Trenin, an expert of the Moscow Carnegie Foundation, asserts that East Asia has been turning into the main center of world politics, including geostrategy. Neither the Baltic nor the Caucasian regions, but the Far East and Baikal areas, will be critical for Russia at the beginning of the twenty-first century. The Russian political elite, traditionally oriented towards the West, has to recognize this.[11]

The more moderate element of the current political class does not share this view. 'The consequences for Russia of following the Eurasian pattern would be catastrophic. Russia would be following advanced countries in a vain attempt to catch up with them', writes political scientist Vyacheslav Nikonov.[12] More importantly, this is the firm position of the presidential administration. Close to it, Sergey Karaganov, the Chairman of the Foreign and Defence Policy Council, characterized the idea of Eurasia as a crazy and empty theory. 'Advanced Asia follows the European path. It has accepted a market economy, rule by democracy and capitalism. There are some countries which refused to do these things, for example African and some Asian countries ('African path', 'Iraqi path'). If you are fond of this model, give it its correct name, 'euroafrican', but not Eurasian.'[13]

The rejection of this Eurasian ideology by the current ruling party does not mean the rejection of a dynamic foreign policy towards Asia. On the contrary, it is considered as extremely significant. Putin and his administration have achieved considerable progress in less than two years in their policy towards Asia. The main improvement is in Russia-China relations, geopolitically highly significant for Russia. China is the key to Siberian and Far East relations. The Russian-Chinese border is more than 4,000 kilometres long. For more than 30 years it was an area of serious military conflicts, but this situation has now been replaced by a non-violent and uncontrollable immigration of Chinese citizens. There is a demographic 'hole' in the Far East: Russia has only seven million people, while the northern Chinese provinces have 400 million. Thousands of Chinese arrive in Russia and settle illegally. There are already a large number of Chinese towns inside the Russian border, and much property has been bought by Chinese people. Russia is under real threat of losing control of Siberia and the Far East. In state-to-state relations, Russia and China signed a comprehensive agreement on partnership and economic cooperation in July 2001. It emphasized that there is no alliance against any third country and it does not include military cooperation.

Russia has begun to participate in regularizing its relations with North and South Korea and has improved its relations with Japan. In September 2000 during Putin's visit to Tokyo, Japan and Russia signed several important documents. Russia agreed to mention as part of these documents the Soviet-Japanese Declaration of 1956 where it was stated that the Soviet Union would hand over to Japan one of the Kurile Islands. There is in practice increasing economic cooperation between the two countries. Russia has become a full member of the Asia-Pacific Economic Co-operation and the ASEAN regional forum.[14]

It seems that current Russian foreign policy is based on the most pragmatic elements of the Eurasia pattern, which are based on geographical considerations. Russia borders on six geopolitical regions: Europe, the Middle East, the Mediterranean, Central Asia, China and the Far East. It must have a strong Asian policy and this is well understood by the current Russian government. For the purposes of this study it is important to conclude that post-Soviet Russian policy towards Asia is not the result of doctrine, but is based on pragmatism, and dynamic policies in this area are balanced by the obvious domination of its European policy.

The years 1999–2001 were controversial as regards Russian-US relations, with attitudes similar to those of the Cold War period, though they combined some elements of partnership with confrontation and disappointment. In addition, there was a sense that time had been wasted, and trust in the future squandered.

The first cause of this was the Kosovo crisis in 1999, which changed the outlook of the Russian political establishment. The nationalistic faction expressed solidarity with 'our Slav brothers' (the Milosevic government), and it even strongly favoured giving it military assistance. But even the more democratic and pro-Western politicians were disappointed by the behaviour of the developed countries. They saw in this an attempt by the great powers to dispense with the leading role of the UN and to appropriate the right to impose their will on those involved in armed conflicts, including sovereign nations. From this position the events in former Yugoslavia have become the very symbol of the new configuration of forces in the world, which is marked by the desire of NATO, led by the US, to demonstrate openly their determination to dominate the international political arena.[15]

The second cause was the US policy of NATO expansion and of the rejection of the ABM Treaty. With the election of President George W. Bush at the end of 2000, America has tended to revert to very firm protection of its national interests. From the very beginning of his presidency he characterized Russia as a direct threat to the West. This was followed by several spy scandals, and the imposition by both sides of restricted visa regulations. However, that retrograde movement has not reached the level of the Cold War. The US and Russia have continued to cooperate in drug control and security problems. Cultural, humanitarian and economic relations are now on a larger scale. The Ljubljana meeting in June 2001 improved personal relations between Bush and Putin. They claim that their countries are not enemies and that they pose no threat to each other. In fact, this meeting took place three months before 11 September 2001.

Current relations with the CIS countries appear as more pragmatic and realistic. Officially they announced their own definite priority, 'The CIS countries are our undoubted priority. Russia will stay the natural nucleus of Commonwealth integration, as is obvious to everybody. However, integration itself is not our own policy. We don't need it as a policy. It has to be really useful for our country and our citizens for us to accept it.'[16]

This approach appears, first of all, a realistic evaluation of the current state of the CIS. The official approach does not differ much from the conclusions of the experts. The latter generally conclude that the CIS is not effective. This is demonstrated by the attempt by the CIS to create a new regional organization with the much more experienced EU. In ten years, EU members have signed 60 agreements, and the CIS countries 1,200 agreements, with recommendations. In the EU countries, 1,500 laws were passed as a direct consequence of the recommendations, but in the CIS countries, none.[17]

Another example is that Russia and Kazakhstan recognize the primacy of international law, while Ukraine and five other countries do not.

Economic integration has made no visible progress. Trade turnover is falling. The CIS share of Russian external trade has fallen from 46 per cent in 1990–1997 to 21 per cent in 2000. The Russian share of CIS trade is 50 per cent. Having 25 per cent of the world's natural resources and ten per cent of world industry, they produce only four per cent of the world's GDP.[18] Thus, the CIS enters the current decade as a disorganized, predominantly political, union, with priority on bilateral relations rather than on integration. We see considerable progress in the movement from doctrine towards pragmatism in that key players recognize the weakness of the CIS. At the same time the importance of good relations with former post-Soviet states is not denied or underestimated, and these are even prioritized among Russia's overall relations. This seems inconsistent with the inefficiency of the CIS.

The following two points are important in the understanding of this conflict. The inefficiency of the present CIS states does not augur well for the future of the CIS. Expert opinion contends that Russia could have had a 20 per cent increase in GNP without one ruble of additional investment, by simply exploiting its existing possibilities of cooperation.[19] Hence, there is a realistic possibility of reintegration. Many analysts have pointed to the following:

> 1. Socio-economic factors: the close economic relations arising from the common industrial complex, which was established and developed from the 1930s to the 1970s. The various functions were dispersed within the organization, necessitating the construction of complementary plants in different regions. Now many are located in different states, but they need to cooperate. As much as 50 per cent of the Russian economic decline in 1992 and 1993 happened because of the breakdown of the necessary economic connections within the former USSR.[20]

> 2. Socio-cultural factors: a common 'civilization' of people with a common history and common traditions; they lived in unity for 70 years; they speak Russian in addition to their indigenous tongue and Russian is the language of interstate communication; there is a similarity of social structures and level of education. There are 25 million Russian and four million Russian-speaking people living in former parts of the USSR. Social security is for them a hard problem because in many of these post-Soviet countries they are not recognized as having full citizenship rights.

> 3. National security factors: Russia still possesses 80 per cent of the Soviet military-industrial complex, but without the complementary

production facilities in the CIS states it can manufacture for itself only 18 per cent of the modern weapons which it needs. The remainder can be produced only with the cooperation of CIS states.[21]

Ten years after the Soviet break-up, however, not all CIS countries want to develop integration within the CIS. Georgia is a leading example of this. Nor are many of them able to participate with adequate efficiency. Russia and Belarus declared a reunification in 1997, but they are still countries with different economies and political systems. The elections to the Russia-Belarus Union Parliament were scheduled to take place in 2002, but, regardless, the parliament's effectiveness is rather doubtful. The adoption of a common currency seems impossible before 2008. Russia has also accepted the birth of a new organization, which is within the CIS and excludes Russia, objecting only to its cooperation in the military sphere. This is GUUAM, consisting of Georgia, Ukraine, Uzbekistan, Azerbaijan and Moldavia. Thus the CIS is really more a 'sleeping beauty' than a real union of states.

Nevertheless, there is a pragmatic solution to this conflict of ideas. The current Russian administration has developed bilateral relations with CIS members. It has also decided to concentrate its main efforts on only those countries which are really determined to participate in integration. The Eurasian Economic Commonwealth became the focus of the current Russian policy as a result of this approach. It started from a customs agreement between Russia and Belarus. In October 2000 Kazakhstan, Kyrgyzstan and Tajikistan joined it. These five countries have established an effective free trade zone between them. They have also progressed in humanitarian relations: they abolished the visa system, considerably simplified the obtaining of citizenship and have clear perspectives of real economic integration. 'Our goal is multilateral cooperation evolving naturally, according to the real needs and mutual interests of the participants.'[22] This declaration seems to be sincere, reasonable and pragmatic.

The third period of Russian post-Soviet policy has therefore been really remarkable. National foreign policy has remained fairly ideological, but the ideology has inevitably changed from the extremes of the Soviet 'world communist revolution' theory, as well as from the 'ally of the West' approach of the initial post-Soviet years. The 'strong Russian state' concept appears as the least ideological in the modern history of Russia. It is ideologically neutral, because it does not involve the idea of any 'enemy of the state'. It turns foreign policy into a more pragmatic policy, based on the criteria of economic efficiency.

If seen from an East–West point of view, Russian foreign policy during the early years of the twenty-first century has been characterized by balancing European and Asian forces. If it is seen from a tripartite US-Europe-Russia perspective, it appeared to be making Europe a priority. Bilateral relations with European countries were considerably strengthened. NATO-Russian relations did not progress. Their movement, however, towards closer cooperation was included in the realistic agenda of discussions between the continental and the Russian political establishments. In fact, that development was initiated by the Russian side. US-Russian relations stayed frozen at the level of March–April 1999, with a tendency to return to the Cold War position, because of the change of president in the US. However, despite this, the drifting apart of Russia and the US up to the end of the summer of 2001 was not similar to the Cold War. It was characterized by less confrontation, and the positive legacy of cooperation during the post-Soviet decade.

Russian policy towards the CIS began to find a middle ground between two ideological extremes: the anti-communist approach valued the idea of a 'civilized divorce', and in the post-communist inertia it was assumed by the former Soviet elite that the CIS would survive and develop spontaneously without any great effort. The current Russian administration is oriented towards the development of mutually beneficial bilateral relations and closer economic and humanitarian cooperation within the Eurasian Economic Commonwealth (Russia, Kazakhstan, Kyrgyzstan, Belarus and Tajikistan).

ANTI-TERROR ALLIANCE: AFTER 11 SEPTEMBER 2001

International relations have completely changed since the attacks of 11 September 2001 and the subsequent war waged by the US against terrorism. Revised domestic and foreign policy priorities have become necessary in all countries. The reaction of Russia is very well-known. Russia supported the US, offered cooperation, important secret information and air corridors for NATO aircraft, and agreed to the establishment of US military bases in Central Asia.

Alternative policies were open to Russia at that time. She could have taken up a passive position, supporting the US morally and expressing sympathy, as China did. Russia could have been positively neutral, helping the US to reach agreement with Uzbekistan and Tajikistan, but itself standing on one side, as did India. Russia went further. It took an active part, stopping short of direct military involvement. There are even some signs of a limited Russian military presence in Afghanistan.

Russia took strong steps towards partnership with the West. The common denominator of the partnership is the fight against terrorism. The main difference from previous years was in Russian-US and Russian-NATO relations. In the first days after 11 September the Kremlin declared a new long-term course of constructive dialogue and cooperation with the West, including the US. It was officially and systematically shaped during Putin's visit to Washington DC in October 2001, and in several meetings with certain European heads of state. Russia has been following this course strictly, despite very serious difficulties. The Russian leadership accepted Washington's decision to abrogate the Anti-Ballistic Missile Treaty, although regarding this political step as a mistake. The Kremlin also suffered quite a strong reaction on cooperation between Western countries and the Central Asian states on military and economic matters. President Putin, however, shocked the world and Russian public opinion by accepting American military involvement in Georgia. The Russian side does not accept all aspects of the Bush concept, but expresses disagreement in a civilized way, as is usual within the Western community of states.

The most amazing change in the approach to the problem of organizing world security is that Russian-NATO relations are not only the focus of general discussions, but have become a matter of detailed political negotiations, which concentrate on the mechanism of Russia's effective participation in NATO activities. 'What limits our move towards the West is the fact that the Western club does not accept us as a member, at least in our general life. The West does not allow us to be too close to it. It is not possible to include Russia in the main structures of the West, (EU and NATO), in the near future, even if we were to desire this very much.'[23] This was said by one of the most reasonable and balanced political analysts in mid-2001.

Less than a year later claimed a certain part of the Russian political establishment claims firmly that Russia must have friendly relations with NATO. To maintain a proper security system Russia has to be united with European countries and the US, within NATO or beside NATO.[24] West and East, in spite of what Rudyard Kipling wrote, now have the chance to meet each other. Russian membership of NATO is no longer seen as impossible. The politics of today involve no discussions about the necessity of integrating Russia and NATO, but only discussions about the level, type and mechanism of this integration. Is it to be the integration of a security system or a wider common activity? What is the best way to shape it? In 2001 cooperation was offered within the formula '19+1', which means that 19 NATO countries would have taken decisions which Russia would have had to accept. Now that formula is replaced in discussions by the format of '20'. It gives Russia the right to participate in decision-making.

At their meeting in Britain in December 2001, Tony Blair and Vladimir Putin discussed possible alternatives. The Russian approach seems flexible enough. Putin spoke about two ways for Russia to participate in NATO decision-making. The first way would be for Russia to define spheres of influence in which she would not participate in NATO decision-making, and spheres of influence in which she would. The second would be to separate two to four problems in which Russia is involved as a full-rights member, without participating in the rest. The first way is better, but Putin declared that Russia is ready to accept either.[25] He has also said several times that Russia can integrate with NATO as deeply as NATO members are ready to accept. 'If NATO is ready to invite Russia to join as a full-rights member in two to three years, Russia might accept this.'[26]

Of course, in this case NATO would have to become a different type of organization. It may have to become the principal instrument of European security. So, with Russia as a participant, it would not remain a defensive military bloc. It would lose this role. Yuly Vorontsov, the former Russian ambassador to the US and a current UN adviser, assumes that NATO will disappear in five years.[27] It has not been accepted that NATO has a future as a security structure for the twenty-first century. 'It is not efficient enough to meet the challenge of providing security in these modern times.' It seems that the furore in Moscow about joining NATO is connected with the phobia of the Russian 'political elite', because the Baltic countries are determined to join this regional organization. 'The Russian President has the much more important task of guaranteeing his country's security in the twenty-first century than to consider the irrational phobias of those politicians who remain mentally in the past century.'[28]

Russia is about to participate in NATO decision-making to some extent: 'President Putin confirmed that Russia is ready to cooperate with NATO to the extent which NATO is ready for itself. If NATO invites Russia to be a full-rights member, I think, Russia may change its position'.[29] 'NATO will disappear in five years.'[30] Russian-NATO relations belong to yesterday's politics. For the purpose of this essay it is important to emphasize that these ideas and discussions are seen as revolutionary, when viewed in the very recent context of when Soviet and post-Soviet Russian policy was doctrinal, and that that doctrine had been completely anti-Western.

Such strong anti-Westernism is not only a conclusive statement, but an explanation of the current controversial discussions among the public and within the Russian political elite. It can be described as 'the unfinished Cold War'. A considerable section of the Russian political elite and, close to it the academic elite, is still oppressed by the legacy of communist days, and cannot expunge the 'image of enemy' from their minds. They are afraid of having too close a relationship with the West, the US and NATO. This tendency towards anxiety appeared several months after 11 September and clearly it has been increasing since. Formerly everybody agreed with the president. At the same time, Seleznev, the Speaker of the Duma, and several leading army officers openly demanded the expulsion of US troops from the 'Russian zone of influence' in Central Asia. There is strong resistance to Putin's agreement with the US on further cuts in strategic nuclear weapons. Even before the Russian opposition to the US-led war in Iraq, a large group of MPs continues to support the Iraqi regime. It is frequently heard that Putin is getting more like another Gorbachev, giving the West too much and never receiving much in return. The opinion that the Russian government went too far in supporting American foreign policy is shared by 48 per cent of the population.[31]

President Putin with his policy of an anti-terrorist coalition and of good relations with NATO and the US, almost like those of an ally, is far ahead of half or even more of the Russian public and political elite. Sergey Karaganov, a complete supporter of the president's policy after 11 September, concluded that there is a considerable gap between the president's views and those of the foreign policy establishment. A recent example was connected with the American involvement in Georgia. Putin publicly supported the American military initiative in the former Soviet republic. The day before this announcement, Russia's reaction appeared to be more negative. Foreign Minister Igor Ivanov telephoned Secretary of State Colin Powell and told him, 'Moscow has well-founded concerns that the direct involvement of the United States military in the fight against terrorism in Georgia could further complicate the situation in the region.'[32] Several days later Ivanov adopted the president's approach.

By the beginning of 2002, then, Russian foreign policy had developed a 'double-rule' within the Russian political class. This is reminiscent to a certain extent of 1993–94, when 'patriotic' opposition to the official pro-Western course of the 'traitors' had been evolving inside the Russian elite, while several years later it appeared as official policy. The tradition of fighting to the last man for 'Great Russia' is still very strong. Doctrine is still a factor in the divergence of a considerable part of the Russian political class in their approach to foreign policy problems. However, this current of opposition lies below the surface and does not represent official Russian policy.

The official Russian foreign policy has three main priorities: the first priority is the importance of the interests of the country itself. Foreign policy has to 'serve' domestic policy, which includes primarily the establishment of efficient security, the raising of living standards and the development of civil society. Russia has to forgo a 'diplomatic presence' because other states wish to behave like superpowers. Russia must use its external resources carefully.[33] The second major priority is non-isolationism: integration into the community of democratic states and international economic structures. The third priority is an active policy in all directions, balanced between West and East, Europe and Asia.

Taken as a whole, this concept is a sign of essential progress on the way from a doctrinaire to a pragmatic approach. Geopolitics is being replaced more by geoeconomics. Concern about internal economic and social problems is a more effective way of protecting national interests and hence of making Russia a really great country without relying on the old concept of a 'Great Russia'. Pragmatism and economic feasibility, less of the euphoria of the 1990s, more common sense, depoliticization of foreign policy and the prospect of its demilitarization. This is the current 'ideology' of Russian diplomacy, as it is seen to be more beneficial for the country in the twenty-first century (as well as, hopefully, for all international relations), than the previous long tradition of doctrinal domination. One of the hardest challenges ahead is to make the course of pragmatism irreversible.

NOTES

1. *Argumenty i facty*, 1 Feb. 2002, p.6.
2. Vladimir Mantusov, *SNG:Economicheskaya kooperatsiya ili pazvod?* (Moscow: OLIMP 2001) p.11.
3. *Argumenty i facty*, 1 Feb. 2002, p.4.
4. Igor Ionov, *Russkaya tsivilizatsiya, 9–19 veka* (Moscow: Prosveshchenie 1999) p.14.
5. *Sovremennie mezhdunarodnie otnosheniya,* (Moscow: OLMA-PRESS 2001) p.486.
6. Vladimir Putin, 'Zadachi Russkoy diplomatii', *Mezhdunarodnaya zhizn* 2, 2002, p.4.
7. Ibid.
8. Andrey Kolesnikov, 'Vozvrashchenie pohishchenoy Evropy', *Izvestia*, 17 Dec. 2001, p.2.
9. Wyacheslav Nikonov, 'Panorama XX1 veka', *Mezhdunarodnaya zhizn* 6, 2001, p.14.
10. Ibid.
11. *Istoriya Rossyi v noveyishee vremya (1945–2001)* (Moscow: Olimp, AST 2001) pp.447–8.
12. Nikonov, 'Panorama XX1 veka' (note 9) p.15.
13. Sergey Karaganov, '"Tretiego puti" ne dano', *Obshchayay gazeta*, 22–28 Nov. 2001.
14. Igor Ivanov, 'Rossia v mirovoy politike', *Mezhdunarodnaya Zhizn* 5, 2001, p.9.
15. A. Kulik (ed.), 'World order after the Balkan crisis. New realities of the changing world', Conference Proceedings, Moscow, 1–2 Nov. 1999, (Moscow: "Dobrosvet" 2000) p.23.
16. Vladimir Putin, 'Zadachi Russkoy diplomatii' (note 6) p.5.
17. Mantusov, *SNG* (note 2) p.38.
18. Ibid. p.22.
19. Ibid. p.25.
20. *Istoriya Rossyi v noveyishee vremya* (note 11) p.431.
21. Ibid. p.432.
22. Vladimir Trubnikov, 'Desyataya godovshchyna SNG', *Mezhdunarodnaya zhysn* 11, 2001, p.12.
23. Nikonov, 'Panorama XX1 veka' (note 9) p.12.
24. Sergey Karaganov, 'Russia-NATO: kontury novogo soyuza?', *Novaya Zhizn*, 10, 28 Feb. 2002, p.10.
25. 'Vizit Prezidenta Putina v Velikobritaniyu', *Diplomaticheskyi Zhournal* 1, 2002, p.64.
26. Karaganov, 'Russia-NATO' (note 24) p.10.
27. Yuliy Vorontsov, 'NATO otomret cherez 5 let', *Izvestia,* 18 March 2002.
28. Andrey Pionkovskyi , 'Pismo angliyskogo druga', *Obshchaya Gazeta*, 22–28 Nov. 2002.

29. Karaganov, 'Russia-NATO' (note 24) p.10.
30. Vorontsov, 'NATO otomret cherez 5 let' (note 27).
31. *Argumenty i facty*, 49/2001, p.20.
32. *International Herald Tribune*, 23 March 2002.
33. Igor Ivanov, *Novaya Russkaya Diplomatiya* (Moscow: OLMA-PRESS 2002) pp.16–17.

Russian Foreign Policy and Its Critics

MARY BUCKLEY

Throughout the history of the Soviet state, and now of the smaller Russian Federation, there have been critical turning points which redirected and reshaped foreign policy. These can be prompted in any state by leadership change, reassessed state interest, domestic political reforms requiring linked foreign policy reforms, the image of the foreign minister, events in the broader global arena or a combination of more than one of these variables.

The events of 11 September 2001 facilitated one such turning point, although arguably President Putin was looking for ways of improving relations with the West anyway after the strained period of NATO intervention in Kosovo. The global fallout from 11 September provided him with an opportunity significantly to realign Russia's foreign policy, despite potential opposition from communists, nationalists and the foreign policy and defence establishments at home. For economic and geopolitical reasons, moreover, it was in his leadership's interest so to do. The subsequent hostage crisis in Moscow between 23 and 26 October 2002 also presented Putin with the opportunity to cement his assertive foreign policy.

Realignment, however, will not necessarily bring with it all expected benefits, such as fast entry into the World Trade Organization (WTO), the destruction rather than storage of US nuclear weapons or an equal vote in all NATO decisions. As in the past, periods of good relations are accompanied by disagreements, strains and, sometimes, crises.

'NEW' FOREIGN POLICY IN THE RUSSIAN FEDERATION

The tottering Soviet Union lost its East European empire in 1989 and suffered an identity crisis as a consequence, made worse by its own collapse in 1991. It became surrounded by newly-independent states – the 'Near Abroad' – with which it had previously shared a federal state. Quite what statehood meant was unclear and Russian academics struggled to define it. Foreign writings such as those of Francis Fukuyama on the 'end of history', the failure of communism and triumph of liberalism uncomfortably rubbed this in.[1]

What Russian leaders had wanted of the US was, moreover, itself confused, unrealistic and even naive. There had been high hopes of support for Russian reforms, backed up by loans. When funds did not match expectations, Russians felt surprised, betrayed, undervalued and even puzzled why they should be left to fend for themselves without the financial prerequisites for success. Despite vulnerability, Russian leaders simultaneously wanted their country to be seen as a 'great power'.

Confusion over Russia's reception by world statesmen was not eased by puzzlement in Russia and abroad about how foreign policy was made in Moscow. The President, ministry of foreign affairs, parliament, reconstituted Security Council after 1992, and presidential advisers all functioned in a disjointed and fractured manner, with unclear delimitations and responsibilities, which did not, and could not, result in a coordinated policy process.[2]

A combination of disappointed expectations in both the US and Russia of each other, topped with unclear delimitations and a lack of liaison and coordination between individuals in the foreign policy process in Russia, exacerbated US-Russian relations. Indeed, one cannot really talk of a clear foreign policy *process* in Russia. There were rather disjointed, discrete *processes* which did not necessarily concur or coincide, but could happen to overlap.

The failure of speedy domestic economic and political reform in Russia was the independent variable that inspired critics in the West to opt for NATO expansion in order to guarantee the security space to the west of Russia. Perceptions in Russia, however, were of betrayal by the West of a past promise and of retreat from partnership. These were deeply aggravated in 1999 by NATO's bombing of parts of the former Yugoslavia.

KOSOVO

NATO intervention in Kosovo, in March 1999, triggered the worst period of US-Russian relations in the history of the new Russian state. Although there were differences in emphasis and nuance of Russian reactions across politicians and parties, the general sentiment was overwhelmingly critical.[3] Yeltsin expressed immediate 'outrage' at 'undisguised aggression'. He pointed out that the UN Security Council had not approved of this action against sovereign Yugoslavia.[4] Defence Minister Sergei Ivanov accused NATO of behaving like a 'world policeman' while Foreign Minister Igor Ivanov hastened to emphasize the importance of stopping aggression by 'purely political means'.[5] Evgenii Primakov, too, talked of the need for 'mutual concessions and compromises'.[6]

Genadii Ziuganov insisted that NATO 'is returning us to the time of Hitlerism' and that 'the USA is establishing a global dictatorship by neo-fascist methods'.[7] Vladimir Zhirinovskii made similar points and set about organizing volunteers to fight alongside the Serbs against NATO.[8] The notion spread amongst nationalists and communists that NATO would bomb Russia next, best captured in a headline in the newspaper *Zavtra*: 'And it will bomb us too.'[9] As many as 98 per cent of the Russian population also expressed views against NATO intervention.[10]

Although Yeltsin made hints about possible Russian military action, these were more rhetoric for nationalist ears than intention, although he did send a few frissons down Western spines.[11] On other matters he was more decisive. Yeltsin halted Primakov's scheduled visit to the US in his new capacity as prime minister, causing a turn-around mid-flight, called for an emergency meeting of the UN Security Council, recalled to Moscow Russia's Chief Military Representative to NATO, suspended Russian participation in the Partnership for Peace and put off talks on the opening of a NATO mission in Moscow. He consistently emphasized that problems in Kosovo could be solved 'only through negotiation' and pointed out that Russia reserved the right to take 'appropriate measures' including 'those of a military nature'.[12]

The Russian defence ministry discussed the new draft military doctrine – designed to replace the earlier one of 1993 – in September. Fresh attention was given to 'potential external and internal threats' to Russia.[13] Ultimately, however, Russia did play a constructive role in Kosovo with Viktor Chernomyrdin, a former prime minister, being sent as a peace envoy and intermediary with Milosevic, albeit criticized by nationalists at home.[14]

In sum, NATO intervention in Kosovo fuelled Russian suspicions of the US's intended world role and was the catalyst for renewed concern about Russia's security interests. The world was seen by many in the defence establishment as a battleground between adherents of unipolarity and multipolarity.

Notwithstanding, however, the increased tensions between the US and Russia, there remained a desire on the part of both leaderships for relations to be different. Each side wanted collaboration with the other, and public opinion reflected this hope, but circumstances were such that strain prevailed. As the months passed, survey data showed a positive turn in attitudes towards NATO and the US. When asked over 18–21 August 1999, 'How do you think relations between Russia and NATO will develop after the Kosovo conflict?', 52 per cent of 1,600 respondents, replied 'gradual normalization'. A much smaller 17 per cent predicted a growth in tension and 25 per cent did not know.[15]

A spiral of wary perceptions of the 'other' between the US and Russia reinforced suspicions about intentions and a growing mistrust, especially after the election of George W. Bush as president. The fact that there was commitment in the US to develop a new anti-missile system, which would act as a national missile defence against 'rogue states' such as Iraq and North Korea, reinforced Russian anger at unipolarity since its consequence would be the US reneging on the 1972 Anti-Ballistic Missile (ABM) Treaty. Russian leaders inevitably protested, opposing any change to the ABM Treaty.[16] Almost a replay of old Cold War tensions also occurred in 2001 when a spy scandal hit the headlines in which a US citizen, Robert Hanssen, was exposed for having sold secrets to the USSR and Russia. The US expelled 50 Russian diplomats and Russia reacted in tit-for-tat style. Looking to cement friendships elsewhere in the world and attempting to make multipolarity as much a reality as was feasible, Russia signed a friendship treaty with China in July 2001.[17]

11 SEPTEMBER 2001 AND WAR IN AFGHANISTAN

The events of 11 September, which caused a wave of genuine sympathy for Americans in Russia, provided an opportunity for US-Russian collaboration and a warming of relations. Bush's comment that 'night fell on a different world' captured the world's horror at the possibility that a different and insidious type of challenge to states was now possible, making everyone vulnerable.[18] By participating in the anti-terrorist coalition, Putin could challenge the marginalization of Russia on the world stage and its downgrading in importance in Washington. He could also point out that Russians had their own terrorist problem in Chechnya about which Western leaders needed to be more sympathetic.

Putin was quick to condemn the attacks on the World Trade Center and on the Pentagon and was ready to enlist Russia in the US anti-terrorist drive. On 24 September, after deliberation, Putin announced that Russia would provide intelligence and airspace for humanitarian aid for Afghanistan and would also support a US military presence in Central Asia. Putin's opposition to NATO expansion became more muted and he increased support for the Northern Alliance in Afghanistan.[19] Although the Kremlin was publicly quiet about military involvement in Afghanistan, and denied it, Russian troops, tanks and military equipment moved to the border in September and surveillance equipment was updated. There were 10,000 border guards under Russian command on the Tajik/Afghan border, and tanks along with several thousand crack troops were sent there from Moscow. The Russian 201st Motorized Rifle Division threw pontoon bridges across the Pyandzh River and established positions inside Afghanistan. Russian troops and air power were fighting the Taliban to defend the bridgeheads. In October, Russian special forces were reported on the ground in Afghanistan. Their task was to pinpoint targets for bombs to destroy Osama bin Laden's mountain strongholds.[20]

As well as offering the US condolences and support, Putin pushed the message that Russia was part of Europe.[21] In fluent German, he told the Bundestag in October that Russia should be incorporated into economic, political and defence structures. Germany had always been more sympathetic to Russia's cause than had the US and the context was a welcome one. Putin was consistent in driving his point across. In October, he told an EU-Russia summit that relations with Russia could indeed improve if NATO took due account of Russia's interests. He indicated that his country might be willing to reassess NATO expansion since a global anti-terrorist coalition was a top priority. Putin gave his agreement to monthly EU-Russia meetings on foreign and defence policy and concurred with a new NATO proposal for widening and deepening relations with Russia.[22]

Putin wanted to stress the importance of respect for Russia's interests and also for Russia's status in the world. There may have been economic problems at home and unresolved issues of national identity, but Putin's leadership was witnessing the beginnings of economic upturn and also greater domestic stability from the growth of political centrism. Under Putin, START II was finally ratified and the Comprehensive Test Ban Treaty was signed, almost daring the US not to renege on the ABM Treaty.[23]

A fanfare for US-Russian relations followed when a summit took place in the US in November 2001. There was progress in agreements to reduce nuclear stockpiles to 1,500 in Russia and to between 1,700 and 2,200 in the US.[24] Bush insisted that no formal treaty was needed, something which Russian leaders subsequently challenged by constant diplomatic chiselling until the US administration agreed to work towards one. Six months later, on 13 May, agreement to sign a formal document was finally announced.[25] This was subsequently done in Moscow on 25 May 2002 amid much fanfare and back-slapping. Not only was there a treaty on arms reductions, but also declarations on strategic and energy cooperation and joint statements on economic relations and on the Middle East.[26]

Putin, then, abandoned the hostile rhetoric against the US and NATO characteristic of Russia in 1999. Any fallout from disagreements over Kosovo was brushed to one side. His priority was for Russia to be seen to be active on the world stage again, cooperating with top leaders and making a difference. He was even calm about the US's withdrawal from the ABM Treaty, saying it no longer surprised him, although it was still a 'mistake'.[27] Putin and Chinese President Jiang Zemin had repeatedly castigated the US for wanting to build a national missile defence system and had shared views on reneging on the ABM Treaty.[28] Now Putin chose to play these down too. It was, however, announced in May that there were preparations in Moscow to renounce the START II accord in response to US withdrawal from the ABM Treaty.[29]

In sum, Putin was being most accommodating about US policies which, up until 11 September, Russian leaders had criticized quite loudly. It would be going too far to say that he reversed them, or dropped them, but now he voiced acceptance of their reality, with respectful disagreement, viewing these disagreements as differences over policy which were insufficient to hold back greater collaboration. In December 2001, a NATO-Russia Permanent Joint Council was set up and US Secretary of State, Colin Powell, went to Moscow to make the point that Russia would be able to participate in NATO's governing bodies even though she was not a member.[30] With some pride, Foreign Minister Igor Ivanov declared that 2001 was 'the year of Russia's return to the international arena as a key player'.[31] Even Defence Minister Sergei Ivanov toned down his usual anti-Western remarks.[32]

Putin's policy inevitably aggravated communists, nationalists and the military establishment at home. Putin was attempting to extract a role on the world stage for Russia as a respected player, secure a place among the G8, end condemnation of his policies in Chechnya, speed entry into the World Trade Organization (WTO), have a greater say in NATO and seal agreements on arms reductions. Although his personal relationship with Bush took a positive turn, with Bush even announcing that he could see Putin's 'soul' in his eyes, and notwithstanding various kind words about Russia from Tony Blair, Jacques Chirac, George Robertson, Silvio Berlusconi and others, nationalists moaned that Putin had not actually managed to extract much that was tangible for Russia in exchange.[33] At best, he won a reversal of the downgrading, suspicion and nonchalance towards Russia in Washington of the early Bush months in office, an initial verbal agreement on arms made into a formal agreement only after huge Russian pressure, and attempts by NATO to improve Russia's relations with it. But realistically, he could not have expected much more, and in some Western eyes was lucky to get this much.

Putin's critics pointed out that Russia's concessions to the West had been huge, but nothing commensurate had been given in return. NATO was still expanding eastwards, now with Moscow's acceptance, the US gave notice that it would definitely be pulling out of the ABM agreement, and to top it all, although US leaders had said that the presence of their troops in Central Asia would be temporary, they were still there even though the Taliban had been defeated and a new regime was in power in Afghanistan. Although, in May 2002 Bush announced amid great fanfare that reductions in US and Russian nuclear arsenals meant that we 'could put behind us the Cold War once and for all' since this was the dawn of 'a new era of US-Russian relationships – and that's important', the Russians had had to pay a price for their much-desired formal agreement.[34] Putin had agreed to the concession that excess warheads could be stored, not destroyed. This meant that at any time, either state could beef up their arsenals again. Had Russia totally sold out to the West, Putin's critics asked?

CRITICS IN RUSSIA

Predictably, Ziuganov dubbed Putin's policies as 'pro-American' and the 'third stage of treason' after Gorbachev and Yeltsin.[35] Putin's closure of bases in Cuba and Vietnam also meant that 'no geopolitical home front will remain for Russia'.[36] Zhirinovskii, more wildly, swung from condemnation to support and back to condemnation again, apologizing for his former 'anti-Americanism', then adopting it again.[37] Other political parties, notably the centrists *Edinstvo* (Unity) and *Edinaia Rossiia* (Unified Russia) and liberal reformers *Yabloko* (Apple) and *Soiuz Pravykh Sil* (SPS – the Union of Right Forces), gave Putin their backing for his participation in the anti-terrorist coalition, albeit with some qualifications and reservations about the consequences.[38]

With time, the main reservations were: first, that the geopolitical map of Central Asia and Eastern Europe would change fundamentally and at Russia's expense; and second, that arms agreements would benefit the US far more than Russia.

Writing in March 2002 in the glossy current affairs magazine, *Rossiskaia Federatsiia Segodnia* (The Russian Federation Today), Professor Boris Usviatsov warned that an embrace by the US could throttle Russia, pointing to the political and military map of Central Asia. With the agreement of Kyrgyzstan and Uzbekistan, the US and France were turning the airport at Bishkek into a main airbase. At the old Soviet aerodrome in Uzbekistan more than 1,500 Americans were stationed and the Pentagon intended to rent it for 25 years. The number of Western troops in Tajikistan, Uzbekistan and Kyrgyzstan added up to more than 10,000.[39] An array of deputies from the Federation Council and the Duma also wrote short pieces about this 'negative', 'worrying' and 'alarming' situation.[40] Usviatsov concluded that 'America does not need a strong and confident Russia' and that Russia should pursue 'strict pragmatism' (*zhestkii pragmatizm*).[41]

Public opinion reflected these fears. An opinion poll of January 2002, showed that 63 per cent of Russians were worried about the US military presence in Central Asia, with 26 per cent of these 'definitely worried' as distinct from 'somewhat worried'. Twenty-four per cent were not worried and 13 per cent did not know.[42] Foreign Minister Ivanov attempted to calm fears, somewhat unsuccessfully, with remarks such as the US military presence there was part of a 'joint rebuff to international terrorism'. He added that it also helped to combat drug trafficking and religious extremism, both of which undermined Russia's security.[43] The implication was that the US presence was, in fact, in Russia's interest.

Putin's softening on NATO expansion also prompted negative reactions, especially since it was widely suspected that any promises of a higher profile for Russia within NATO would not be accompanied by voting power. In February 2002, NATO offered to form a new NATO-Russia Council (NRC), thereby replacing the Permanent Joint Council (PJC). Russia could send an ambassador, but enjoy no veto.[44] Foreign Minister Ivanov said it was not clear to him how the new 20 differed from the previous PJC, other than cosmetically. Defence Minister Sergei Ivanov argued for consensual decision-making as did the military, who wanted an equal say in matters of European security.[45] Russia kept pressing for equal partnership in NATO concerning European security matters and for a full vote.[46]

In April, Igor Ivanov reported that new agreement on the NRC was being reached, thereby granting Russia participation 'in the development, approval and implementation of decisions'.[47] Now the NRC would be considered 20, or *dvadtsatka* to the Russians. This was subsequently discussed at the NATO meeting of foreign ministers in Reykjavik in mid-May and formalized on 28 May near Rome at a signing ceremony.[48] Public opinion about NATO in the run-up to the agreement remained sceptical. In April 2002, 33 per cent of respondents thought it was 'in Russia's interests' to get closer to NATO, while 37 per cent considered it went 'against' and 30 per cent were unsure.[49]

There were also divided views about the meaning of the final arms agreement between Bush and Putin. Rhetoric aside, all Russia had really received was a formal document rather than a verbal agreement about what was happening anyway. Putin put on a brave face about his inability to get Bush to destroy all US warheads with the afterthought that Russia would not necessarily destroy all of hers either.[50]

A roundtable that convened in Moscow in April 2002 to discuss the six months since Russia joined the anti-terrorism coalition saw a span of views. General Leonid Ivashov, now deputy director of the Academy of Geopolitical Problems, was blunt, saying that there was no real partnership. As he put it, 'In my opinion, there wasn't and there couldn't be any partnership. It was just an emotional reaction to the September 11 tragedy.' By adjusting Russian policy to that of the US, 'we just wanted to solve a series of Russian problems' and the elite may have 'naively hoped to improve its personal image'. Good partnership was unlikely due to differences in economic, military and geopolitical interests. The notion that Russian-US relations would improve radically was, in Ivashov's perception, just an 'irrational hope'.[51]

Realistically, Aleksandr Shabanov, deputy chair of the Duma's Foreign Affairs Committee, pointed out that the US had always followed its own political course and 'has such a dominant position in the world in every way.

How can you have equal relations with such a supreme power? Of course it's impossible. We shouldn't have illusions and even think about it. Present-day Russia and its elite have to accept it.'[52] Shabanov observed that the US would not change its track just to meet Russia's needs.

Aleksei Arbatov, now deputy chair of the Duma Defence Committee and in the Yabloko faction, observed, 'we are rightly against NATO enlargement, but what can we offer in exchange to the Europeans for their security? Absolutely nothing'. He advised against bad relations with the US but felt that Russia should not stay with an 'America-centric' policy and instead orient itself to a mix of countries like Japan, India, South Korea and the EU states, who sometimes criticize the US.[53]

Musing on anti-Americanism, Arbatov suggested that a good way to fight against such passions would be to 'imagine how we would have behaved if what happened in the US had happened in Russia. I believe we would have behaved in a tougher way and that we would respect less the interests of other countries'. He also admitted that 'we'd like to be at the same level as the US and the West, but inside our country we are not behaving according to Western standards'.[54] Arbatov cited as examples the lack of press freedom and human rights violations in Russia's war in Chechnya.

Also, pointedly, Viacheslav Nikonov of the Politika Foundation think-tank, surmised that Russia lacked a cohesive strategy for relations with the West since Russian leaders did not grasp what they wanted from the US. He believed that 'our political elite, with their incessant ambitions, are continually getting all huffy with the Americans even in matters that the Americans don't have anything to do with'.[55] The Russian defeat in figure skating at the 2002 winter Olympic Games was one such example.

Nikonov, however, pointed out the benefits of good relations with the West. First, they meant that 'you don't have to waste all your energy defending yourself against the West'. Second, 'it is prestigious' and 'what's more, it gives you the chance to be a member of some clubs'. He regretted that the West would not let Russia into some of its 'exclusive clubs, but we are allowed to take part in the G8 meetings'. Third, 'you can count on investments, even if at the same time you need to build up a good climate for investments in the country. This is a domestic task, but also a foreign policy task.'[56]

Indeed, many in Russian elites had anticipated that cooperation with the US after 11 September would bring economic benefits. Aleksandr Livshits, a former defence minister and deputy premier and since founder of an economic policy think-tank, drew attention to dashed hopes. He interpreted new steel tariffs as aimed at protecting US domestic industry and as trying to destroy the Russian steel market. Livshits cynically stressed that Russia had been discussing its status as a market economy with the US for seven or eight years. Yeltsin had said 'Bill, where's our status?' and Clinton had lifted the Jackson-Vanik amendment for Kazakhstan but not for Russia.[57] This differing treatment clearly festered.

Former president of the USSR, Mikhail Gorbachev, had also become vocal about US-Russian relations before this roundtable had convened. He noted that Putin had been the first to telephone Bush on 11 September and that Russia was being extremely helpful in giving information, coordinating work with other states, delivering humanitarian aid to Afghanistan and supplying the Northern Alliance with weapons. All this was in Gorbachev's view 'the right policy'.[58]

But Gorbachev warned that not everyone in Russia interpreted this in the same way. There were some who thought with the categories of 'old thinking' and others who asked whether it was good for the most powerful state in the world 'to bomb destitute Afghanistan'. A third group were saying that, 'Look we supported America in her difficult hour, but will she come to meet us halfway on an important problem for us?' Russians did want something back from America in return.[59]

Recent opinion polls on attitudes towards the US have yielded differing results. In March 2002, across 44 regions, one poll showed that just 17 per cent of Russians saw the US as a 'friendly' state. A large 71 per cent thought otherwise.[60] A poll in late March saw 37 per cent of respondents seeing the US as an 'ally' and a similar 38 per cent branding the US an 'opponent'. Twenty-five per cent did not know.[61] These two polls, however, were conducted shortly after the Olympic Games controversy. In late April, another poll, also conducted by the All-Russian Centre for the Study of Public Opinion, indicated that four per cent of Russians felt 'very good' about the US and 55 per cent 'basically good'. Twenty-six per cent felt 'bad' and seven per cent 'very bad'. Eight per cent were undecided.[62] Fluctuations appear to occur quite readily in response to the most recent international developments.

Although the bombing of Iraq provoked hostile criticisms in Russia, wavering was evident by November 2002. Initially, in February 2002, Defence Minister Sergei Ivanov was quick to respond to Bush's remarks about an 'axis of evil'. Russia did not intend to brand North Korea, Iraq and Iran in this manner.[63] In March 2002, however, Ivanov did express concern that Iraq might be developing nuclear weapons and made it clear that Russia supported international monitors going into Iraq.[64] In March, the US and Russia agreed upon a list of goods that could be supplied to Iraq without UN sanction.[65]

Public opinion also showed strong opposition to Russia participating in a US operation to topple Saddam Hussein. In a survey of March 2002, just one per cent of respondents backed Russian involvement in this. Fourteen per cent felt Russia could 'support but not participate', 42 per cent wanted

Russia to stay on the sidelines but remain a US ally in the anti-terrorist coalition, 16 per cent thought Russia should oppose the US and offer diplomatic help to Iraq and four per cent propounded military help to Iraq. A reasonably large 23 per cent was undecided.[66]

As Bush's determination to take on Iraq grew, and against the backdrop of debates about fresh UN resolutions to tackle Iraq and fears of unilateralism triumphing over multilateralism, a similar poll was conducted. In September 2002, just two per cent of respondents in a nationwide survey felt that Russia should participate alongside the US if Bush began a military operation to overthrow Saddam Hussein's regime and 19 per cent backed 'support but not participate'. These were just tiny increases over the March percentages. At one percentage point lower, 41 per cent favoured staying on the sidelines but remaining in the anti-terrorist coalition and two points higher than before, at 18 per cent, wanted to oppose the US and help Iraq. Just two per cent advocated helping Iraq militarily and 18 per cent did not know what Russia should do.[67]

Faced in September 2002 with a slightly different question of 'Can an American military operation in Iraq be justified if Saddam Hussein does not accede to the demands of the UN Security Council regarding controls on production of weapons of mass destruction in Iraq?', eight per cent of respondents said 'definitely' and 20 per cent 'probably'. A higher 14 per cent thought 'definitely not' and a more robust 31 per cent declared 'probably not'. Thus results showed 28 per cent with positive responses and a higher 44 per cent with negative ones. A large percentage – 28 per cent – did not know. There was growing hesitation among the public about what was the appropriate action.[68]

TERRORIST ACTS INSIDE THE RUSSIAN FEDERATION

Putin's resolve to fight international terrorism was fuelled by terrorist attacks in 2002 inside Russia. The first, in Kaspiisk, Daghestan, occurred on 9 May, and received little attention worldwide.[69] By contrast, the second captured world headlines when, on 23 October, 50 armed Chechens seized a theatre in Moscow and held around 800 people hostage. These are both discussed in some detail in other essays in this collection.[70] It is important here, however, to draw attention to the relevance of such attacks to the formulation of contemporary Russian foreign policy.

Putin reaffirmed his resolve to combat terrorism and insisted that Russia would make no '"understandings" with terrorists nor surrender to their blackmail'. Putin attempted to link the attack of 23 October to world terrorism by declaring that there was no doubt that it had been planned in 'foreign terrorist centres. They originated the plan and recruited the perpetrators'.[71] The leader of the theatre siege, Movsar Baraev, dismissed this when a group of journalists was admitted into the theatre on 24 October. Putin nonetheless stepped up his commitment to combating world terrorism with the pledge that Russia would use its army to this end and that:

> ...if anyone uses weapons of mass destruction or the equivalent against our country, Russia will respond with measures commensurate with the threat wherever terrorists, the organizers of their crimes, and their ideological and financial supporters might be.[72]

Related instructions were issued to the General Staff.

In the aftermath of the crisis, Putin likened it to the attacks in New York and called it Russia's 11 September. The magazine *Itogi* gave the message that 11 September and 23 October would together 'set out the global vector of development for the entire international community'.[73] Putin portrayed Russia alongside the US on the global stage as a leader in tackling global terror. Soon after the crisis, Putin met with heads of security agencies to discuss new anti-terrorism measures and ordered a revision of Russia's national security policy.[74] There was talk in Moscow of a 'Putin doctrine' as Russian officials drafted a new security concept.

Putin's foreign policy has become decidedly more aggressive and is now justified in terms of battling international terrorism. His assertiveness was evident when he insisted that because Denmark permitted the World Chechen Congress on its territory, a scheduled meeting with the EU there on Kaliningrad should convene elsewhere. Putin's government pressed Denmark to extradite Chechen separatist envoy Akhmed Zakaev and declared that it would also call for Qatar, Turkey and Georgia to hand over other terrorists.[75]

Riding high on his re-emphasized foreign policy platform of tackling global terrorism, Putin also escalated military activity in Chechnya with 'broad-scale, tough and targeted' operations.[76] This renewed campaign came a week after the Kremlin had said it would reduce troops in Chechnya. Defence Minister Ivanov also called for greater flexibility for the armed forces in dealing with terrorism and announced, somewhat Soviet-style, that:

> We've been receiving more and more information that on the territory of the Chechen Republic, and not just there, preparations are being made for committing more terrorist acts. In several populated areas, recruiting is going on, in this case, for suicide bombers, turning them into zombies.[77]

Putin's and Ivanov's recent proclamations have come in for heavy criticism from human rights activists.[78] Oleg Orlov, head of the Memorial, for instance, stresses that the war has been intensifying over recent months and the announcement of a reduction in troops had been just a public relations device for the West.[79]

Putin's general policy towards Chechnya, according to sociologist and socialist Boris Kagarlitsky, has not changed 'one iota'. The difference is that Russia now links itself more closely to US rhetoric about terrorism, so Russia is not acting alone. Kagarlitsky believes that Bush is happy to see an analogy to his actions because Moscow will be less able to criticize Washington's objectives, namely military intervention in Iraq. He argues that the 'war on terrorism' has become a slogan that is 'an ideological skeleton key that can be used to justify any actions that might seem dubious from the perspective of international law and democratic norms'.[80] Iakov Ettinger of Moscow's Bureau for Human Rights also expressed the view that the US supported Putin in his hostage crisis and said it may list organizations connected to Chechen separatists on its terrorist list in return for a Russian vote of support concerning Iraq in the UN Security Council. Indeed, Putin did support UN Resolution 1441 on Iraq, calling it an acceptable compromise. Ettinger noted that European countries, by contrast, are the ones in Moscow now branded as soft on terrorism for their criticisms of war in Chechnya and of war against Iraq.[81]

The strong link between domestic and foreign policies, evidenced by the impact of the Moscow hostage crisis upon Putin's war on international terrorism and, in turn, the latter used as a justification for more military action and not negotiation over Chechnya, has had a dual effect in Russia. Putin's popularity remains strong and support for his efforts in Chechnya is growing. But human rights organizations are becoming more uneasy and very critical, especially of a new package of amendments passed to Russia's restrictive press law.[82]

With long historical memories, some Russians have started making the link between the state having to fight terrorism today, and the Tsarist state of the nineteenth century and early twentieth century having to battle to put it down. By the end of 2002, the line that 'Russia has often suffered from terror' was circulating in Moscow.[83] This was cast as a justification for a firm foreign policy stance today.

CONCLUSIONS

Although the events of 11 September 2001 offered Russia a chance to return to the world stage and to play its part in the coalition against terrorism, that part did not guarantee the delivery of all items on Putin's agenda. Although there appeared to be a better understanding for a while of the situation in Chechnya and greater sympathy for Russia's difficulties there, criticisms of human rights abuses inflicted by Russia's troops returned, expressed in the EU, US and UN.[84]

Although the hostage crisis in Moscow in October 2002 again won Putin favour in the West, sceptics of his policy in Chechnya have not altered their view even if Washington has struck a deal for backing on Chechnya in return for support on Iraq. At a meeting with the EU in November 2002 to discuss the Russian enclave of Kaliningrad, Putin showed irritation at questions about Russian military tactics in Chechnya and described the rebels as 'religious extremists and international terrorists'.[85] Chris Patten, the EU external relations commissioner, said exchanges on the issue were 'lively' and there was no 'meeting of minds', although agreement on Kaliningrad was reached.[86]

Although the US needed bases in Central Asia from which to launch its war in Afghanistan, it was galling to many Russians that a Western military presence that was not in a hurry to leave was now in states that were not long ago part of the erstwhile Soviet empire and were now in the CIS. US military instructors were also in Georgia providing training in counter-terrorism.

To those Russians sensitive to the fact that Russia has for centuries been surrounded or dominated by enemies and hostile states, be it rule by the Mongols from around 1200 for two and a half centuries or Western interference after the 1917 revolution, Western encroachment coming from the east first and then the south felt uncomfortable, even though the US was meant now to be a friend. Russia's profile may have grown in world politics as a consequence of Putin's reactions to 11 September, then 23 October, and with them some influence, but most of the goods that Putin wanted to be delivered to Russia in return have yet to come. At best, tiny possibilities for Russia are opening in diplomacy, NATO and world trade, with the Jackson-Vanik amendment not yet overturned. Even though the US Senate on 22 May passed a non-binding resolution for normal trade relations with Russia, the amendment was not lifted due to a dispute with Russia over US poultry imports. For domestic nationalist critics, the Jackson-Vanik amendment was now part of the political football of a chicken war.[87] In May 2002, however, the WTO director-general predicted that Russia would be able to join before September 2003 and, in June, the US government finally recognized Russia as a fully-fledged market economy.[88]

And the US superpower remained, almost inevitably, the leader in a world that was unipolar given its overwhelming military superiority, not matched by the EU or any other region. It is not in Bush's leadership style, unlike Clinton's, to be modest about this. Although the US would like as stable a world as possible, and Russia does have a role to play in helping to create this, as seen in Putin's attempts to broker peace over Kashmir between India and Pakistan, it remains the fact that Russia needs the US more than the latter needs the former.[89] Putin, however, is casting his call for a new security concept not just as a response to terrorism but also as a 'reply to NATO'.[90] In many respects, the realist approach to international relations still obtains.

Soviet and Russian relations with the US have been characterized by various periods of enmity, hostile perceptions, crisis, warming, cooperation, goodwill, competition, renewed mistrust, deteriorating relations, tension and again warming in transition to renewed cooperation. Moreover, no period of good relations, whether during Khrushchev's 'peaceful coexistence', détente under Brezhnev, 'new thinking' in Gorbachev's leadership or a pro-Western slant under Yeltsin when Kozyrev was foreign minister, was entirely 'good'. Each of these periods simultaneously endured some strains and tensions with the US. The same obtained between Clinton and Yeltsin and now between Bush and Putin. One tension appeared suddenly in March 2002 when a leaked report suggested that Russia was one of seven states against which the US had contingency plans for a nuclear strike. A flurry of diplomacy ensued to calm nerves and anger.[91]

The system factor of either 'state socialist' or 'in transition to capitalism' does not necessarily wipe out this blend of 'good' marred by 'strain', although it may carry the potential to reduce it. Friendly overtures by Yeltsin and Putin have been accompanied by invective from communists and nationalists against the West, to such an extent under Yeltsin that the Russian president felt compelled to remove Kozyrev and nominate Primakov in his place. The variable of 'ideologically divided society' continues to exert pressure on any leader in relations with the West. This was the case under Gorbachev and Yeltsin and it will continue to impinge on Putin so long as society is divided. The growth of political centrism may, to some extent, dilute the extremes, but Russian centrism itself has a strain of nationalism which acts as a brake on automatic cooperation with the US. Its defining characteristics are not just Russian interests first but a desire for Russian greatness to an extent currently beyond Russia's economic and military means.

A blend of naive pride about what Russia *should* be on the world stage, mixed with lingering humiliation about the implosion of the USSR and loss of empire, topped with hope for future redress of these apparent injustices to long-suffering Russia, makes for unrealistically heightened sensitivities in a global environment of other histories, political cultures and power realities.

The material prerequisites for the dreams of Russia's nationalists to be realized are wanting. At best, Putin's pragmatism may ensure that Russia gets the best international deal that it can in a competitive global context in which Russia can call few shots. The future success of this pragmatism, however, depends upon Putin being able to carry his government, foreign policy, military and defence establishments, parliament and citizens with him. It also hangs, to his chagrin, not just on his concessions to the West, but also on the will of President Bush. Westernizing Russians may want to be equal partners with the US, and even adopt US anti-terrorist rhetoric, but this is not a realistic goal without material back-up.

NOTES

Gratitude is owed to Drummond Bone, former principal at Royal Holloway, for his kind granting of sabbatical leave.

1. Francis Fukuyama, *The End of History and the Last Man* (Harmondsworth: Penguin 1989) p.29.
2. Alex Pravda, 'The Politics of Foreign Policy', in Stephen White, Alex Pravda and Zvi Gitelman (eds), *Developments in Russian Politics 4* (London: Macmillan 1997) pp.208–26; Margot Light, 'Post- Soviet Russian Foreign Policy: The First Decade', in Archie Brown (ed.), *Contemporary Russian Politics: A Reader* (Oxford: OUP 2001) pp.419–28.
3. For fuller discussion, refer to Mary Buckley, 'Russian Perceptions', in Mary Buckley and Sally N. Cummings (eds), *Kosovo: Perceptions of War and Its Aftermath* (London: Continuum 2002) pp.156–75. Note the typographical error in this source that names Defence Minister Sergei Ivanov wrongly as Igor Sergeev.
4. *Rossiiskaia Gazeta*, 26 March 1999, p.2.
5. *Krasnaia Zvezda*, 8 April 1999, p.1; *Vremia MN,* 26 March 1999, p.2.
6. BBC, *Summary of World Broadcasts* (SWB), SU/3492, 25 March 1999, B/4.
7. *Pravda*, 26–29 March 1999, p.1.
8. *Argumenty i Fakty*, no. 14 (April 1999) p.4; *Rossiiskaia Federatsiia Segodnia,* no. 13, 1999, p.2.
9. *Zavtra*, April–May 1999, p.2.
10. *Argumenty i Fakty* (note 8) p.4.
11. *Rossiiskaia Gazeta* (note 4) p.2.
12. Buckley, 'Russian Perceptions', in Buckley and Cummings (eds) (note 3) p.161.
13. Ibid. pp.168–70.
14. Ibid. p.162.
15. Joint Project of the Centre for Public Policy, University of Strathclyde and the Russian Centre for Public Opinion and Market Research at: www.RussiaVotes.org/.
16. www.guardian.co.uk/russia/article/0,2763,578472,00.html.
17. Vlad Sobell, 'Russia Turns West', *The World Today* 57/11 (Nov. 2001) pp.18–19.
18. Quoted in *The Economist*, 27 Oct.–2 Nov. 2001, p.22.
19. For a useful summary, see Sobell, 'Russia Turns West' (note 17).
20. For reports see: www.guardian.co.uk/international/story/0%2C555510%2C00.html; www.hindustantimes.com/nonfram/041001/dlame65.asp; www.csmonitor.com/2001/1015/p13s1-wosc.html; www.newsmax.com/archives/articles/2001/10/3/101626.shtml; www.rediff.com/us/2001/sep/29ny8.htm.
21. www.rferl.org/newsline/2001/10/031001.asp.
22. www.guardian.co.uk/waronterror/story/0,1361,653073,00.html.
23. Buckley, 'Russian Perceptions', in Buckley and Cummings (note 3) p.171.
24. *The Independent,* 14 Nov. 2001, p.8.
25. BBC News, 13 May 2002, 22.00 hours.
26. *Izvestiia*, 26 May 2002, p.1; *Moskovskii Komsomolets*, 25 May 2002, p.1; *Nezavisimaiia Gazeta*, 24 May 2002, p.1; *Krasnaia Zvezda*, 25 May 2002, p.1; www.vip.lenta.ru/26.05.2002.
27. Radio Free Europe/Radio Liberty (RFE/RL) *Newsline*, 5/236, part 1 (14 Dec. 2001) p.1.
28. RFE/RL, *Newsline*, 5/220, part 1 (20 Nov. 2001) p.2.

29. RFE/RL, *Newsline*, 6/97, part 1 (24 May 2002) p.2.
30. RFE/RL, *Newsline*, 5/232, part 1 (10 Dec. 2001) p.2.
31. RFE/RL, *Newsline*, 6/1, part 1 (3 Jan. 2001) p.2.
32. *Krasnaia Zvezda*, 13 Sept. 2001, p.1; RFE/RL, *Newsline* 5/229, part 1 (5 Dec. 2001) p.1.
33. Genadii Ziuganov, 'V Vashingtone voskhishcheny, v Moskve negoduiut': www.kprf.ru/komment.htm.
34. BBC News, 13 May 2002, 22.00 hours; *The Guardian*, 14 May 2002, p.1.
35. Ziuganov, 'V Vashingtone' (note 33).
36. www.zavtra.ru/cgi//veil//data/zavtra/01/415/11.html, p.1.
37. *Rossiiskaia Federatsiia Segodnia*, no. 21, 2001, p.5; www.ldrp.ru/Vistup_vvzh/vistup_2001_ 10_29_soiuzmolod.htm, p. 2; RFE/RL, *Newsline*, 5/229, part 1 (5 Dec. 2001) pp.1–2.
38. *Rossiskaia Federatsiia Segodnia*, no. 21, 2001, pp.5–6, 20–21; www.sps.ru/sps/16637.
39. Boris Usviatsov, 'Ob'iatiia po-Amerikanskii', *Rossiskaia Federatsiia Segodnia*, no. 5, 2002, pp.58–60.
40. 'Tochka Zreniia na Problemy Chlenov Soveta Federatsii i Deputatov Gosudarstvennoi Dumy', Usviatsov (note 39) pp.58–60.
41. Usviatsov (note 39) p.60.
42. Nationwide VCIOM survey, 25–28 Jan. 2002, N=1600, at: www.RussiaVotes.org.
43. RFE/RL, *Newsline*, 6/51, part 1 (18 March 2002) p.3.
44. RFE/RL, *Newsline*, 6/50, part I (15 March 2002) p.2.
45. RFE/RL, *Newsline*, 6/47, part I (12 March 2002) p.2; RFE/RL, *Newsline*, 6/50, part 1 (15 March 2002) p.2. For earlier arguments, see *Nezavisimoe Voennoe Obozrenie*, no. 43 (265), 23 Nov. 2001, p.1.
46. RFE/RL, *Newsline*, 6/50, part 1 (15 March 2002) p.2.
47. RFE/RL, *Newsline*, 6/71, part I (16 April 2002) p.1.
48. *The Independent*, 29 May 2002, p.10.
49. Nationwide VCIOM surveys, 19–22 April 2002, N=1603 at: <www.RussiaVotes. org>.
50. RFE/RL *Newsline* (note 44) p.2.
51. <www.rferl.org/nca/features/2002/04/04042002081008.asp, p.1>
52. Ibid.
53. Ibid. pp.2–3. See also: <www.strana.ru/stories/01/10/08/1714/68634.html>.
54. Ibid.
55. Ibid. p.2.
56. Ibid.
57. Ibid.
58. Mikhail Gorbachev, 'Ot kolitsii protiv terrora – k spravedlivomu mirovomu poriadku' in *Rossiiskaia gazeta* at: <www.rg.ru/Anons/arc_2001/1020/1.shtm>.
59. Ibid.
60. RFE/RL *Newsline* 6/46, part I (11 March 2002) p.2.
61. Nationwide VCIOM surveys, 22–25 March 2002, N=1600, at: <www.RussiaVotes.org>.
62. Nationwide VCIOM surveys, 19–22 April 2002, N=1603, at: ibid.
63. RFE/RL *Newsline* 6/23, part I (5 Feb. 2002) p.1.
64. RFE/RL *Newsline*, 6/51, part 1 (18 March 2002) p.3.
65. RFE/RL *Newsline*, 6/60, part 1 (29 March 2002) p.1.
66. Nationwide VCIOM surveys, 22–26 Feb. 2002, N=1600, at: <www.RussiaVotes.org>.
67. Ibid., 20–23 Sept. 2002, N=1600 at: <www.RussiaVotes.org>.
68. Ibid.
69. RFERL, *Newsline* 6/86, part 1 (9 May 2002) p.1; ibid, 6/87, part 1 (10 May 2002) p.1; ibid. 6/88, part 1 (13 May 2002) p.2.
70. *Izvestiia*, 24 Oct. 2002, p.1; *Izvestia*, 25 Oct. 2002, p.1.
71. Ibid., pp.1–2, 25 Oct. 2002.
72. RFERL, *Newsline* 6/204, part 1 (29 Oct. 2002) p.1; *Izvestiia*, 31 Oct. 2002.
73. www.rferl.org/nca/features/2002/11/05112002161104.asp; *Itogi*, 5 Nov. 2002.
74. *Izvestiia*, 28 Oct. 2002. See also: www.rferl.org/nca/features/2002/1030102002150931.asp.
75. Ibid. For discussion of 'crisis' in relations with Denmark, see *Izvestiia*, 3 Nov. 2002.

76. www.rferl.org/nca/features/2002/11/04112002154629.asp.
77. Ibid. For an interview with Ivanov on how to tackle terrorism, see *Izvestiia,* 4 Nov. 2002.
78. Ibid., p.2.
79. Ibid.
80. www.rferl.org/nca/features/2002/11/05112002161104.asp.
81. Ibid.
82. www.rferl.org/nca/features/2002/11/01112002180338.asp.
83. *Izvestiia,* 1 Nov. 2002.
84. RFE/RL *Newsline,* 6/74, part I (19 April 2002) p.2.
85. *The Guardian,* 12 Nov. 2002, p.16.
86. Ibid. For Russian coverage, see *Izvestiia,* 13 Nov. 2002.
87. RFE/RL, *Newsline,* Vol. 6, No. 96, part I, 23 May 2002, p.1.
88. RFE/RL *Newsline,* 6/99, part 1 (29 May 2002) p.2; Ibid. 6/106, part 1, (7 June 2002) p.1.
89. *The Independent,* 3 June 2002, p.8.
90. *Itogi,* 5 Nov. 2002; *Nezavisimaia gazeta,* 6 Nov. 2002. For a critical view that 'NATO is not everyone', see *Pravda,* 12 Nov. 2002.
91. RFE/RL *Newsline,* 6/48, part I (13 March 2002) p.1.

NATO Enlargement and Eastern Opinion

IAN MCALLISTER AND STEPHEN WHITE

The collapse of communist rule throughout Eastern Europe at the end of the 1980s placed new challenges before governments and publics. East and West had been moving together as the decade advanced, and the Paris Charter, signed in November 1990, was generally agreed to mark the formal end of the Cold War. On 1 July 1991, the Warsaw Treaty Organization was wound up; and by the end of the year Russia, under its first post-communist president, Boris Yeltsin, was calling for a much broader association with the Western states which had formerly been the USSR's military and political antagonists. He saw the Western countries, Yeltsin told the UN Security Council, 'not just as partners, but as allies', and the Camp David Declaration that he concluded with US President George Bush shortly afterwards referred to the 'friendship and partnership' on which their new relations were based.[1]

The end of the Cold War, in fact, left many issues unresolved and posed some that were entirely new. Russia, though post-communist, was still a nuclear power, and its future political direction was uncertain. The other Soviet republics moved to divest themselves of nuclear weapons, but they had still to make a choice between the security systems of their former NATO opponents and an alliance with their Russian neighbour. Three of the post-communist states collapsed into their constituent republics, and there were challenges to national boundaries throughout the region. How could Western countries abandon their long-standing security alliances in these circumstances? The nature of security, in any case, had changed. It was no longer a confrontation between two military alliances: there were new groupings of allies, within and across the East-West divide, and there were new concerns about nuclear safety, transnational crime and other forms of 'soft security'.

Beyond these policy issues were wider questions of perception and identity. 'Europe', after all, was a community of shared values, not just an area within which there should be free movement of labour and capital; and it was a military alliance that extended across both sides of the Atlantic. Did citizens in the newly post-communist states think of themselves as part of this system of values, and natural allies of the 'other democracies'? Or were they more likely to feel part of a Slavic community, based on language, culture and family associations, if no longer ideology? Equally, who were their 'friends' and who were their 'enemies' in these new circumstances? Were Europe's post-communist citizens concerned about their security environment, or was there a greater sense of assurance now that the hostile confrontation of the Cold War years had ended? And did their views, in either event, have any implications for public policy in states that were still authoritarian if no longer Marxist-Leninist?

These are the issues we seek to explore in this essay, basing our account upon several bodies of evidence gathered in Russia, Ukraine, Belarus and Moldova ten years after the formal end of communist rule. With colleagues, we conducted more than a hundred interviews at decision-making level among ministry officials, presidential staffers, parliamentary committees, party leaders, businessmen and policy advisors. In addition, we commissioned 18 focus groups, one of them in each country with junior officers. We examined the documentary evidence, including defence and security doctrines where they existed. But our primary source here is a set of nationally representative surveys conducted in each of our four countries – Russia, Ukraine, Belarus and Moldova – in the first half of 2000, and in Russia alone in the summer of 2001. Fuller details are provided in an appendix.

Our surveys took place a year after NATO had conducted a military offensive in the Balkans, and about a year after it had incorporated three former communist countries – the Czech Republic, Hungary and Poland – as full members. There had, admittedly, been a 'Partnership for Peace' that had eventually embraced all of the countries of the region; Russia had agreed a 'founding act' with the alliance in May 1997, and Ukraine a 'charter for a distinctive partnership' in July 1997. But NATO's new security concept, adopted in the spring of 1999, appeared to hold out a much more ambitious role for the alliance in the future, with a membership that might extend still further (including former Soviet republics and not just former communist countries), and with a sphere of activity that might take its peacekeeping forces well outside the territory of its members and possibly into former Soviet space. The implications of this more far-reaching doctrine were not lost on many of the decision-makers we interviewed.

Our surveys also took place before the atrocities of 11 September 2001 and the establishment of an international alliance dedicated to the conduct of a 'war on terrorism'. The Russian president's position had clearly moved much closer to that of his Western counterparts, particularly in the sharing of intelligence data; but official spokesmen warned against extending the campaign to other countries, and even the existing degree of cooperation was enough to arouse deep misgivings within a traditionally-minded high command. It was easy enough, moreover, for a Russian president to change a policy stance; it was much less clear that there had been a deeper reorientation of popular attitudes across the entire region. Our concerns here are with popular attitudes before 11 September, but we return to the issue in our conclusion.

First of all we ask: How did ordinary citizens in our four countries view their security environment? And then: What were their attitudes towards NATO itself, as a security threat or, for some, an organization they should try to join?

THE SECURITY ENVIRONMENT

We asked, first of all, if our respondents thought there was any reason to fear a military attack within the coming five years. Not many did so, although there was less complacency in Russia than in Ukraine, Belarus or Moldova. In Russia alone, where we asked the same question in 2000 and 2001, just four per cent thought an attack was 'very likely', and 20 per cent thought it was 'likely'. But a much larger 56 per cent thought any attack was 'unlikely', and a further 19 per cent thought it was 'very unlikely'. In Belarus, Moldova and Ukraine, similar numbers thought an attack was likely or a possibility, but still larger proportions – about a third – thought a military attack was 'very unlikely'. Overall, three times as many thought a military attack was unlikely as thought it was likely, and more than five times as many thought it was very unlikely as thought it was very likely to take place.

A 'threat', of course, could come from any quarter. And so we asked our respondents if 'any of the following countries could be a substantial threat to [their country's] security'. There was some variation in the responses that were available in each of our four countries. In Ukraine, Belarus and Moldova we asked about the potential threat from Iran, and in Russia about the threat from Iraq. Equally, we did not ask a question that directly related to a perceived threat from NATO in Belarus, Moldova or Ukraine. We repeated our questions in Russia in the summer of 2001, and it is these figures that are reproduced in Table 1 (see p.51). They differed very little from those that emerged when we asked our questions for the first time in the early months of 2000.

Perhaps the clearest conclusion is that, ten years after the end of the Cold War, the US is still seen as the greatest potential threat to the security of post-communist Europe. The US, moreover, was seen as the most serious potential threat not just in Russia, but in each of our four countries. In Russia, NATO was thought to represent almost as serious a threat, but it was clearly a related one (over two-thirds of those who thought NATO was a 'big threat' took the same view of the US, and vice versa). In Russia alone we asked about the potential security threat from non-Russian minorities within the state itself. Not surprisingly, in the light of the bombings of civilian buildings in the late summer of 1999 and the continuing Chechen war, the risk was seen as very real, and hardly less than the potential threat from the US and NATO. But domestic insurgency is a problem that is specific to Russia (internal differences in Moldova have for the moment been resolved by de facto secession), and elsewhere in the region security was normally conceived in terms of external aggression.

The next most serious threat across the region, though less clearly in Russia than in the other three countries, was Iran or Iraq (Iraq was asked in Russia only, and Iran only in Belarus, Moldova and Ukraine). In Russia, no more than about a fifth of our respondents saw Iraq or China as a potential threat; China shares the world's longest land border with the Russian Federation, and there are long-standing patterns of association with both countries across the communist and post-communist periods. In the other three countries, rather larger proportions (up to a third or more) saw Iran as a potential threat. Indeed, in these three countries Iran consistently ranked second as a potential security threat, after the US and ahead (in Belarus, well ahead) of any threat from their Slavic neighbour.

Finally, there was some threat from the rest of Europe, from the EU and its individual members, or from other post-Soviet republics; but the level of threat was much lower than in the case of the US and NATO, or even Iran/Iraq and China. Belarusians, who lost nearly a third of their population in the Second World War, had perhaps the most reason to be apprehensive about Germany, and about the EU of which Germany is the largest and most important member. Russians, at the other extreme, were less concerned about a threat from Western Europe, and they were less concerned about the threat from Ukraine and Belarus than either Ukrainians or Belarusians were about the threat from Russia. Most concerned of all about the threat from other former Soviet republics were the Moldovans; but there were special circumstances, in that our survey was limited to the area under the control of the Chisinau government. Accordingly, it excluded the self-styled Dniestr Republic in the north of the national territory, where government still rested upon the force of Russian arms at the time of our survey.

Overall, there were distinctive threat profiles across the region. Russians were more concerned about their traditional adversary, the US, and about the NATO alliance it dominated; after that, their concerns were more domestic than external. Ukrainians, Belarusians and Moldovans shared the concern about the US, and were relatively more worried about the other states that might represent a potential threat to their security, including Iran, China and Western Europe as well as Russia itself. Their responses were what might have been expected from smaller states with a different

TABLE 1
SOURCES OF SECURITY THREATS, 2000–2001
(PER CENT SAYING 'BIG' OR 'SOME THREAT')

	Belarus	Moldova	Russia	Ukraine
US	50	46	47	41
NATO	n.a.	n.a.	44	n.a.
Non-Russians	n.a.	n.a.	45	n.a.
Iran/Iraq	36	33	19	35
China	27	31	22	29
Germany	24	23	10	18
EU members	22	16	17	15
Russia/Ukraine	12	31	8	25
(N)	(935)	(884)	(2,000)	(1,447)

Source: Authors' surveys, 2000 and (in Russia) 2001; further details are included in the appendix.
Notes: The question wording was: 'Do you think any of the following countries could be a substantial threat to the security of [country]'? Respondents in Russia were allowed to select Iraq, but elsewhere Iran; Russians were allowed to select Ukraine, but in the other countries respondents were invited to select Russia.
n.a. = not asked. Estimates exclude 'don't knows' and refusals.

geopolitical location, and less powerful armed forces. Their geopolitical location, at the western end of the former Soviet area, also made it more realistic for them to consider a military, or other forms of, association with the member countries of NATO and the EU.

These were responses for whole societies; but were there important variations by gender, age, political orientation or (particularly in Ukraine) region? We set out the evidence in Table 2.

There was a high degree of consistency, first of all, in the proportion in each of our four countries which perceived some degree of threat to their

TABLE 2
THREAT PERCEPTIONS, SOCIO-ECONOMIC STATUS AND IDEOLOGY
(ZERO-ORDER CORRELATIONS WITH THREAT PERCEPTIONS)

	Belarus	Moldova	Russia	Ukraine
Gender (male)	.09**	.03	.00	.02
Age (single years)	-.09**	.00	.01	-.07**
Tertiary education	.01	.04	-.01	.03
Urban resident	.02	.00	-.03	.05*
Ideology				
Left	.07**	.04	n.a.	-.02
Centre	.04	.05	n.a.	.08**
Right	.05	.03	n.a.	.02
(N)	(1,090)	(1,000)	(1,940)	(1,590)

Source: as for Table 1.
Notes: * statistically significant at p<.05, ** p<.01.
Threat perceptions are the number of threats mentioned by each respondent.

own security. Just over four out of every ten respondents thought none of the countries we listed in Table 1 represented a potential threat to their security, the proportion varying from 41 per cent in Belarus and Russia to 42 per cent in Moldova and 47 per cent in Ukraine. At the other end of the scale, between three and eight per cent mentioned all six countries as threats, with the highest level of concern among Moldovan respondents. The average number of threats mentioned varied from 1.4 in Russia and Ukraine to 1.7 in Belarus and Moldova.

There were few associations, however, between threat perceptions and socio-economic status or ideology. Men were more likely to mention threats in Belarus, but not in any of the other three countries; the young saw more threats in Belarus and Ukraine; and city dwellers saw more threats in Ukraine. But the findings were more notable for the absence than the presence of strong patterns, with the partial exception of age. Ideology, too, played only a limited role in shaping threat perceptions, despite the legacy of the Cold War. In Belarus it was those on the left who were more likely to see a threat to their security, while in Ukraine it was those in the centre, and in Moldova (we have no comparable data for Russia) ideology had no statistically observable impact at all.

THE NATO DIMENSION

The US and the NATO alliance were clearly regarded throughout the region as the most substantial threat to the security of individual countries. None of our four countries, however, had been a member of the alliance, and none had ever been attacked by its member nations. How clearly, in these circumstances, did ordinary people across the region perceive it? Did they even understand what the alliance was? We asked respondents in each case if they could tell us, giving them four options: (i) a trading bloc, (ii) a United Nations peacekeeping agency, (iii) a US-led military alliance including the countries of Western Europe (the 'right' answer); or (iv) anything else. We asked a similar question about the EU, inviting our respondents to choose its headquarters from a list of five European capitals. About a third were able to identify the EU headquarters, not many more than might have been expected to select it randomly; but about half were able to identify NATO as a military alliance. This meant, by the same token, that about half of our respondents – slightly more outside Russia – were unable to answer, or misinformed.

We asked other questions about NATO enlargement: both the enlargement that had taken place, and the further enlargement, perhaps including some former Soviet states and not just former communist states, that was under discussion at the time of our survey. The responses we obtained are set out in Table 3 (see opposite).

We asked, first, if the incorporation of the Czech Republic, Hungary and Poland had represented a threat to the security of the four countries within which we conducted our investigation. About a third of our Russian respondents saw some reason to be concerned, and about a fifth of our Belarusians, but levels of concern elsewhere in the region were much lower. Close to half of our Moldovan and Ukrainian respondents, indeed, saw no risk to their security whatsoever from the incorporation of the new members, although in the case of Ukraine it involved a state with which they share a common border.

What if the alliance expanded further, including former Soviet republics and not simply the countries of Central and Eastern Europe? There were greater levels of concern in almost every case (compare the upper and lower panels of Table 3), and particularly in Russia, where NATO action may already have 'aggravated East-West relations by raising the perceived level of threat for those whose predispositions are to view Western actions benignly'.[2] Russians were still likely to see no serious threat to their security in the enlargement of the alliance that had already taken place. But almost half of our Russian respondents saw some threat to their security in a further enlargement. Belarusians were also divided, although less evenly, and

TABLE 3
ATTITUDES TO ENLARGEMENT, 2000–2001 (PERCENTAGES)

(A)   *Attitudes to Czech, Hungarian and Polish membership*

	Belarus	Moldova	Russia	Ukraine
Major threat	5	3	6	2
Some threat	20	15	29	7
Not much threat	44	27	28	36
No threat	31	55	37	42
(N)	(866)	(812)	(1,943)	(1,266)

(B)   *Attitudes to further enlargement*

	Belarus	Moldova	Russia	Ukraine
Major threat	8	5	14	5
Some threat	29	10	31	13
Not much threat	38	29	26	36
No threat	25	57	29	46
(N)	(825)	(768)	(1,941)	(1,213)

Source: as Table 1.
Note: The question wording was (A) 'After the collapse of the Soviet Union the Czech Republic, Hungary and Poland joined NATO. Do you think this represents a threat to the security of our country?'; (B) 'Do you think that if other East European countries, including former Soviet republics [in Russia: the Baltic republics], also joined NATO, it would represent a very big/fairly big/not very big/no threat at all to the security of our country?'

substantial numbers were unable to form an opinion. Moldovans and Ukrainians, once again, were the least concerned; more than three-quarters saw no reason to regard a future enlargement of NATO as a threat to their security, and there were more who had no opinion than who were opposed to it.

If those who resisted the further enlargement of NATO were the 'opponents of NATO', what kind of people were they? Older, less educated communist supporters, or a more representative cross-section of the population? We set out our evidence in Table 4, which relates the numbers that saw further expansion as a 'major threat' or 'some threat' to a range of social and attitudinal characteristics. The results suggest that a variety of factors are consistently significant, the most important of which is the perception of a security threat: the more security threats that are mentioned, the greater the probability of seeing NATO enlargement as a threat. The effect of such perceptions in Belarus is particularly important, perhaps because of its proximity to the main NATO countries; indeed, the impact of this single measure is more important in shaping views about NATO in that country than either the socio-economic or the ideology variables combined.

Age is an important factor in three of the four countries examined, the exception being Moldova. Older respondents, reflecting their socialization in the Cold War years, are significantly more likely to oppose NATO enlargement, net of other factors. The remaining socio-economic variables

TABLE 4
NATO ENLARGEMENT, SOCIO-ECONOMIC STATUS
AND SECURITY THREATS (STANDARDISED REGRESSION COEFFICIENTS)

	Belarus	Moldova	Russia	Ukraine
Gender (male)	-.04	-.11**	-.01	-.12**
Age (single years)	.12**	.01	.08**	.14**
Tertiary education	-.07*	-.01	.02	-.09**
Urban resident	.01	.01	.02	-.08**
Ideology				
Left	.07*	.03	n.a.	.07**
Centre	-.11**	-.02	n.a.	-.09**
Right	-.06*	-.10**	n.a.	-.16**
Security threats	.34**	.13**	.23**	.09**
Constant	7.54	7.37	6.32	7.66
Adj R-squared	.14	.03	.06	.10
(N)	(1,090)	(1,000)	(1,940)	(1,590)

Source: as for Table 1.
Notes: ** Statistically significant at p<.01, * p<.05.
          Ordinary least squares regression analysis showing standardised (beta) coefficients predicting the probability of viewing NATO enlargement as a threat. The dependent variable combines the two items in Table 3.

are less consistent: being female is associated with the perception of NATO as a greater threat in all four countries, but the effect is statistically significant in only two, Moldova and Ukraine. And tertiary education is associated with pro-NATO views in Belarus and Ukraine, but not in Moldova or Russia. Finally, ideology influences views in the expected directions, with those placing themselves on the left opposing NATO enlargement, those on the centre and right taking the opposing view.

But as well as those who opposed further enlargement, there were those who were unconcerned by it; and similarly, there were those who favoured membership as well as those who disliked it. We asked, straightforwardly, if any of our respondents favoured the idea of membership; our results are set out in Table 5. The picture is a very varied one. By a substantial margin, our Moldovan respondents were the most enthusiastic about membership: less, it would seem, because of any concern about their security than because of a wish to associate as closely as possible with the rich Western countries and their international organizations, and perhaps to balance the Russian military presence in Transdnistria. Elsewhere, a very substantial minority of our respondents thought there was something to be said for membership, but there were considerable and varying levels of uncertainty (even among those who favoured membership substantial numbers confessed they had no idea what NATO was, and another proportion identified it incorrectly). Ukrainian opinion was evenly balanced; Belarusians were more opposed than favourable; and our Russian respondents were still more likely to be opposed, although here as elsewhere there was substantial support for both positions.

Who were the NATO supporters? On the evidence of our surveys, they were in many ways the inverse opposite of those who thought the further enlargement of the alliance would prejudice their security interests. Across our four countries, social characteristics such as gender, age and education made relatively little difference: the most substantial effects were in

TABLE 5
ATTITUDES TO NATO MEMBERSHIP, 2000–2001 (PERCENTAGES)

	Belarus	Moldova	Russia	Ukraine
Strongly positive	8	30	6	16
Positive	35	46	35	34
Negative	35	16	41	29
Strongly negative	22	8	18	21
(N)	(729)	(789)	(1,868)	(1,145)

Source: As for Table 1.
    The question wording was 'In your opinion, if [country] became a member of NATO, would it be very good/quite good/not very good/very bad?'

Ukraine, where youth and higher living standards were associated with higher levels of support for membership. In general, there were much clearer associations with a series of attitudinal dimensions: left-right self-placement, party family, Soviet nostalgia, and support for membership of the EU, all in the expected direction. For instance, supporters of EU membership were about three times as likely as the sample as a whole to support membership of NATO, but those who regretted the demise of the USSR were about three times as likely to be opposed.

A NEW RELATIONSHIP?

Formally, NATO and its Eastern counterparts are negotiating a new relationship, within the context of a commitment on the NATO side to further expansion. A new relationship of this kind will not be submitted to a popular vote in Russia or the other former Soviet republics, and it is unlikely to figure prominently in future elections in those countries. There may, indeed, be some domestic advantage for Russian leaders from a new relationship with the Western alliance if it leads to a greater willingness to take Russian interests into account in international decision-making, and if it moderates foreign criticism of the Russian government's conduct in Chechnya. The post-communist nations, as in the communist period, have centralized political systems within which elite choices are decisive – at least in the short term.

There is little evidence, at the same time, that popular attitudes have shifted significantly in a Western direction, at any rate in Russia. The survey evidence over the entire period since 1990 shows that Russians were most hostile towards the US in the summer of 1999, in the immediate aftermath of the NATO bombing campaign in Kosovo; but there was only a short-term improvement after 11 September, and by the spring of 2002 there was more popular hostility towards the US than there had been at any point in the first half of the 1990s.[3] The patterning of opinion is also unlikely to have shifted noticeably from the position that we have set out here: with older respondents, for instance, considerably more hostile towards NATO enlargement and towards the possibility of their own country's membership.

We have argued elsewhere that public opinion may best be seen as a 'veto group' in such matters.[4] Attitudes to NATO are part of a wider debate about the future orientation of the post-communist countries: towards integration with each other (a 'Slavic choice'), or towards integration with the West (a 'Western choice'). Issues of this kind are rarely posed in national elections, but this owes much to the fact that each of these positions has a substantial constituency that is committed to its support, and which would vigorously resist a choice in the other direction. Relations with

NATO appear to fit within the same framework, although constituencies of supporters and opponents are less distinct. In turn, it is likely that domestic opinion will impose limits upon the extent to which the Russian president and his counterparts in Slavic Europe will be able to commit themselves entirely to the Western alliance that was for so long their global enemy.

APPENDIX

Nationally representative surveys were conducted in each of the four countries – Belarus, Moldova, Russia, Ukraine – using a common questionnaire and a well-established local agency.

Our survey in Belarus was conducted by Novak under the direction of Andrei Vardomatsky. Fieldwork took place between 13 and 27 April 2000. There were 62 sampling points, and 90 interviewers conducted face-to-face interviews in respondents' homes. The total number of interviews was 1,090, using the agency's normal three-stage stratified sampling model to secure representation of the resident population aged 18 and over. All seven of the country's regions were included.

In Moldova our survey was carried out by Opinia under the direction of Tudor Danii, in association with Socis of Kyiv. Fieldwork took place between 12 and 19 February 2000. The universe for the study was the resident population of Moldova aged 18 and over, excluding residents of the Pridnestrovskii region and the city of Bender in the self-declared republic of Transdnistria, which is disproportionately Russian in population. A multi-stage stratified sample was constructed in accordance with Opinia's normal practices; 111 interviewers were employed, who conducted 1,000 face-to-face interviews in respondents' homes. In addition, 37 monitors checked all stages of the fieldwork.

In Russia our surveys were conducted by the All-Russian Centre for the Study of Public Opinion (VTsIOM), in association with the Centre for the Study of Public Policy at the University of Strathclyde. Fieldwork took place between 19 and 29 January 2000 and between 17 June and 3 July 2001. In the former case, the universe was the resident population of the Russian Federation aged 16 and over, and 2,003 interviews were conducted on a face-to-face basis in respondents' homes (our results are based on the 1,940 interviews that took place with those aged 18 and over). A four-stage stratified sample was constructed in accordance with the agency's normal practices. Interviews took place in 107 primary sampling units in 38 of the 89 subjects of the Federation; 193 interviewers were employed, and 16 per cent of the interviews themselves were monitored by agency supervisors. In the latter case the universe consisted of Russian Federation residents aged 18 and over, excluding soldiers, convicts and those of no fixed address.

Interviews took place in 195 primary sampling units in 42 different subjects of the Federation; 197 interviewers were employed, yielding a total of 2,000 interviews. VTsIOM field supervisors controlled 15 per cent of interviews with 147 callbacks at the respondent's household and 152 were checked by telephone. The sample was weighted according to gender, age and education to align it with the population as defined by the state statistical office.

In Ukraine our survey was conducted by the Kyiv International Institute of Sociology under the direction of Vladimir Paniotto and Valeriya Karuk. The questionnaire was piloted between 28 and 31 January and fieldwork took place between 18 February and 3 March 2000. A four-stage stratified sample was constructed, and 110 primary sampling units were employed. A total of 125 interviewers took part; they conducted 1,600 interviews on a face-to-face basis in respondents' homes of which ten per cent were subject to a check by supervisors, yielding a valid total of 1,590.

NOTES

We acknowledge in each case the support of the UK Economic and Social Research Council through grant L213252007 to Stephen White, Margot Light and John Löwenhardt.

1. See Stephen White, *Russia's New Politics* (Cambridge: CUP 2000) p.222.
2. William Zimmerman, 'Survey Research and Russian Perspectives on NATO Expansion', *Post-Soviet Affairs* 17/3 (July–Sept. 2001) p.260.
3. See VTsIOM, *Press-vypusk No. 8*, 3 April 2002: www.wciom.ru/wciom/new/press/press020404_htm, accessed 23 April 2002.
4. Stephen White, Ian McAllister, Margot Light and John Lowenhardt, 'A European or a Slavic Choice? Foreign Policy and Public Attitudes in Post-Soviet Europe', *Europe-Asia Studies* 54/2 (March 2002) pp.181–202.

A Bumpy Road to An Unknown Destination?
NATO-Russia Relations, 1991–2002

MARTIN A. SMITH

This essay traces the evolution of the NATO-Russia relationship from 1991 to 2002. The approach adopted is to divide this period into six distinct phases. These illustrate the complexities of the relationship and also help to bring out the core underlying themes that have marked relations over their first decade.

The distinct phases in NATO-Russia relations since 1991 have been, first, a fragile honeymoon lasting from the end of 1991 to the late summer of 1993. This was followed by a noticeable deterioration over 1994 and 1995 and then attempts to construct a new 'special relationship'. These efforts were seriously challenged, but not permanently ruptured, during the Kosovo crisis of 1998–99. Following the Kosovo settlement of June 1999, a slow, deliberate policy of gradual restoration and development of relations was pursued by the Russian side. This was still being applied when the events of 11 September 2001 ushered in expectations, in some quarters, of more dramatic and qualitative enhancements. The discussions that follow will examine and discuss each of these phases in turn before overall themes in the relationship are identified and briefly assessed in the conclusion.

FRAGILE HONEYMOON

In December 1991, Russian President Boris Yeltsin chose to make relations with NATO the subject of his first significant foreign policy initiative. He dispatched a letter to the leaders of NATO governments, then meeting in Brussels, declaring that 'today we are raising the question of Russia's membership of NATO' as a 'long-term political aim'.[1] Viewed as a piece of political theatre, this initiative certainly succeeded. It caught international attention and made headlines worldwide, especially in the NATO countries. In substantive terms, the general Western attitude to the Yeltsin letter was that the Russian government did not really intend to join NATO. Rather, the letter was seen as a strong political and diplomatic signal to the effect that the new Russian state saw good relations with NATO and its members as a key foreign policy priority. Thus, no specific Western answer was given to what was considered to be the purely hypothetical question of Russian membership. In the short term, the Yeltsin letter played an important role in creating the 'honeymoon' atmosphere in relations with NATO, right at the start of Russia's independent existence.

This did not mean that Russian leaders were prepared to accept everything that NATO might consider doing. Enlargement was a potential bone of contention from an early stage, even for supposed liberals in the Russian leadership. During 1992 and the first half of 1993, potential tensions over this issue remained latent. In the late summer of 1993, however, NATO enlargement suddenly broke cover as an issue. Ironically, the debate was initiated by President Yeltsin. On an official visit to Poland in late August, he agreed to a joint declaration with the then Polish president, Lech Walesa, which included the statement that:

> The presidents touched on the matter of Poland's intention to join NATO. President L. Walesa set forth Poland's well-known position on this count, which was met with understanding by President B. N. Yeltsin. *In the long term, such a decision taken by a sovereign Poland in the interests of overall European integration does not go against the interests of other states, including the interests of Russia* [emphasis added].[2]

Yeltsin's apparent endorsement of Polish aspirations to NATO membership (repeated in the case of the Czech Republic on a visit to Prague immediately following his Polish tour) was instrumental in transforming the political landscape. Hitherto, outside Central Europe the debate, insofar as it had existed, had been conducted largely amongst analysts and think tanks with little obvious impact on policy-makers. After August 1993, however, enlargement was to become increasingly the dominant theme in the whole NATO-Russia relationship. The apparent green light from the Russian president was seized upon by Central European leaders, and sympathetic officials within NATO governments, most especially in the US.

Why had Yeltsin signed up to the Warsaw Declaration? It is crucial to note the significance of the exact wording of the agreed text. This stated, as noted, that Polish accession to NATO 'in the interests of overall European integration' would not threaten Russia's interests. The Russian foreign ministry subsequently bemoaned the frequency with which Western officials and commentators chose to overlook this qualification when asserting that Russia had simply assented to NATO enlargement per se. In a commentary published in *Segodnya* in early September 1993, foreign ministry official Vyacheslav Yelagin set out the ministry's basic line. This was, first, one opposing the *rapid* enlargement of NATO membership, while recognizing that former Warsaw Pact states had the right to join if they so chose. Second, according to Yelagin, the foreign ministry's preference was for 'strengthening and improving such structures as Conference on Security and Co-operation in Europe [CSCE] and the North Atlantic Cooperation Council', that is, bodies within which Russia had a seat. Finally, implicit in Yelagin's argument was that Russia, as a great power, should develop some kind of special relationship with NATO *before* any enlargement into Central Europe was considered.[3]

In mid-September 1993, President Yeltsin addressed a letter to the US, Germany, France and the UK, setting out similar views on the future of European security. Its core message was that 'security must be indivisible and must rest on pan-European structures'. Otherwise, he asserted, there was a risk of 'neo-isolation of [Russia] as opposed to its natural introduction into the Euro-Atlantic space'.[4]

There is also some evidence of disappointment amongst Russians in the political leadership that Yeltsin's original December 1991 signal had not, as they saw it, been picked up and acted upon by NATO. Some, it seems, had taken the idea of eventual Russian membership seriously. Sergei Karaganov, a member of Yeltsin's Presidential Council, argued that NATO enlargement into Central Europe alone 'means a strengthening of a nation's opposition here and also geopolitical isolation of the country, so what we are offering – why not Russia. Russia has asked for membership two years ago.'[5]

Yeltsin himself, although not reiterating the Russian membership theme, indicated that he expected a better response from NATO.[6] As he put it in his September 1993 letter, 'we favor a situation where the relations between our country and NATO would be by several degrees warmer than those between the Alliance and Eastern Europe'. NATO leaders could not have asked for a clearer statement of what the president wanted: a 'special relationship', which elevated Russia's status above that of NATO's other eastern interlocutors and so recognized its status as a great power.

DETERIORATION

There were three main reasons why official Russian attitudes towards NATO grew more suspicious during 1994 and the first half of 1995. Prominent was a belief that Russia had been duped about the true nature and aims of the Partnership for Peace (PfP) scheme, which NATO members had unveiled at a January 1994 summit meeting.[7]

A crisp summary of the major concerns of the opponents of PfP was provided by political scientist Vladislav Chernov in an article in *Nezavisimaya Gazeta* in February 1994. He argued that:

- The PfP's 'motive force' was made up 'primarily of the anti-Russia sentiments of our former friends'.
- The PfP was a subterfuge designed to 'ensure a US military presence in Poland and Hungary'.
- Given a focus within PfP on bringing former Soviet and Central European armed forces up to NATO standards, the programme would work to the detriment of Russian arms manufacturers who had traditionally dominated the market in these regions.[8]

Despite internal opposition, in early spring 1994 it appeared as if the proponents of Russia's joining PfP were gaining the upper hand in its domestic debates. That it did not do so was due principally to the use of NATO airpower against Serb forces in Bosnia – the second reason why Russia's relations with NATO deteriorated.

Although NATO had formally stood ready to use airpower in support of UN relief and protection efforts in Bosnia since the previous summer, its first serious threat to do so was not made until February 1994. The first actual air strikes took place three months later, at pretty well exactly the time that had been pencilled in for a PfP signing visit by the Russian foreign minister to NATO Headquarters.

However, it is important to note that the use of airpower in Bosnia did not induce Russia – or at least the Russian foreign ministry – to scrap efforts to cooperate with NATO. Rather, Foreign Minister Andrei Kozyrev stated that 'we are interested in much more serious relations with NATO than a mere framework document, so that surprises and unilateral measures, especially military ones, can be ruled out in those zones where we must cooperate very closely'.[9]

In June 1994, following a half-yearly NATO foreign ministers' meeting, an important diplomatic signal was sent to Moscow in the final communiqué. It was stated that 'our relationship with Russia, *including in appropriate areas outside the Partnership for Peace*, will be developed over time' [emphasis added].[10] This was a key concession. Hitherto, NATO members had always insisted that no special side deals were possible with individual partners over and above the PfP. They had now accepted a breach in this principle, in order to finally persuade the Russian government to sign up.

The basis of the new compromise was a formula which came to be known as 'no vetoes, no surprises'. Under this, the Russians accepted that new consultative arrangements would not accord them the status of full participants, with veto rights, in NATO decision-making. In return, NATO members agreed that they would not make major decisions without consulting Russia first. What the Russian government had uppermost in its mind when pressing for 'no surprises' was a desire to ensure that it would have plenty of warning should NATO decide to proceed with enlargement.

In December 1994 things went awry. Andrei Kozyrev, who had been due to meet his NATO partners to set the seal on the detail of the new links and programmes, pulled out at the last minute. He objected to the inclusion in the communiqué issued at the meeting of NATO foreign ministers, which had just taken place, of a commitment to 'initiate a process of examination inside the Alliance to determine how NATO will enlarge, the principles to guide this process and the implications of membership'.[11] This, argued Kozyrev, violated the principle of 'no surprises', as Russia had not been forewarned about it. Unconvinced by NATO protestations that what had been set in train was a technical study process without any wider implications, Kozyrev stated that a 'hasty and unwarranted expansion of the alliance is not to Russia's liking'.[12] Thus, the perception that NATO was trying to covertly initiate an enlargement process was the third reason why tensions developed in its relations with Russia.

During the early summer of 1995, the US floated a new formula to try to overcome the impasse. In a speech in London, the then US Ambassador to NATO, Robert Hunter, stated that 'at NATO, we are ready to give Russia a voice, but not a veto over Alliance decisions'.[13] The prospect of an enhanced input into NATO deliberations helped to pave the way, finally, for the Russian government to agree to complete its accession to PfP, which it did at the end of May – nearly 18 months after the scheme was first unveiled.

Russia's accession was accompanied by agreements giving it the 'voice' promised by the Americans. The agreed *Areas for Pursuance of a Broad, Enhanced NATO/Russia Dialogue and Cooperation* included, most significantly, provision for '"16+1" discussions in the North Atlantic Council, Political Committee or other appropriate Alliance fora (timing and topic(s) to be agreed in advance)'.[14] This went beyond anything offered to any other non-NATO member. By early 1997, the 16+1 consultative format had reportedly been used on 'two dozen' occasions[15] and there can be little doubt that its existence helped to draw some of the sting from NATO-Russia relations from mid-1995.

The other key factor in this context was the de facto decision made by NATO members in mid-1995 not to proceed with enlargement until after the Russian parliamentary and presidential elections scheduled for December 1995 and June 1996 respectively. No public announcements on a moratorium were made, but it was reported that private assurances had been given to Foreign Minister Kozyrev.[16]

When this de facto moratorium was in effect, both sides showed a willingness to adopt a flexible and pragmatic approach in the expectation that *eventual* NATO enlargement was now inevitable. During 1996, Yevgeny Primakov, who had succeeded Kozyrev as Russia's foreign minister, laid out the conditions under which NATO enlargement into

Central Europe could be accepted by Russia. Primakov's demands were, first, that no nuclear weapons or supporting infrastructure of any kind should be stationed on the territory of new members. Second, the eastward movement of NATO military infrastructure per se should be kept to a minimum, or preferably not happen at all.[17]

The US suggested upgrading NATO's institutional relations with the Russians still further in 1996. In early September, then Secretary of State Warren Christopher declared that, in future, 'Russia's cooperation with NATO should be expressed in a formal charter. This charter should create standing arrangements for consultation and joint action between Russia and the alliance...The charter we seek should give us a permanent mechanism for crisis management so we can respond together immediately as...challenges arise.'[18]

This was a major concession because the Russians had long pressed for their relationship with NATO to be formalized in a document; preferably legally binding, but at least one that was accepted by both sides as politically binding. Hitherto, NATO member states had resisted this and had restricted the relationship, outside PfP, to the level of declaratory statements of intent.

At the December 1996 meeting of NATO foreign ministers, as already mentioned, the effective moratorium on NATO enlargement proceeding was ended. Two concessions were offered to the Russians. NATO members had devised what came to be known as the 'three nos' formula. This addressed the issue of nuclear weapons specifically. It was stated that NATO had 'no intention, no plan, and no reason to deploy nuclear weapons on the territory of new members nor any need to change any aspect of NATO's nuclear posture or nuclear policy – and we do not foresee any future need to do so'.[19] Realistically, this was as far as NATO members could go without conceding a Russian veto over their future nuclear posture.

On the issue of further enhancements to the institutional relationship with Russia, the December 1996 NATO communiqué confirmed the US proposal that this 'could take the form of a Charter'. The practical thrust was towards an evolutionary development of the existing 16+1 consultations, supplemented by more 'military liaison and cooperation'. The task now facing NATO and Russian negotiators was to get this enhanced relationship off the ground, preferably before NATO finally decided to open its doors to new members.

A SPECIAL RELATIONSHIP?

Beginning in January 1997, Yevgeny Primakov and then NATO Secretary-General Javier Solana held talks on developing the new relationship promised at the NATO meeting the previous December. However, neither side made a serious attempt to tie the other down to agreed interpretations of how a new consultative arrangement would actually work in practice. This made more likely the possibility of mutual misperceptions and subsequent disenchantment when the time came for the two sides to try and put the new arrangements into practice. A special summit meeting of NATO members plus President Yeltsin was arranged for Paris in May 1997 in order to sign the ponderously-titled *Founding Act on Mutual Relations, Cooperation and Security between NATO and the Russian Federation*.

At face value, the *Founding Act* gave the Russians a good deal. NATO offered an additional element to its December 1996 'three nos' pledge. It was stated that 'it has no intention, no plan, and no reason to establish nuclear weapon storage sites on the territory of [new] members'. By disavowing any intention of constructing nuclear weapons infrastructure on new members' soil, NATO was, to all intents and purposes, ruling out the possibility of moving nuclear weapons there even in the event of heightened tension or crisis. It was also stated that 'in the current and foreseeable security environment, the Alliance will carry out its collective defence and other missions by ensuring the necessary interoperability, integration, and capability for reinforcement rather than by additional permanent stationing of substantial combat forces'.[20]

A new 'NATO-Russia Permanent Joint Council' (PJC) was created. This was, so it had been said, intended to be 'a council of 17',[21] and so more inclusive than the existing 16+1 consultative arrangements which, by definition, presupposed that Russia was an institutional outsider. The PJC was to meet regularly at either ministerial or ambassadorial level and, to that end, Russia was to establish a mission to NATO headed by an ambassador. In this respect its level of representation would be on a par with that of the NATO members themselves. The underlying purpose of the PJC, it was grandly declared, would be to 'build increasing levels of trust, unity of purpose and habits of consultation and cooperation between NATO and Russia'.

In sum, the *Founding Act* did give Russia a special relationship with NATO in the sense that its level of representation and rights of consultation were greater than those accorded to any other non-member state. Institutionally, its representatives would sit in the PJC on equal terms, at least formally, with their NATO counterparts.

There was a crucial proviso, however; that the 'provisions of this Act do not provide NATO or Russia, in any way, with a right of veto over the actions of the other nor do they infringe upon or restrict the rights of NATO or Russia to independent decision-making and action'. Thus, Russia had merely consolidated, in the buzz-phrase of the time, 'a voice, but not a veto' in NATO deliberations. The Act detailed 'specific areas of mutual interest' which could be placed on the agenda at PJC meetings. The list was broad. Yet, the very fact that the scope of the PJC had been limited at all meant that, in future, NATO members could and would keep controversial items off the agenda.

The initial response to the signing of the *Founding Act* was markedly cool in some quarters in Russia, where the decision to sign was interpreted as a defeat.[22] In countering such accusations, the Yeltsin government argued that everything depended on the way in which things worked out in practice. As the presidential press spokesperson put it, NATO and Russia were at 'the beginning of the struggle in interpreting the agreement'.[23]

In the US, meanwhile, some worried that the Russians had been given too much; a veto de facto if not de jure. Former Secretary of State Henry Kissinger was the best-known exponent of this view. He argued that 'in practice, NATO Council sessions and Permanent [Joint] Council sessions will tend to merge. The free and easy "family atmosphere" of existing institutions will vanish.'[24] Joseph Biden, a leading US Senator, expressed a similar view:

> The practical effect of being in the same building, the same proximity, the same circumstances, is that women and men are not going to get up from this consultative group in room B after having talked about something that the Russians raised...and then walk down to room A where the [NATO] Council is meeting and say, Now, I am not going to consider what was just said in there.[25]

These concerns, plus reported unease among some European NATO members about giving Russia 'wide scope for joint decisions',[26] prompted the Clinton administration to change tack. Whereas in the period up to the Paris summit, the accent had been on the extent to which NATO-Russia relations might develop,[27] now the message was significantly more restrictive. Testifying to the Senate Foreign Relations Committee, Thomas Pickering, the then Under-Secretary of State for Political Affairs, and a former US ambassador to Russia, avowed that, in the Clinton administration's view:

> The PJC is a consultative mechanism, and...consultation in diplomatic parlance means just that, talking together. It does not mean a situation in which you are obliged to negotiate. It does not mean you are in a situation where you are obliged to make a decision...In cases where the Russians might suggest subject matter on which there is no NATO position, it is clearly provided that NATO is not required to undertake any such discussion and certainly can, if it wishes and chooses to make such a discussion, first agree among itself, its members, as to what its position is.[28]

The clarity that Pickering claimed was, in fact, not as evident in the text of the *Founding Act* as he suggested. The document only derivatively provided a right for NATO to, in effect, veto attempts by the Russians to raise topics that NATO members did not want to talk about. It was stated that 'consultations will not extend to internal matters of either NATO, NATO Member States or Russia', leaving open the definition of 'internal matters'. All told, from the autumn of 1997, the 'struggle in interpreting' the *Founding Act* was joined. Subsequently, restrictive Western interpretations gained the upper hand, with consequent disenchantment becoming evident on the Russian side.

To be fair, there are also grounds for doubting whether the Russians were prepared to engage constructively in the spirit of the enterprise. The very first scheduled meeting of the PJC in July 1997 was postponed (for one day). This occurred because the Russian representatives raised eleventh hour objections to the chairing arrangements, despite the fact that these had been set out in the *Founding Act*, to which President Yeltsin had affixed his signature two months previously.[29] During the first six months of PJC meetings, the Russian representatives reportedly threatened to walk out twice: over the US decision to sign security agreements with the Baltic States and American policy towards Iraq respectively.[30] The Russian government also displayed a persistent reluctance to conclude an agreement on the opening of a NATO military liaison mission in Moscow, also provided for by the *Founding Act*.[31]

On the NATO side, the member states quickly developed an approach to PJC meetings that contributed significantly to these falling some way short of the aspiration to 'build trust, unity of purpose and habits of cooperation'. In reviewing the first two years of PJC activity in July 1999, Peter Trenin-Straussov noted that NATO members had been forming positions in advance of meetings and presenting their Russian interlocutors with faits accomplis. As a result, according to Trenin-Straussov, 'the Russians for their part, soon discovered that dealing with individual NATO member states outside the PJC was more effective and satisfying'. In consequence, 'the PJC quickly turned itself into a talking shop for rather stale dialogue'.[32]

By early 1999, there seemed little doubt among informed observers that the PJC had not yet succeeded in placing NATO-Russia relations on a significantly more cooperative or institutionalized footing. Virtually every commentary on the PJC and the *Founding Act* by then habitually referred to problems and limitations. Trenin-Straussov called the PJC a 'disabled child'.[33] A report prepared for the NATO Parliamentary Assembly, meanwhile, argued that NATO's 'dialogue with Russia remains thinly rooted'.[34] Dmitri Trenin wrote, with studied understatement, that 'the two years of the PJC's operation have not left particularly good memories, or a good working model for progressively closer cooperation'.[35]

THE KOSOVO CRISIS

To many, the Kosovo crisis posed the greatest threat to NATO-Russia relations since the end of the Cold War. The main focus of the discussions in this section will be on determining the actual extent to which relations really were breached and damaged during this crisis, both at the time and over the longer term.

The Yeltsin government's immediate response to the commencement of the NATO air campaign against the Federal Republic of Yugoslavia (FRY) on 24 March 1999 was to sever its structural links with the institution. Much was made of this in both the Russian and Western media, where it was frequently suggested that Russia had 'broken off links with the West'. In reality the Russian action was carefully calibrated and targeted and it did not amount to anything so drastic. Most significantly, Russia withdrew its mission to NATO and halted participation in the PJC.

Equally important, however, was what the Russian government did *not* do. It resisted calls from the Communist Party among others to terminate its military presence in Bosnia as part of the ongoing NATO-led Stabilization Force (SFOR) there.[36] On the wider diplomatic front, the Russian government continued to maintain normal relations with all NATO governments, including the US.

There were three main reasons behind this policy of *limited* disruption of relations. First, the Yeltsin government felt that it could not afford – literally – to take any action which might jeopardize the financial and economic support which it received from Western countries and via international institutions and agencies such as the International Monetary Fund.[37] Second, there was an underlying fear of being isolated – or rather in this case of Russia isolating itself. President Yeltsin expressed this clearly one month into the bombing: 'In spite of NATO's aggressive actions, we cannot break with the Western countries', he said, 'we cannot lead ourselves into isolation because we are in Europe and no one will kick us out of Europe.'[38] In some quarters, finally, there was a sense of impotence, that there was nothing Russia could do to stop the bombing. A 25 March editorial in *Izvestia* summed up this feeling in stating that 'a break with America, a break with NATO would be far more costly for us than for the West. So we have to grin and bear it. The more vigorously we shake our fists, the stupider we're going to look.'[39]

In his first official response to the initiation of the bombing, Yeltsin, whilst announcing the suspension of relations with NATO in the areas noted above, was careful to keep the door open in one particularly important area. He stated that 'Russia [was] prepared to continue working closely' with leading NATO members in pursuit of a diplomatic settlement.[40] The best opportunity for Russia to avoid being isolated or marginalized and demonstrate that it was not completely impotent lay in the diplomatic sphere. Thus it was scarcely surprising that Russian leaders concentrated their energies on efforts to broker a diplomatic settlement.

In order to assess the nature and extent of the influence that Russia had on the terms of the final settlement, agreed by the Milosevic government in the FRY in June 1999, it is necessary first of all to consider NATO's own starting point. In a statement released after a NATO Council meeting on 12 April, the member states set out five demands which President Milosevic was expected to meet before the bombing could be called off. They were:

- A verifiable end to Serb military action and repression in Kosovo.
- The withdrawal from Kosovo of Serb military, police and paramilitary forces.
- The stationing in the province of an 'international military presence'.
- The unconditional and safe return of refugees and displaced persons and 'unhindered access to them by humanitarian aid organizations'.
- Willingness to work on a settlement of the political status of Kosovo.[41]

Two days after these five points were agreed, a 'German peace plan' was unveiled. Actually this description, although widely used in the media, was inaccurate on two counts. The proposals did not amount to a 'plan' as such. Rather, they were presented as a series of suggested steps by which a settlement might be reached. Second, the proposals were not exclusively German. They had been agreed jointly by German and Russian diplomats. The key importance of Russian involvement was repeatedly stressed on the German side, although it suited the Russians to have the proposals presented formally by Germany in order to increase the chances of a positive reception within NATO.[42]

The principles upon which the eventual settlement was based were agreed at a meeting of foreign ministers of the Group of Eight (G8) countries on 6 May. Use of the G8 forum in itself reflected a concession to Russian (and German) wishes. The G8 principles incorporated the 12 April NATO demands but amplified them in significant ways. In so doing they also reflected important elements of the 14 April Russo-German proposals. The key additions were:

- The 'international presences' to be deployed in Kosovo following a Serb withdrawal should be both 'civil and security'. NATO's 12 April statement had spoken only of 'an international military presence'.
- Further, these presences should be 'endorsed and adopted by the United Nations'. A UN role had not been identified by NATO on 12 April, but it was a key feature of the Russo-German proposals.

- The G8 statement agreed on the 'establishment of an interim administration for Kosovo to be decided by the Security Council of the United Nations'. This adopted another important element of the Russo-German proposals. It had not been mentioned by NATO on 12 April.
- The 'demilitarization of the UCK' (i.e., the Kosovo Liberation Army) was identified as an integral part of an overall political settlement. Again, the 12 April NATO demands, which had been exclusively directed at the Serbs, had been silent on this. It had, though, featured in the Russo-German proposals.[43]

Overall as Dov Lynch has noted, the G8 proposals, of which the elements mentioned here were all incorporated into the settlement agreed with the Serbs in June 1999, 'contained important elements of success for Russia'.[44] One key issue was not resolved before Milosevic accepted the G8/NATO demands. This was the nature and extent of a Russian military presence, working with NATO, in post-settlement Kosovo. Russian negotiators had accepted that the international security presence should be NATO-led and this was incorporated into UN Security Council Resolution 1244, passed on 10 June 1999, which put into place the agreed settlement.[45] The specific question of Russian participation was effectively set aside for subsequent consideration, in order to prevent it from holding up the overall settlement.[46] What happened next demonstrated that, for all their diplomatic cooperation since the end of April, substantial underlying distrust remained between Russia and NATO in mid-1999.

On the day after Resolution 1244 was passed, some 200 Russian troops detached themselves from the Russian contingent in SFOR in Bosnia. They undertook a pre-emptive march to the airport in Pristina, the provincial capital of Kosovo, arriving before the first contingents of NATO troops from the newly-formed Kosovo Force (KFOR). The most likely explanation for this headline-grabbing move is that the Russians wished to ensure that they had some actual military presence, however small, in the heart of Kosovo from the start and were not frozen out completely by NATO. This 'worked' to the extent that NATO and Russia subsequently negotiated an agreement providing for substantial Russian participation in KFOR; and under a command structure whereby it was possible for the Russian government to assert that it was not simply placing its forces 'under NATO'.[47]

By June/July 1999, it was clear that NATO-Russia relations had survived the Kosovo crisis essentially intact, if far from in rude health. There certainly did exist a substantial element of mistrust. Already, however, Russian relations with the NATO institution and its military structures were being restored, apropos of the agreement on Russian participation in KFOR. The prevailing Russian view was possibly best summed up in *Vremya MN* at the beginning of July. It opined that:

> During the Balkan war, Russia made the most important choice in our country's recent history. We didn't ally ourselves with NATO, but, thank God, we didn't become its enemy either. Now, Russia and the West can become partners who may not have any reason to love each other, but have to work together if only because there's no getting away from each other.[48]

PHASED RESTORATION

On 23 July 1999, the PJC met for the first time since before the start of the NATO bombing campaign. The Russian side was at pains to make clear, however, that this meeting did not wipe the slate clean and signal a return to business as before. It was emphasized that the PJC had been reactivated solely for the purpose of discussing issues 'in a clearly defined sphere: interaction within the framework of KFOR'.[49] A moderate upgrading was announced two months later when the Russian government decided to send back its chief military representative to NATO. However, it declared that this signalled no change to its basic approach of restricting contacts.[50]

Yet there was a view, widely expressed by Russian political leaders, that Russia would have to learn (again) to live with NATO as a principal actor on the European stage. As Foreign Minister Igor Ivanov expressed it in October 1999, 'like it or not, NATO is a reality in today's international arena, primarily in Europe but also in the world in general'.[51] Four months later, former prime and foreign minister Yevgeny Primakov expressed a similar view: 'we have to talk, as NATO is a real force and this should be taken into account'.[52]

Boris Yeltsin announced his resignation at the end of 1999 having, it was widely assumed, manoeuvred his preferred successor, Vladimir Putin, into pole position for the forthcoming Russian presidential election. Putin wasted little time, early in 2000, in making clear his interest in moving relations with NATO forward. In February 2000 the two sides agreed to 'intensify their dialogue in the Permanent Joint Council...on a wide range of security issues'.[53] In other words, consultations within the PJC would, henceforth, take place on other issues, in addition to those relating to KFOR. *Segodnya* asserted that 'it's safe to say that the crisis in Russia-NATO relations has been overcome, or almost overcome'.[54]

Putin also sent a signal that he wished to go further; in a television interview that he gave to the UK interviewer Sir David Frost. In response to a question about possible Russian membership in NATO, he replied 'why not?' This was strikingly reminiscent of the approach taken in the letter that

President Yeltsin had addressed to NATO members in December 1991. The signalling nature of Putin's remark was widely accepted, both inside Russia and among NATO members,[55] though little of substance was done by NATO in acting upon it.

A degree of disenchantment on the Russian side with the perceived lack of substantial NATO follow-up may help to explain why relations subsequently developed a certain testiness. It appeared that, for every 'good news' story coming out of Russia from a NATO point of view, less welcome developments soon followed. At the beginning of 2001, for example, agreement on opening a NATO information office in Moscow was reached against a backdrop of press speculation that Russia had begun to deploy theatre nuclear weapons in Kaliningrad, on the borders of Poland and Lithuania.[56] In July, Putin told an international press conference that, while 'we don't consider NATO hostile...we don't see any reason for its existence'.[57]

11 SEPTEMBER 2001

Following the 11 September terrorist strikes on the US, it seemed initially as if their effect would be felt more in confirming already existing Russian objectives rather than in ushering in anything dramatically new. In late September, Vladimir Putin was quoted in some press reports as calling on NATO to admit Russia to membership; an echo of his interview with Frost 18 months previously.[58]

The main thrust of Putin's effort at this time appears to have been to take advantage of Western – especially US – interest in constructing the broadest possible international coalition for the impending 'war on terrorism' in order to persuade NATO members to respond more dynamically than hitherto to his signals in favour of enhanced relations and more cooperation. Following a meeting with NATO Secretary-General Lord Robertson in early October, Putin was quoted as saying that 'we have got the impression that our signals in favour of closer cooperation have been heard'.[59] Positive mood music was also picked up at a PJC meeting at the end of September.[60] Thus far, however, there had been little more than words.

The prospects of this situation changing seemed promising in November 2001. Secretary-General Robertson used a visit to Russia that month to propose a new forum to the Russian government – the 'Russia-North Atlantic Council' (RNAC). This new body, he explained:

> Would involve Russia having an equality with the NATO countries in terms of the subject matter and would be part of the same compromising trade-offs, give and take, that is involved in day-to-day NATO business. That is how we do business at 19.... We build

consensus. So the idea would be that Russia would enter that. That would give Russia a right of equality but also a responsibility and an obligation that would come from being part of the consensus-building organization.[61]

Russia was being offered the prospect of some joint decision-making powers. However, pivotal issues remained to be clarified. One question was whether the RNAC proposal was, in fact, a product of the impact of 11 September at all. A strong case can be made that something like it would have appeared in any event as a result of the decision taken by NATO members in June 2001 to proceed with a second round of eastern enlargement. As *Noviye Izvestia* somewhat archly commented in November: 'NATO makes conciliatory gestures toward Moscow every time it prepares to admit new members'.[62]

NATO foreign ministers formally endorsed the RNAC proposal at their meeting in December 2001. They stated that the aim of establishing a new council would be to 'identify and pursue opportunities for joint action at 20', by creating 'new, effective mechanisms for consultation, cooperation, joint decision, and coordinated/joint action'. Significantly, by promising to create 'new, effective mechanisms', NATO members seemed to be tacitly admitting that the existing arrangements, based on the PJC, had been substantially *ineffective*.

The NATO ministers were careful to establish parameters. 'NATO', they stated, 'will maintain its prerogative of independent decision and action at 19 on all issues consistent with its obligations and responsibilities.'[63] Given the extension and development of NATO's 'obligations and responsibilities' since the end of the Cold War, this stipulation could potentially be interpreted elastically to exclude virtually anything of potential interest and concern to the institution's Russian interlocutors.

The NATO position reportedly hardened further in the early months of 2002, under pressure from a divided Bush administration in the US.[64] Nevertheless, NATO foreign ministers did agree, in May 2002, to create what was now called the 'NATO-Russia Council' (NRC) to replace the existing PJC. According to press reports, the NRC would give Russia co-decision-making rights in nine issue areas including significant ones such as military crisis management, counter-terrorism, non-proliferation of weapons of mass destruction and theatre missile defence. This provoked enthusiastic media commentary. *The Times* in London called the NRC 'the most far-reaching change in the North Atlantic alliance since NATO was founded in 1949'.[65]

Important provisos were, reportedly, included in the new arrangement. One was a so-called 'retrieval' mechanism. This would allow NATO members to withdraw an issue from discussion in the NRC if the prospects for consensus being reached with the Russians looked poor.[66] It opened the door to potential disagreements over who should decide when such an impasse had been reached. There was also ambiguity over whether or not NATO members would reserve the right to formulate common positions in advance.[67] This, as noted above, had been one of the main complaints from the Russian side about the workings of the PJC as it evolved.

The NRC idea was not dramatically new. Rather, it seemed like an attempt to relaunch the NATO-Russia relationship on a basis not too dissimilar to what was, officially at least, set out in the 1997 *Founding Act*. That had come unstuck, principally because neither the NATO members nor the Russians had been prepared to invest sufficient political capital or effort into really shifting their mutual relations onto a qualitatively new footing. In 2001–02, they decided to try again.

Regardless of the ultimate success or otherwise of the NRC, it still seems clear that the specific impact of the events of 11 September 2001 on the NATO-Russia relationship has been limited. It cannot fairly be asserted that the RNAC/NRC proposal – or something like it – would not have been put forward anyway, given that NATO members had decided in June 2001 that they were going to proceed with further enlargement. NATO members also seemed to want to hedge the NRC, to the extent that it risked becoming the PJC under another name. In 2002, it still appeared that the substance – or lack of it – of NATO-Russia relations was essentially unscathed by the events of 11 September.

CONCLUSION

Two issues were implied in the title of this study. First, have NATO-Russia relations since 1991 proceeded along a 'bumpy road'? It is certainly true that they have had their ups and downs, as the discussions above have made clear. The bottom line, however, has been that at no time since 1991 has either side been prepared to see relations terminated completely. The closest they have come was at the outset of the NATO air operations against the FRY over Kosovo in March 1999. However, the Russian government's response was not a protracted sulk. Rather, it successfully manoeuvred itself into a position where it could play a key role in the diplomacy that ultimately brought the bombing to an end. NATO members, for their part, tacitly encouraged this development.

The second issue raised by this study's title is concerned with the ultimate goals of the relationship. Neither side has established any, at least in a formal or declaratory sense. This absence can be most clearly seen on the Russian side by the failure to definitively either accept or reject the possibility of NATO membership. NATO, meanwhile, has not decided how much it is really prepared to open up to Russian input and participation. The extent to which it did so between 1991 and 2002 was relatively limited and tactically motivated (by a desire to defuse active Russian opposition to enlargement), rather than the product of strategic vision.

On present evidence, therefore, the road ahead for NATO-Russia relations is likely to remain bumpy, and the destination unknown. This does not mean, however, that the relationship lacks a kind of underlying stability. There may have been a dearth of *stated* overall goals and objectives, but actions speak louder than words. The actions of NATO members and Russian leaders since 1991 clearly point towards the conclusion that, though the road ahead may be bumpy and uneven, the need to maintain a workable NATO-Russia relationship is now largely unquestioned by mainstream policy-makers on both sides. The process has become the goal.

NOTES

The views expressed here are personal and should not be construed as representing the views or policy of the British government, Ministry of Defence or the Royal Military Academy, Sandhurst.

 1. B. Johnson, 'History "Turns Inside Out" as Russia Asks to Join NATO', *Daily Telegraph*, 21 Dec. 1991.
 2. English language translation in *BBC Summary of World Broadcasts* EE/1778 (1993) p.A/8.
 3. *Segodnya*, 14 Sept. 1993: translated in *The Current Digest of the Post-Soviet Press* (hereafter *CDPSP*) XLV/37 (1993) pp.16–17.
 4. For the text of the letter see 'Russian President Boris Yeltsin's Letter to US President Bill Clinton', *SIPRI Yearbook 1994* (Oxford: SIPRI/OUP 1994) pp.249–50.
 5. *Newsnight*, 27 Oct. 1993. In *Foreign Broadcast Information Service* FBIS-SOV-93-209 (1993) p.13.
 6. It has been alleged subsequently that informal approaches were made by senior Russian officials during the early 1990s to ascertain whether Russian membership of NATO was indeed possible. Reportedly, the US responded negatively. Question from Senator Wellstone to Ambassador Thomas Pickering, Senate Foreign Relations Committee Hearings, Oct. 1997. *The Debate on NATO Enlargement* (Washington DC: US Senate Committee on Foreign Relations Oct./Nov. 1997): http://frwebgate.access.gpo.gov/.
 7. PfP is an umbrella term for programmes of military-to-military contact and cooperation involving NATO members and non-member states in Europe. Active participation is an essential requirement for states seeking to join NATO. In 2002, 27 non-NATO states were involved in PfP.
 8. *Nezavisimaya Gazeta*, 23 Feb. 1994: *CDPSP* XLVI/8 (1994) p.11.
 9. *Segodnya*, 15 April 1994: *CDPSP* XLVI/15 (1994) p.9.
10. *Press Communiqué M-NAC-1(94)06* (Brussels: NATO 1994): www.nato.int/docu/comm/49-95/c940609b.htm.
11. *Press Communiqué M-NAC-2(94)116* (Brussels: NATO 1994): www.nato.int/docu/comm/49-95/c941201a.htm.
12. *Segodnya*, 3 Dec. 1994: *CDPSP* XLVI/48 (1994) p.18.
13. R. Hunter, 'European Security Architecture Needs Russia to be Complete', *Official Text* (London: US Information Service 1995) p.7.
14. *Areas for Pursuance of a Broad, Enhanced NATO/Russia Dialogue and Cooperation* (Brussels: NATO 1995): www.nato.int/docu/comm/49-95/c950531a.htm. The '16' were the then 16 NATO members.

15. A. Pierre and D. Trenin, 'Developing NATO-Russian Relations', *Survival* 39/1 (Spring 1997) p.7.
16. P. Almond, 'Russia Agrees to Military Pact with the West', *Daily Telegraph*, 1 June 1995.
17. See, *inter alia*, J. Thornhill, 'Russia Hints at NATO Compromise', *Financial Times*, 12 March 1996; A. Gimson, 'Russia Eases Tone on NATO Expansion', *Daily Telegraph*, 5 June 1996 and I. Karacs, 'Russians Pull Back from Confrontation with NATO', *The Independent*, 5 June 1996.
18. W. Christopher, 'A New Atlantic Community for the 21st Century', *Department of State Dispatch* 7/37 (1996): http://dosfan.lib.uic.edu/ERC/briefing/dispatch/1996/html/Dispatchv7no37.html.
19. *Press Communiqué M-NAC-2(96)165* (Brussels: NATO 1996): www.nato.int/docu/pr/1996/p96-165e.htm.
20. *Founding Act on Mutual Relations, Cooperation and Security between NATO and the Russian Federation* (Brussels: NATO 1997): www.nato.int/docu/basictxt/fndact-a.htm.
21. This phrase was attributed to the then German foreign minister, Klaus Kinkel. See 'Wooing a Bear', *The Economist*, 14 Dec. 1996, p.47.
22. *Izvestia*, 28 May 1997: *CDPSP* XLIX/21 (1997) p.5; *Nezavisimaya Gazeta*, 27 May 1997: *CDPSP* XLIX/22 (1997) pp.10–11.
23. Quoted in *Russia and European Security* (Document A/1722) (Paris: Assembly of the Western European Union 2000): www.assembly-weu.org/en/documents/sessions_ordinaires/rpt/2000/1722.html.
24. Senate Foreign Relations Committee, *The Debate on NATO Enlargement* (see note 6). See also K.-H. Kamp, 'The NATO-Russia Founding Act: Trojan Horse or Milestone of Reconciliation?', *Aussenpolitik* 4 (1997) pp.320–1.
25. Senate Foreign Relations Committee, *The Debate on NATO Enlargement* (note 6).
26. 'Wooing a Bear' (note 21).
27. Following the successful conclusion of the Solana-Primakov negotiations in May, an unnamed NATO 'source' was quoted as saying that 'we have…told the Russians that this agreement is just the beginning and that, as the relationship improves, their role could become even more significant'. See M. Evans, 'Deal Grants Russians Unique NATO Access While Denying Veto', *The Times*, 17 May 1997.
28. Senate Foreign Relations Committee, *The Debate on NATO Enlargement* (note 6).
29. Kamp, 'The NATO-Russia Founding Act' (note 24) p.324.
30. I. Isakova, 'The NATO-Russian Relationship One Year After: Next Steps After First Enlargement?', *RUSI Journal* 143/5 (Oct. 1998) p.16.
31. *NATO-Russia Relations and Next Steps for NATO Enlargement* (Document AS277PCED-E) (Brussels: NATO Parliamentary Assembly 1999): www.nato-pa.int/publications/comrep/1999/as277pced-e.html.
32. P. Trenin-Straussov, *The NATO-Russia Permanent Joint Council in 1997–1999: Anatomy of a Failure* (Berlin: Berlin Information Center for Transatlantic Security 1999): www.bits.de/public/researchnote/rn99-1.htm.
33. Trenin-Straussov, *The NATO-Russia Permanent Joint Council* (note 32).
34. NATO Parliamentary Assembly, *NATO-Russia Relations and Next Steps for NATO Enlargement* (see note 31).
35. D. Trenin, 'Russia-NATO Relations: Time to Pick up the Pieces', *NATO Review* 48/1 (2000) p.21.
36. The Communist leader, Gennady Zyuganov, had called for this on the day after air operations were launched. *Sovetskaya Rossia*, 27 March 1999: *CDPSP* 51/12 (1999) p.5.
37. M. Smith, *Russian Thinking on European Security after Kosovo* (Camberley: Conflict Studies Research Centre 1999) p.6.
38. Quoted in D. Lynch, 'Walking the Tightrope': The Kosovo Conflict and Russia in European Security, 1998–August 1999', *European Security* 8/4 (Winter 1999) p.70.
39. *Izvestia*, 25 March 1999: *CDPSP* 51/12 (1999) p.9.
40. *Rossiiskaya Gazeta*, 26 March 1999: *CDPSP* 51/12 (1999) p.3.
41. 'The Situation In and Around Kosovo' *(Press Release M-NAC-1(99)51)* (Brussels: NATO 1999): www.nato.int/docu/pr/1999/p99-051e.htm. These demands were reiterated,

unchanged, at the NATO 50th anniversary summit in Washington DC in late April.
42. I. Daalder and M. O'Hanlon, *Winning Ugly: NATO's War to Save Kosovo* (Washington DC: Brookings 2000) pp.165–6; B. Posen, 'The War for Kosovo', *International Security* 24/4 (2000) p.67. For the text of the proposals see *Kosovo Peace Plan* (London/Washington DC: British American Security Information Council 1999): www.basicint.org/peaceplan.htm.
43. *Statement by the Chairman on the Conclusion of the Meeting of the G8 Foreign Ministers on the Petersberg* (Univ. of Toronto 1999): www.g7.utoronto.ca/g7/foreign/fm990506.htm.
44. Lynch, 'Walking the Tightrope'(note 38) pp. 75–6.
45. *Resolution 1244 (1999)* (NY: United Nations 1999): www.un.org/Docs/scres/1999/99sc1244.htm.
46. Daalder and O'Hanlon, *Winning Ugly* (note 42) pp.172–3.
47. For the text of the agreement and associated attachments see *Agreed Points on Russian Participation in KFOR* (Brussels: NATO 1999): www.nato.int/kfor/resources/documents/helsinki.htm.
48. *Vremya MN*, 5 July 1999: *CDPSP* 51/27 (1999) p.8.
49. WEU Assembly, *Russia and European Security* (note 23).
50. *Trud*, 8 Sept. 1999: *CDPSP* 51/36 (1999) p.20.
51. *Nezavisimaya Gazeta*, 12 Oct. 1999: *CDPSP* 51/41 (1999) p.3.
52. Quoted in E. MacAskill, 'NATO and Russia Re-establish Ties as Tensions Ease', *The Guardian*, 17 Feb. 2000.
53. *Joint Statement on the Occasion of the Visit of the Secretary-General of NATO, Lord Robertson, in Moscow on 16 February 2000* (Brussels: NATO 2000): www.nato.int/docu/pr/2000/p000216e.htm.
54. *Segodnya*, 17 Feb. 2000: *CDPSP* 52/7 (2000) p.19.
55. See, *inter alia*, *Izvestia*, 7 March 2000: *CDPSP* 52/10 (2000) p.5; *Kommersant*, 7 March 2000: *CDPSP* 52/10 (2000) p.5; 'The Fist Unclenched', *The Times*, 6 March 2000.
56. G. Whittell and M. Evans, 'Putin "Redeploys Nuclear Arms on Baltic Coast"', *The Times*, 4 Jan. 2001.
57. A. Lagnado and G. Whittell, 'Putin Composure Slips Over Chechnya Claim', *The Times*, 19 July 2001.
58. R. Boyes, 'Putin Is Impatient for NATO Welcome', *The Times*, 27 Sept. 2001.
59. Quoted in C. Bremner, 'Russia and West to Work More Closely on Security', *The Times*, 4 Oct. 2001.
60. *Kommersant*, 28 Sept. 2001: *CDPSP* 53/39 (2001) pp.6–7.
61. *Press Conference with NATO Secretary-General, Lord Robertson, 22 November 2001* (Brussels: NATO 2001): www.nato.int/docu/speech/2001/s011122b.htm.
62. *Noviye Izvestia*, 20 Nov. 2001: *CDPSP* 53/47 (2001) p.21.
63. *Press Communiqué M-NAC-2(2001)158* (Brussels: NATO 2001): www.nato.int/docu/pr/2001/p01-158e.htm.
64. See K. Bosworth, 'The Effect of 11th September on Russia-NATO Relations'. Paper presented to the annual conference of the British Association for Slavonic and East European Studies, Cambridge, April 2002, pp.12–13.
65. 'The New Alliance', *The Times*, 15 May 2002.
66. I. Traynor, 'Russia and NATO Reach Historic Deal', *The Guardian*, 15 May 2002.
67. For differing views about what NATO members had agreed on this score see, *inter alia*, M. Evans, 'Russia to Move into NATO HQ', *The Times*, 15 May 2002 and J. Dempsey and R. Wolffe, 'In from the Cold', *Financial Times*, 15 May 2002.

Strategic or Pragmatic Partnership? The European Union's Policy Towards Russia Since the End of the Cold War

GRAHAM TIMMINS

INTRODUCTION: THE EUROPEAN UNION, RUSSIA AND THE
CONCEPT OF STRATEGIC PARTNERSHIP

The end of the Cold War in 1989–91 has compelled both the European Union (EU) and Russia to reposition themselves within the European political environment.[1] Where the EU is concerned, the removal of the post-war ideological rift that divided the European continent for almost half a century provided the opportunity to extend eastwards its founding purpose of generating order. For Russia, the end of the Cold War represented the loss of empire and the need to undertake a painful process of coming to terms with the loss of superpower status. In recognizing the importance of Russia to the creation of a pan-European political order, the EU has highlighted the need for a strategic partnership between itself and Russia.[2]

The main policy tool adopted by the EU in its relations with Russia is the Partnership and Cooperation Agreement (PCA) which was signed in 1994 and supplemented by the Common Strategy on Russia launched in 1999. Put in broad terms, the EU's objective is to develop dialogue mechanisms, which will result in constructive engagement with the post-communist regime in Moscow and generate a sense of shared norms and values. As the Commissioner for External Affairs, Chris Patten, commented during his visit to Moscow in January 2001, the EU is the result of a 'common vision and a common will' based around the principles of an open society, the market, rule of law, press freedom and human rights and, as such, 'it should not be surprising that we seek to project the same principles and values externally'.[3]

However, the idea that the EU can engage Russia in a strategic partnership, given its recent past and the legacy that remains, has attracted criticism in the academic literature. At the risk of over-simplification, the key issue is that, whereas the development of the EU is increasingly motivated by post-Westphalian patterns of sovereignty and the desire to extend a normative foreign policy agenda eastwards, Russia remains locked into a realist interpretation of international relations with its central foreign policy objective being the maintenance of traditional state sovereignty and reduction of US influence in Europe.[4]

As a consequence, and even where the EU and Russia are willing to engage in the rhetoric of partnership and cooperation, as Vahl suggests, there is an 'absence of strategic substance' to support the claim of strategic partnership. Furthermore, in addition to the divergences in foreign policy that exist, Vahl argues that both the EU and Russia are preoccupied with their respective internal agendas. With the EU focusing on its dual agenda of deepening and widening and Russia concentrating on economic reform and addressing instability on its southern borders, 'both the problems and opportunities seem too small or too distant to warrant real and deep commitments'.[5] The purpose of this essay is to outline the development of EU-Russian relations since the end of the Cold War, to evaluate the extent to which a clear strategic direction in EU policy towards Russia can be identified and to consider the basis for partnership as the EU attempts the construction of, in the words of Commission President Romano Prodi, 'a wider European area of peace, stability and prosperity, a new European order, a pax Europea between equal partners'.[6]

BUILDING PARTNERSHIP AND COOPERATION: THE EU AND RUSSIA BEYOND THE COLD WAR

Formal relations between the then European Community (EC) and the Soviet Union prior to the ending of the Cold War were minimal, with Moscow viewing the EC as little more than an economic appendage to the US-led Western alliance. On the occasions that EC-Soviet relations were raised, Moscow's intention in broad terms was to generate greater international credibility for the Soviet-led trading community, the Council for Mutual Economic Assistance (CMEA). Given the EC's preference for bilateral relations with CMEA states, talks failed to progress beyond the initial exchanges until Mikhail Gorbachev's rise to power in March 1985.[7] The signing in June 1988 of a *Joint Declaration on the Establishment of Official Relations Between the European Economic Community and the Council for Mutual Economic Assistance* was, therefore, a genuine breakthrough and owed much to Gorbachev's vision of a new integrated Europe or 'common European home'.[8] The Declaration allowed for bilateral links between the EC and CMEA states and a Trade and Cooperation Agreement with Russia, which followed in December 1989. However, Gorbachev's reform programme had unleashed a political tidal wave that began by sweeping away Soviet power in Eastern Europe in the autumn of 1989 and eventually in the Soviet Union itself in 1991.

The EC responded to events in Eastern Europe by heading a multilateral aid and technical assistance programme, 'Operation PHARE' (*Pologne et Hongrie assistance à la reconstruction économique*), which was launched in December 1989 and initially aimed at Poland and Hungary but was rapidly broadened out to cover the majority of post-communist states in Central and Eastern Europe. A year later at the Rome European Council summit in December 1990 the EC recognized the need to develop a similar programme for the Soviet Union (which became the Commonwealth of Independent States or CIS in January 1992) and in December 1991 the TACIS (Technical Assistance to the Commonwealth of Independent States) programme was launched.[9] During 1991–99, €4.2m was provided via TACIS of which €1.3m, or 30 per cent, went to Russia directly with cross-border regional programmes comprising another €1.2m (27 per cent). Of this amount, the priority areas have been nuclear safety and the environment (20 per cent of total TACIS funding), public administration reform, social services and education (15 per cent) and restructuring state enterprises and private sector development (14 per cent).[10]

It was also agreed at the Luxembourg European Council summit in June 1991 that the Commission would commence exploratory negotiations with the Soviet Union with a view to a major agreement that would extend cooperation beyond the economic and into the political and cultural spheres. The official demise of the Soviet Union in December 1991 strengthened the resolve of the EC and in June 1994 a bilateral 'Partnership and Co-operation Agreement' (PCA) was signed between the now European Union and Russia with the specific objectives being:

- to provide an appropriate framework for the political dialogue between the Parties allowing the development of close relations between them in this field;
- to promote trade and investment and harmonious economic relations between the Parties based on the principles of market economy and so to foster sustainable development in the Parties;
- to strengthen political and economic freedoms;
- to support Russian efforts to consolidate its democracy and to develop its economy and to complete the transition into a market economy;
- to provide a basis for economic, social, financial and cultural cooperation founded on the principles of mutual advantage, mutual responsibility and mutual support;
- to promote activities of joint interest;
- to provide an appropriate framework for the gradual integration between Russia and a wider area of cooperation in Europe;
- to create the necessary conditions for the future establishment of a free

trade area between the Community and Russia covering substantially all trade in goods between them, as well as conditions for bringing about freedom of establishment of companies, of cross-border trade in services and of capital movements.[11]

As far as Russia's immediate objectives were concerned, the PCA established a basis for EU-Russian trade and was perceived as a means by which it could gain access to European and global markets and compensate for the collapse of its traditional markets, not least in the Central and Eastern European region. The political undertakings attached to the PCA were, Timmermann suggests, a necessary compromise but were seen as secondary to the potential economic gains.[12] But at first glance it was not immediately apparent what economic benefits the EU would derive from the PCA.

Despite Russian claims to regional power status, the economic asymmetries between the EU and Russia are striking. Russia has approximately one tenth of the EU's GDP and while the EU is Russia's most significant trading partner, comprising 40 per cent of its imports and 33 per cent of its exports, Russia's economic importance to the EU in manufacturing terms is negligible with Russian goods comprising just two per cent of EU exports and three per cent of its imports.[13] The perceived gains of the PCA to the EU would be phrased predominantly in political terms by providing a structured dialogue through which the EU could seek to influence the post-communist agenda in Russia. Institutional arrangements for two summits each year between the President of the Commission and Council Presidency with the President of the Russian Federation, an annual ministerial cooperation council and cooperation committees comprising nine sub-committees covering aspects of the PCA were agreed and a link between the European Parliament and Russian Duma established.[14]

The contents of the PCA signed with Russia and other CIS states in 1994 were not too dissimilar to the Europe Agreements which had been signed with the Central and Eastern European states from 1991 onwards. The decision taken at the Copenhagen European Council summit in June 1993 to invite membership applications from Central and Eastern Europe and the subsequent accession negotiations have been an effective means by which the EU has been able to export its normative agenda eastwards.[15]

However, this strategy has been successful precisely because the Central and Eastern Europe states have set entry into Western institutions as the benchmark of their success in navigating the challenges of the post-communist transformation process. The political significance of the variable terminology employed was that membership of the EU for the PCA signatories would not be an option, at least not in the immediate future. Gower refutes the suggestion that closing down any expectation of Russian

EU membership from the outset was a conscious decision taken in Brussels. Rather, 'this distinction does not seem to have been a deliberate act of discrimination against Russia but merely a recognition on the part of the EU that, whereas the ECE states have pressed strongly for a commitment to eventual accession to the Union, there has been no evidence that Russia has had a similar goal'.[16] However, whether the EU would have invited a membership application from Russia had Moscow shown any interest is doubtful. Russia's reluctance to take on the normative obligations of EU membership together with the socio-economic factors involved in absorbing a state with Russia's demographic size and complexity into the EU makes it very unlikely that membership would be considered as a credible option.

The signing of the PCA came at a time when Russia was moving away from its Western policy and the more Slavophilic 'Russia First' platform was beginning to exercise growing influence on political thinking in Moscow.[17] Russian military intervention in Chechnya in 1994 and the subsequent escalation of military hostilities in the region amidst widespread international condemnation and accusations of human rights violations were consequences of Russia's shift in foreign policy and provided a watershed in EU-Russian relations in that they exposed the political limitations of the PCA as a means of influencing Russian behaviour. As Gower highlights, The PCA is built upon an assumption of common values including 'a commitment to political and economic freedoms, the promotion of international peace and security and respect for democratic principles and human rights as defined in the Helsinki Final Act and the 1990 Charter of Paris for a New Europe' and included provision for 'unilateral action by one party if it believes that the other has failed to fulfil its treaty obligations'.[18]

The Chechen conflict, therefore, provided a major test whether the EU would assert the political conditionality clause of the PCA; that ratification was suspended suggests that this is a test the EU passed. It was only towards the end of 1996, following Boris Yeltsin's announcement of a military withdrawal from Chechnya, that discussions could be resumed leading to ratification and implementation in December 1997. An interim agreement was, however, signed in February 1996 which facilitated implementation of the trade clauses in the PCA and provoked the suggestion of an EU realpolitik. But as Haukkala argues, 'the European Union showed a great deal of consistency in condemning the war and in applying political pressure on Russia in order to solve the crisis'.[19]

TOWARDS GREATER PRAGMATISM IN THE EU-RUSSIAN RELATIONSHIP: A TALE OF TWO STRATEGIES

The Chechen conflict was just one of several tensions that had been mounting between the EU and Russia following the signing of the PCA. During 1997 the EU had finalized its thinking on how it wished to structure the accession negotiations with the Central and Eastern European applicant states and talks began in London in March 1998. Russia at this time was suffering from a damaging collapse of the rouble and was quickly waking up to the soft (i.e. non-military) security agenda in Europe and the impact that enlargement would have on its economic interests in the Central and Eastern European region. A further source of tension was the role of NATO in the emerging European security architecture. NATO had overtaken the EU enlargement agenda in the late 1990s when expansion was agreed in principle at the NATO summit in Brussels in January 1994 and led eventually to the entry of the Czech Republic, Hungary and Poland into NATO in March 1999. The Russian government had issued its first military doctrine in November 1993 whereby NATO expansion was judged as being 'to the detriment of the interests of the Russian federation's military security'.[20]

NATO's Partnership for Peace initiative launched in January 1994 which included Russia and the *Founding Act on Mutual Relations, Cooperation and Security between NATO and the Russian Federation* in May 1997, which established a Permanent Joint Council, went some way towards addressing the Russian desire for consultation but was generally deemed to be insufficient. Moreover, when NATO launched Operation 'Allied Force' against the Federal Republic of Yugoslavia in March 1999 without a UN mandate and without giving the Russian government prior notification, Yeltsin responded by suspending cooperation with NATO.[21] But if the NATO-led intervention into Kosovo in 1999 had proven to be a pivotal event in US-Russian relations, the same was true of the US-European transatlantic relationship.

Christopher Hill's seminal article on the 'capability-expectations gap' in European foreign policy in 1993 suggested that considerable progress was required if the discrepancies that existed between the rhetoric and reality surrounding the EU as an international actor were to be bridged.[22] Kosovo came as a stark contrast to the bold statement in 1991 by Luxembourg's foreign minister, Jacques Poos, at the start of the Balkan crisis that 'this was the hour of Europe not the hour of the Americans'.[23] Furthermore, following the Commission's optimism in 1992 surrounding the newly-established Common Foreign and Security Policy (CFSP), the majority of external observers since have offered a more measured assessment of the EU's track record to date. As Rees comments, the intergovernmental disputes leading up to the Maastricht European Council summit in 1991, where the CFSP was established, and since have left the EU 'weak and divided in the face of testing security issues'.[24]

The *Declaration on Strengthening the Common European Policy on Security and Defence* (ESDP) agreed at the European Council summit in Cologne in June 1999 whereby the EU would develop 'the capacity for autonomous action, backed up by credible military forces, the means to decide to use them, and a readiness to do so, in order to respond to international crises without prejudice to actions by NATO'[25] together with the appointment of the former NATO secretary-general, Javier Solana, as the inaugural high representative for the CSFP who would work as part of a troika with the commission president and secretary-general of the Council signalled a new determination to establish the EU as a credible international actor. But if the Cologne Declaration represented a growth in the importance of hard security thinking within the EU, the ESDP should not be taken as a movement away from the soft or civilian power agenda.[26]

At the Amsterdam Council summit in June 1997 the EU had indicated in somewhat innocuous terms its decision to introduce a new CFSP policy instrument in the guise of common strategies, which would be implemented where 'the Member States have important interests in common'.[27] One such common interest was the need to address the growing tensions in the West's relations with Russia. The *Common Strategy of the European Union on Russia* which set out a vision for EU-Russian relations and welcomed 'Russia's return to its rightful place in the European family in a spirit of friendship, cooperation, fair accommodation of interests and on the foundations of shared values enshrined in the common heritage of European civilization'[28] became the first of the EU's common strategies and set out two key strategic goals:

- a stable, open and pluralistic democracy in Russia, governed by the rule of law and underpinning a prosperous market economy benefiting alike all the people of Russia and of the European Union;
- maintaining European stability, promoting global security and responding to the common challenges of the continent through intensified cooperation with Russia.[29]

The background to the Common Strategy on Russia had originally emanated from a Commission communication in 1995 and had been drafted in the wake of the Russian intervention in Chechnya. As Haukkala outlines, the communication was aimed at developing a 'mutually beneficial partnership' between the EU and Russia and set out the following priorities:

1. The further involvement of the Russian Federation in the

development of the European security architecture, the overriding aim being to avoid new divisions in Europe;

2. The further development of democratic norms, institutions and practices, and the respect for human rights, individual liberties;

3. Further progress towards economic reform and encouragement of European Community/Russia economic interaction in order to ensure Russia's economic liberalization and establishment of the market economy; and its growing participation in a wider European zone of prosperity, and the world economic system;

4. The intensification of bilateral and multilateral cooperation in other fields, *inter alia* justice, home affairs and crime prevention, and crisis prevention and management;

5. The extension of open and constructive dialogue at different levels and in various fora, covering all matters of common interest.[30]

The communication eventually led to an Action Plan which was adopted in May 1996 and coincided with the first signs that EU pressure on Moscow in regard to Chechnya was starting to show progress and with Russia's entry into the Council of Europe in February 1996. The common strategy, however, was announced just ahead of the NATO intervention in Kosovo. Far from announcing a new dawn in EU-Russian relations, the common strategy came at a time when EU-Russian relations were at their lowest point since the end of the Cold War.

A critical reading of EU policy towards Russia at this point would argue that too many concessions were being made to Moscow and too much credibility afforded to Russia's claims to be part of the democratic community by the EU in return for little progress in the way of tangible reform. Moreover, as Haukkala comments, it was not altogether clear where the strategic direction in the common strategy lay. 'First, a strategy, in order to be successful, has to express clear aims and objectives for future action. Second, a strategy has to provide clear ways and means how these objectives shall be reached in the first place and what to do in case things do not go as they have been planned.'[31] The common strategy in this sense put forward various intentions and preferred outcomes without clearly stating how they were to be achieved. Much, then, can be said for the parallels that Danilov and De Spiegeleire draw between the course of the European integration process in the post-war period and policy towards Russia in their suggestion that 'functional impulses' best explain EU policy towards Russia:

> The strategy is distinctly European: it is quite long-term; incrementally integrationist; multi-dimensional; multi-level (sub-national, national and supra-national); and both functional and

institutional. It closely mirrors the neo-functionalist logic that has served Western Europe so spectacularly well over the past half century; economic integration 'spilling over' in political and eventually in security integration. Thus the European approach to the 'Russian security question' has been basically (and characteristically) indirect: to assist the country's painful transformation process across the board, in the hope that at some point in time this will also yield security benefits.[32]

In much the same way that the Chechen conflict obstructed ratification of the PCA, the common strategy was hindered by the restart of hostilities when Chechen forces entered Dagestan in August 1999. While on this occasion, the EU demonstrated initial sympathy for the Russian position, by the time of the EU-Russia summit in Helsinki in October 1999 it was clear that relations had become strained as the EU attempted to apply political pressure to Russia to seek a political solution to the conflict. The EU *Declaration on Chechnya* at the Helsinki European Council summit in December 1999 condemned the bombing of the Chechen capital, Grozny, and finished with an emotional plea that:

> Russia is a major partner for the European Union. The Union has constantly expressed its willingness to accompany Russia in its transition towards a modern and democratic state. But Russia must live up to its obligations if the strategic partnership is to be developed. The European Union does not want Russia to isolate herself from Europe.[33]

The declaration was followed up in January 2000 by proposals for a series of trade sanctions against Russia.

However, as Haukkala argues, despite the political rhetoric and threat of economic sanctions, the EU found itself powerless to influence events as Russian forces continued their offensive on Grozny and in February 2000 eventually captured the Chechen capital. Of more importance was the growing realization in Western capitals that EU pressure in relation to the Chechen issue was in danger of provoking a major breakdown in EU-Russian relations and prompted the development of a new, more pragmatic approach towards Moscow.[34]

The need for a more constructive dialogue between the EU and Russia was reciprocated in Moscow. The end of the Cold War had compelled Russia to redefine its identity and relations with the rest of Europe. President Boris Yeltsin had attempted to balance Russian foreign policy between the pragmatic, pro-Western lobby, which recognized Russia's reliance upon Western financial aid and integration into international markets, with the more bellicose Slavophile tendencies, which argued for a more distanced position towards the West. The consequence was, not too surprisingly, an erratic foreign policy and it was not until Vladimir Putin replaced Yeltsin as Russian president in March 2000 that a more consistent policy line could be discerned.[35]

In his 'Russia at the turn of the millennium' speech released on 31 December 1999 Putin acknowledged the 'material and mental' damage of the Soviet-type system to Russian society and signalled a policy agenda of societal reconciliation, state reform and greater economic efficiency. In framing this agenda within the context of the need for deeper integration into the global economy, Putin set Russia's direction down the Westernizing rather than the Slavophile path.[36] In response to the EU Common Strategy on Russia, Moscow produced its own *Russian Medium-Term Strategy for Development of Relations with the European Union* in October 1999. This document was instructive in so far that it provided the first clear statement that Russia had no aspiration to become a member of the EU:

> Partnership between Russia and the European Union will be based on the treaty relations, i.e., without an officially stated objective of Russia's accession to or 'association' with the EU. As a world power situated on two continents, Russia should retain its freedom to determine and implement its domestic and foreign policies, its status and advantages of an Euro-Asian state and the largest country of the CIS, independence of its position and activities at international organizations.[37]

Russian strategic interest in its relations with the EU was identified as the development of a collaborative pan-European security defence identity which 'could counterbalance, *inter alia*, the NATO-centrism in Europe', the strengthening of economic relations leading to 'a Russia-European Union free trade zone' and including an energy dialogue, the fostering of EU support for Russia's entry into the World Trade Organization (WTO), increased political dialogue on a wide range of political, economic and technical issues and technological cooperation, all of which would lead to 'a united Europe without dividing lines and the interrelated and balanced strengthening of the positions of Russia and the EU within an international community of the 21st century'.[38]

The Russian foreign policy line towards the EU was reaffirmed in June 2000 with the publication of *The Foreign Policy Concept of the Russian Federation,* which highlighted Russian involvement in the developing European security architecture and broader recognition of the EU-Russian economic relationship:

> Of key importance are relations with the European Union (EU). The ongoing processes within the EU are having a growing impact on the dynamic of the situation in Europe. These are the EU expansion,

transition to a common currency, the institutional reform, and emergence of a joint foreign policy and a policy in the area of security, as well as a defense identity. Regarding these processes as an objective component of European development, Russia will seek due respect for its interest, including in the sphere of bilateral relations with individual EU member countries. The Russian Federation views the EU as one of its main political and economic partners and will strive to develop with it an intensive, stable and long-term cooperation devoid of expediency fluctuations.[39]

The period between 1994 and 1999 was a turbulent episode in the development of EU-Russian relations but an instructive one during which the EU and Russia moved towards a better mutual understanding of each other's foreign policy agendas. This has provided a basis for future cooperation.

THE SANTA DE FEIRA EUROPEAN COUNCIL SUMMIT 2000 AND THE EU'S WIDER EUROPE AGENDA

At the EU-Russia summit in Moscow in May 2000 the new climate of 'constructive dialogue' in EU-Russian relations was clearly evident with Russia pledging to seek a 'political solution' to the situation in Chechnya and reaffirming its position as a 'constructive, reliable and responsible partner in working towards a new multipolar system of international relations, based on strict implementation of international law'. The EU for its part noted the 'latest developments' in Chechnya and underscored 'the importance of cooperation between European Union and Russia in the framework of the PCA and on the basis of the two strategies'.[40] The Santa de Feira European Council summit in June 2000 was, therefore, a major turning point in EU-Russian relations in that it was the first summit of the post-Yeltsin era and came at a time when the EU was revising its position on enlargement and developing its wider Europe agenda which would address relations with those states unlikely to become members in the near future.

Haukkala argues that the pragmatic dimension to EU-Russian relations was unambiguously given in the summit statement where it was agreed that 'a strong and healthy partnership must be maintained between the Union and Russia'.[41] The key areas of attention emerging at this time were, and remain: (i) the ESDP; (ii) enlargement and cross-border cooperation; and (iii) economic relations including the energy dialogue.

The European Security and Defence Policy (ESDP)

High on the agenda was the evolving ESDP. In formulating the Common Strategy on Russia, the EU's intention had been to ameliorate Russian fears of marginalization and to engage Russia in further dialogue as a means of encouraging economic and political liberalization. The Common Strategy had undertaken to 'examine the possibility of creating a permanent EU-Russia mechanism for political and security dialogue' which would 'develop joint foreign policy initiatives with regard to specific third countries and regions, to conflict prevention and to crisis management especially in areas adjacent to Russia, on the Balkans and the Middle East'.[42] This commitment was reaffirmed at the May 2000 summit and it was suggested that 'Russia may be invited to participate in future crisis management operations'.[43]

Alongside this development, the first trilateral ministerial meeting between the EU, Russia and the US had taken place in Lisbon in March 2000 and acted to quell Western concerns that Russia was attempting to split the transatlantic alliance by playing the 'European Card'. What the trilateral meetings, the ESDP and developments in EU-NATO relations since 1999 suggest is an increasingly sophisticated understanding of the European security architecture as all three parties move beyond the Cold War security agenda.[44]

Following the terrorist attacks on the US in September 2001, the EU and Russia issued a *Joint Declaration on Stepping up Dialogue and Cooperation on Political and Security Matters* at the EU-Russia summit in Brussels in October 2001. This was designed to address 'issues of mutual interest, such as increasing international security and crisis prevention and management in Europe, non-proliferation and disarmament, conventional weapons exports, the OSCE, the United Nations and combating international terrorism',[45] which provided Russia, on paper at least, with consultation rights on ESDP that were in effect superior to those enjoyed by the non-EU NATO member states.[46] Russia had undoubtedly won this concession as a consequence of the terrorist attacks. In his speech to the German Parliament on 25 September 2001, a week prior to the EU-Russia summit, Putin condemned the attacks but pointed to the lack of international cooperation between Russia and the West as a contributing factor to the rise of international terrorism:

> What do we lack nowadays for effective cooperation? Despite all the positive achievements of the past decades, we have not yet managed to work out an effective mechanism for cooperation. The coordinating agencies, established so far, do not give Russia any real opportunity to participate in the process of preparing and adopting decisions. Today, decisions are frequently taken essentially without our participation, and only afterwards are we insistently asked to approve them.... Not so long ago, it appeared that soon a truly common house would be built on the [European] continent, a house in which Europeans would not be divided into eastern and western, or northern and southern

lines. Yet, these 'fault lines' will continue to exist. And this primarily because we have still not yet been able to free ourselves for good from many of the stereotypes and ideological clichés of the Cold War.[47]

The latest development is the Russian-proposed initiative of an ESDP Action Plan put forward at the EU-Russia summit in May 2002 which seeks to further develop EU-Russian military cooperation It came at the same time as Russia and NATO were establishing a new partnership at the Reykjavik NATO summit in May 2002.[48] While EU member states were willing to go along with Russia on the idea of an Action Plan, it is unlikely to yield anything tangible in the foreseeable future until greater internal consensus on EU defence policy is achieved.[49]

Enlargement and Cross-Border Cooperation

The entry of Austria, Finland and Sweden into the EU in January 1995 had opened up a new chapter in EU-Russian relations and had resulted in a common border for the first time. The geopolitical significance of this development was taken on board and the Northern Dimension gained its first public recognition at the European Council summit in Luxembourg in December 1997 and coincided with the implementation of the PCA. A Commission communication on the 'Northern Dimension for the Policies of the Union' was released at the Vienna European Council in December 1998 and a year later, in December 1999 at the Helsinki European Council summit, the Commission was asked to draw up an Action Plan. It was agreed at the EU-Russia summit in May 2000 that increased work was necessary in order 'to combat transnational threats, including those of extremism and terrorism, organized crime, trafficking of drugs and human beings, smuggling of weapons, and money laundering' together with the broader Northern Dimension agenda designed to support 'mutually beneficial cross border cooperation' in economic, environmental, social and cultural matters.

The *Action Plan for the Northern Dimension in the External and Cross-Border Policies of the European Union* was adopted at the Feira European Council summit in 2000 and came at a particularly significant time as preparations for the enlargement into Central and Eastern Europe were gathering pace. As has already been outlined, Russia has become increasingly aware of the soft security agenda and has repeated its concerns regarding the economic impact of enlargement on numerous occasions. The Commission presented its final progress reports on the accession negotiations in November 2002 and accession of the ten successful applicant states has been set for 1 May 2004.

It is highly unlikely that Russia will receive the consultation rights on enlargement it seeks. Agreement on the Common Economic Space (CES), however, will undoubtedly provide a means by which the EU can negotiate a compensation package to go some way towards addressing Russian concerns. As was agreed at the May 2002 EU-Russia summit, 'the pending EU enlargement will open new prospects for our relations but at the same time will possibly create new problems, including in the sphere of trade, economic cooperation and human contacts. We agree to discuss more actively the essence of the Russian concerns in the framework of the PCA.'[50]

A more problematic issue is that of the Russian enclave of Kaliningrad on the Baltic Sea between Poland and Lithuania which, following enlargement, will be encircled by the EU. The EU made it clear at the EU-Russia summit in May 2002 that it would not countenance visa-free travel between Russia and Kaliningrad. This statement provoked an inevitable protest from Moscow and it remains to be seen whether the agreement on this sensitive issue will be reached at the EU-Russia summit in Autumn 2002 which puts in place special provision for transit for Russian nationals between Russia and the Kaliningrad enclave will provide a long-term solution. Again, the most likely outcome is an agreement on Kaliningrad which will be encompassed within the CES.

Economic Relations and the Energy Dialogue

Although the PCA sets out a free trade zone as the end goal of the economic relationship between the EU and Russia, it is questionable whether this would be in the interests of either party at present. The EU would be confronted with cheap agricultural and heavy industrial imports, which it has so far been able to prevent using anti-dumping legislation. Where Russia is concerned, opening up what remains largely a Soviet-style economy would unleash damaging competitive pressures. Russia's key foreign economic objective is membership of the World Trade Organization (WTO). Having applied to join GATT (General Agreement on Tariffs and Trade), the predecessor to WTO, in 1993, Russia's application was suspended until the WTO was formed in 1995. The perceived benefits are: (i) greater access to international markets; (ii) greater domestic competition and, as a consequence, efficiency; (iii) an increase in foreign direct investment; and (iv) legal recourse to settle trade disputes.[51]

The EU has given its formal support for Russian WTO membership and in the course of 2002 recognized Russia as a market economy. A further stepping stone towards Russia achieving WTO membership was the decision taken at the EU-Russia summit in May 2001 to establish a Common European Economic Area (later referred to as the Common Economic Space - CES) by 2003. The creation at the October 2001 summit of a 'High-Level Group to elaborate a concept for a closer economic relationship between Russia' represented a raising of the rhetoric but has so far yet to yield any real progress.[52]

A more tangible area of mutual interest is the energy dialogue, which was initiated at the EU-Russia summit in October 2000 and presents the opportunity for Russia to assert a degree of linkage between energy exports and the CEES. In promoting itself as an advanced industrial economy, Russia is keen to avoid a developing world profile where its exports are based predominantly around the exploitation of natural resources. However, the extent to which Moscow is prepared to use the energy dialogue as a means of encouraging a more diverse trading relationship with the EU needs to be balanced against its dependency on the EU for foreign trade and investment.

CONCLUSION: FUTURE PROSPECTS FOR THE EU-RUSSIAN RELATIONSHIP

There is still much ground to be covered before it can be claimed that the EU speaks with one voice on international affairs, and whether a fully coherent and consistent policy line towards Russia exists within the Western capitals of Europe remains open to question.[53] Russia presents the EU with a major challenge and the extent to which a stable and durable relationship can be established will be an indication of the EU's growing maturity as an international actor. Although both parties can talk about common interests, there is still considerable ground to be covered in developing a shared normative basis for the relationship and distinct differences can be identified in terms of foreign policy goals. Russia's central concern remains that of gaining a place at the 'European table' and establishing its claim to regional power status.

Though the former of these two objectives has to some extent been achieved, Russia still has much to do in addressing its internal economic agenda. In this sense, the economic impact of EU enlargement into Central and Eastern Europe and delays in joining the WTO will be future sources of tension. It can, therefore, be suggested that pragmatic incrementalism rather than strategic partnership best accounts for the current state of EU-Russian relations and is not an assertion that should be taken necessarily as a criticism.

In return for Russia's place at the table, the EU has demonstrated success in sweetening the pill of enlargement and in stabilizing cross-border relations. The energy dialogue will also no doubt result in real benefits in time as will the more long-term socialization process as Russia is coaxed towards a 'Western model' of norms and values. As such, rather than EU policy being a means of stabilizing Russia, the development of relations with Moscow has reduced the extent to which its new-found eastern neighbour can act as a source of instability within the EU. This is the case now as it stands and will become a more significant factor once enlargement takes place. But if the EU demonstrates incremental tendencies, the same is undoubtedly true of Russia and little else can be realistically expected given the tremendous changes to the political climate of Europe which have taken place in recent years. Although there remains considerable doubt regarding the extent to which the EU and Russia are able to interact in any meaningful way within a framework of strategic partnership, it remains the case that neither sees its interests as best served in marginalizing the other.

NOTES

1. This article is based on research papers presented at the Centre for Russian, Soviet and Central and East European Studies annual conference in St Andrews, 2002, and the British Association for Slavonic and East European Studies annual conference in Cambridge, 2002, and represents the initial stage of a project on *EU-Russian Relations Beyond The Cold War* which is being funded by the European Commission via the Jean Monnet project. My thanks go to all those who took the time to comment on my work and also to an anonymous reviewer. I would also like to thank Patrick Child, Torsten Wöllert and Diego de Ojeda in the European Commission, Carl Hartzell in the European Council and Andrey Avetisyan, of the Russian Mission to the EU in Brussels, for granting me interviews in June 2002.
2. *Common Strategy of the European Union on Russia*, June 1999. Available at: http://europa. eu.int/comm/external_relations/ceeca/com_strat/index.htm.
3. Chris Patten, 'The EU and Russia: The Way Ahead', speech delivered 18 Jan. 2001: www.europa.eu.int/comm/external_relations/news/patten/speech_01_11.htm.
4. Hiski Haukkala, *Two Reluctant Regionalizers? The European Union and Russia in Europe's North* (Helsinki: The Finnish Institute for International Affairs Working Paper No. 32, 2002) pp.8–9.
5. Marius Vahl, *Just Good Friends? The EU-Russian 'Strategic Partnership' and the Northern Dimension* (Brussels: Centre for European Policy Studies, Working Document No. 166, 2001) p.2.
6. Romano Prodi, Speech at EU-Russia Summit, Moscow, 29 May 2000: http://europa. eu.int/comm/external_relations/russia/summit_29_05_00/prodi_speech_29_05_00.htm.
7. See Peter van Ham, *The EC, Eastern Europe and European Unity* (London: Pinter 1993) for a detailed summary of the EC-CMEA relationship.
8. Mikhail Gorbachev, *Perestroika: New Thinking for Our Country and the World* (London: Collins 1987) pp.194–5.
9. *Rome European Council Presidency Conclusions, 15 and 15 December 1990*: www.europarl. eu.int/summits/previous_scan.htm.
10. See the European Commission External Relations website: http://europa.eu.int/comm/ external_relations/ceeca/tacis/index.htm.
11. *Partnership and Cooperation Agreement*, 1994, Article 1, p.7, taken from European Commission: External Relations website: http://europa.eu.int/comm/external_relations/ russia/pca_legal/index.htm.
12. Heinz Timmermann, 'Relations Between the EU and Russia: The Agreement On Partnership and Co-operation', *Journal of Communist Studies and Transition Politics* 12/2 (June 1996) p.219.
13. Haukkala (note 4) p.4.
14. See the overview of the EU's relations with Russia taken from European Commission: External Relations website: http://europa.eu.int/comm/external_relations/russia/intro/ index.htm.
15. For two particularly interesting accounts of the normative debate surrounding the eastern

enlargement process, see Frank Schimmelfennig, 'The Community Trap: Liberal Norms, Rhetorical Action, and the Eastern Enlargement of the European Union', *International Organization* 55/1 (Winter 2001) pp.47–80; and John O'Brennan, 'EU Enlargement to Central and Eastern Europe: A Normative Reading', *Political Science Forum* 1/1 (2002) pp.163–86.

16. Jackie Gower, 'Russia and the European Union', in Mark Webber (ed.), *Russia and Europe: Conflict of Cooperation?* (London: Macmillan 2000) p.72.

17. Hiski Haukkala, *The Making of the European Union's Common Strategy on Russia* (Helsinki: The Finnish Institute of International Affairs, Working Papers No. 28, 2000) pp.7–8.

18. Gower, 'Russia and the European Union' (note 16) p.74.

19. Haukkala, *Making of the European Union's* (note 17) p.8. See also Christopher Hillion, 'Partnership and Cooperation Agreements between the European Union and the New Independent States of the Ex-Soviet Union', *European Foreign Affairs Review* 3 (1998) pp.399–420.

20. *Izvestia*, 18 Nov. 1993: CDPSP XLV/46 (1993), p.12.

21. NATO-Russian relations are discussed in more detail in Martin A. Smith and Graham Timmins, 'Russia, NATO and the EU in an Era of Enlargement: Vulnerability or Opportunity?', *Geopolitics* 6/1 (Summer 2001) pp.73–81.

22. Christopher Hill, 'The Capability-Expectations Gap or Conceptualizing Europe's International Role', *Journal of Common Market Studies* 31/3 (1993) pp.305–28.

23. 'War in Europe', *The Economist*, 6 July 1991, p.11.

24. G. Wyn Rees, 'Common Foreign and Security Policy and Defence: A Lost Opportunity?' in Philip Lynch, Nanette Neuwahl and G. Wyn Rees (eds.), *Reforming the European Union: From Maastricht to Amsterdam* (London: Longman 2000) p.177. A full investigation of the international role of the EU is beyond the scope of this article. However, for two recent studies, see Brian White, *Understanding European Foreign Policy* (Basingstoke: Palgrave 2001); and Hazel Smith, *European Union Foreign Policy: What it Is and What it Does* (London: Pluto 2002).

25. *Cologne European Council Presidency Conclusions, 3 and 4 June 1999*: Annex III: European Council Declaration on Strengthening the Common European Policy on Security and Defence. Available at: www.europarl.eu.int/summits/kol2_en.htm.

26. The concept of the EU as a civilian (i.e. non-military) power was first credited to Francois Duchene in the early 1970s. See 'Europe's Role in World Peace' in Richard Mayne (ed.), *Europe Tomorrow* (London: Fontana 1972) and 'The European Community and the Uncertainties of Interdependence' in Max Kohnstamm and Wolfgang Hager (eds.), *A Nation Writ Large? Foreign Policy Problems before the European Communities* (London: Macmillan 1973). For a more contemporary discussion of this concept, see Ian Manners, 'Normative Power Europe: A Contradiction in Terms?', *Journal of Common Market Studies* 40/2 (2002) pp.235–58.

27. The Treaty of Amsterdam amending the Treaty on European Union and the Treaty establishing the European Community, 1997, article J.3(2). See Andrew Duff (ed.), *The Treaty of Amsterdam: Text and Commentary* (London: Sweet and Maxwell 1997) pp.111–19 for a thorough discussion of the changes to the CFSP implemented in the Amsterdam Treaty.

28. *Cologne Presidency Conclusions, 3 and 4 June 1999* (note 25).

29. Ibid., p.14.

30. Commission of the European Communities, 'The European Union and Russia: The Future Relationship', COM (95) 223 final, 31 May 1995, 5.2. cited in Haukkala, 2000 (note 17) p.9.

31. Haukkala, 2000 (note 17) p.11.

32. Dmitry Danilov and Stephan De Spiegeleire, >*From Decoupling to Recoupling: Russia and Western Europe: A New Security Relationship?* (Paris: Institute for Security Studies of the Western European Union, Chaillot Paper No.31, 1998) p.26 (taken from website version at: www.weu.int/institute/chaillot/chai31e.html) and Stephan de Spiegeleire, *Recoupling Russia: Staying the Course. Europe's Security Relationship with Russia* (Brussels: IISS/Centre for European Policy Studies (CEPS) European Security Forum, 14 Jan. 2002) p.1, taken from website version at: www.eusec.org/spiegeleire.htm.

33. *Helsinki European Council, Presidency Conclusions* Annex 2 – Declaration on Chechnya, 10 Dec. 1999, cited in Haukkala, 2000 (note 17) pp.34–5.
34. Haukkala, 2000 (note 17) p.38. Haukkala's argument here is that the member states, especially the bigger ones, used EU statements to condemn Russian military action in the Caucasus region but adopted more moderate positions in bilateral relations as a means of limiting political damage.
35. For a more detailed discussion of Russian foreign policy under Yeltsin, see Mike Bowker, 'The Place of Europe in Russian Foreign Policy' in Mark Webber (ed.), *Russia and Europe: Conflict or Cooperation?* (London: Macmillan 2000) and Laura Richards Cleary, 'Russia: Caging the Bear?' in Martin A. Smith and Graham Timmins (eds), *Uncertain Europe: Building a New European Security Order?* (London: Routledge 2001).
36. Vladimir Putin, Russia at the Turn of the Millennium Speech, 31 Dec. 1999. Available in translation at: www.government.gov.ru/english/statVP_engl_1.html.
37. *The Russian Medium-Term Strategy for Development of Relations with the European Union*: www.eur.ru/eng/neweur/user_eng.php?func=apage&id=53.
38. Ibid.
39. *Foreign Policy Concept of the Russian Federation, 2000*: www.bits.de/EURA/EURAMAIN.htm#Rfpoldoc.
40. *Joint Statement, EU-Russia Summit, Moscow, 29 May 2000*: http://europa.eu.int/comm/external_relations/russia/summit_29_05_00/index.htm.
41. *Santa Maria de Feira European Council Presidency Conclusions, 19 and 20 June 2000*. Cited in Haukkala (note 17) 2000, p.40.
42. Ibid., p.28.
43. *Joint Statement, EU-Russia Summit* (note 40).
44. The issue of EU-NATO relations and the impact this has had on the formulation of Western policy towards Russia is beyond the scope of this essay. The author and Martin A.Smith are currently working on a research project examining the EU, NATO and Russia which will be published by Routledge in 2003.
45. *Joint Statement, EU-Russia Summit, Brussels, 3 October 2001*: Annex 4 – Joint Declaration on stepping up dialogue and cooperation on political and security matters. Available at: http://europa.eu.int/comm/external_relations/russia/summit_10_01/dc_en.htm
46. The relevance of Russian consultation rights on ESDP were brought to my attention by Kara Bosworth. See 'The Effect of 11th September on Russia-NATO Relations', paper delivered at the British Association for Slavonic and East European Studies Annual Conference, Cambridge, April 2002.
47. Vladimir Putin, speech to German Parliament on 25 Sept. 2001: www.pegmusic.com/putin-in-germany.html.
48. *Financial Times*, 15 May 2002.
49. As was pointed out to me during an interview in Brussels, the ESDP remains essentially an internal policy tool of the CFSP and, as such, cannot be negotiated externally with Russia in a manner Moscow would prefer.
50. EU-Russia Summit, Moscow 29 May 2002: http://europa.eu.int/comm/external_relations/russia/summit_05_02/state.htm.
51. Alan Jones and Grahame Fallon, 'Exploring Attitudes Towards Russia's Proposed Membership of the WTO', research paper presented at the University Association for Contemporary European Studies Annual General Conference, Belfast, 2002.
52. EU-Russia Summit, Brussels, 3 Oct. 2001.
53. Despite the absence of public disagreement, some degree of divergence between EU policy and the bilateral policies of the member states towards Russia can be anticipated. Disaggregating EU policy towards Russia remains a relatively under-researched question and the extent to which Germany plays a pivotal role in developing and determining the EU policy line is a key issue in this context and will provide the next stage in my own research.

Exploitation of the 'Islamic Factor' in the Russo-Chechen Conflict Before and After 11 September 2001

JOHN RUSSELL

> Never will we appear submissive before anyone,
> Death or Freedom – we can choose only one way
> *(Chechen National Anthem, Verse 4)*[1]

The hyperbole and rhetoric of these lines, though not unusual in the discourse of self-determination and national identity, have taken on sinister new associations since 11 September 2001, and reverberate anew as the world assesses the resolution of the Moscow hostage crisis. The events of 11 September, retrospectively, appear to have justified Russia's longstanding claim that the West was not only underestimating the 'plague of the twenty-first century' – international (Islamic) terrorism[2] – but also ignoring the existence of 'an arc of Islamic fundamentalism from Kosovo to the Philippines'.[3]

Russia sought and gained a support role in America's war against terrorism in Afghanistan, taking every opportunity since the World Trade Center attacks to present its conflict with the Chechens, which it has always characterized as a counter-terrorist operation, as a key component of the coalition's overall struggle with Islamic insurgents, ranking in importance with that of Israel against the Palestinians and the West against the Taliban and al-Qaeda.[4] Western leaders have responded by toning down significantly their criticism of Russian actions in Chechnya, acknowledging tacitly President Putin's carte blanche in dealing with not only the Chechen rebels, but also the civilian population in the war zone.[5] In the perception of many of its citizens, Russia has been restored to its predestined role as the first line of defence in the 'clash of civilizations', defending the Western way of life against the threat of, traditionally the 'Yellow' but now, the Islamic 'Green' Peril'.[6] Since 11 September this claim is no longer dismissed in the West as mere post-Great Power posturing.

In that the attacks on New York and Washington facilitated Russia's attempt to join the US as a strategic partner in the war against international Islamic terrorism, their timing worked very much to Putin's advantage. As the conflict dragged on throughout 2000 and 2001 with no victory in sight, public opinion in Russia was beginning to turn against the war in Chechnya.[7] Although the levels of support among the Russian public have not regained those of the early months of the conflict in 1999, Putin's newly found status as an ally of Bush, Blair and other Western leaders has consolidated his personal popularity ratings.[8] In October 2002, following a period during which polls declared that the Russian public was almost two to one against a continuation of the war in Chechnya, the Moscow theatre siege and Putin's tough stand in resolving it led to a surge in support for the President's policy of seeking a military solution.[9]

This essay examines the impact of 11 September on the 'Islamic factor'[10] in the Russo-Chechen war primarily from the Russian perspective, but taking into account the views of the West, and seeks to establish the degree to which changes in public attitudes influenced the options perceived to be left open to the Chechen separatists. It traces the battle, therefore, for the hearts and minds of the public in Russia and the West and, by extension, in Chechnya itself. It builds on an earlier examination of the crude stereotyping and demonizing of the Chechens, in which I described how, in the course of two brutal wars, Russian popular stereotypes of the Chechens had been manipulated in such a way as to replace a generally positive perception of the noble and free mountain man – the *dzhigit* – into, first, a dangerous and bloodthirsty criminal (bandit) and, subsequently, into a crazed and fanatical terrorist of an Islamic fundamentalist persuasion.[11]

Finally, in the light of the attacks on New York and Washington, and, subsequently, of the Moscow theatre siege, it seeks to determine what exit strategies, other than bombing their way to victory, are open to the Russians in Chechnya.[12]

It may be argued that Russia has not fundamentally changed its policy towards Chechnya post-11 September, but merely exploited the changed international atmosphere to emphasize even more the Chechens' links with Islamic fundamentalists of al-Qaeda and the Taliban.

Russian public opinion had already been won over as a result of the Moscow apartment bombs of September 1999. This is demonstrated by the fact that although neither the political, nor military leaders of Russia, in their zeal to eradicate such 'terrorists', appear to dwell overlong on the distinction between ordinary Chechen civilians and the 'terrorists' hidden in their midst, this inconsistency has by no means met with the overwhelming disapproval of the Russian public during this second war. To win over Western opinion, Russia sought to 'absolutize' its conflict with the Chechens by consolidating the image of all those who take up arms to oppose its policies as Islamic terrorists and, therefore, as a component of the war on international terror launched by the US in the wake of the September attacks. This would appear to have paid off, at least at the level of heads of state, when President Bush required that Chechen leader Asian Maskhadov choose, in effect, between the Arab commander Khattab (in Chechnya) and Putin,[13] in a situation in which a democratic plebiscite would prefer, in all likelihood, a third option.

The role of the Russian media in maintaining and consolidating public support for the conflict in Chechnya during the second war was critical. During the first Chechen war an independent Russian media ensured that a just and lasting resolution of the conflict was kept on the agenda on behalf of a sceptical Russian public. By the start of the second war, Russian generals and politicians had learnt the utility of a tame and dependent press, safe in the knowledge of a public thirst for revenge against the Chechens, in particular, and Islamic fundamentalists in general.[14] Just as the first war influenced the development of Islamic culture across the Russian Federation,[15] the Moscow bombs of September 1999 and the events of 11 September 2001, have affected attitudes towards all Muslims in the former Soviet Union.[16] A political analyst at the Hoover Institution at Stanford University claims that: 'The September 11 terrorist attacks in the United States and Putin's support for the US-led war against terrorism is interjecting new and potentially explosive tension back into Russia's inter-ethnic relations.'[17]

To examine these shifts in Russian popular attitudes, I propose to distinguish between factors stemming from historical aspects of the Russo-Chechen relationship and those that have been attributed to the Chechens subsequently, especially since 11 September. A key component of this will be the legitimate self-perceptions and aspirations of the Chechens and their misinterpretation, sometimes through ignorance, but oft-times through design, by the Russians.

The most deep-rooted of these historical aspects were largely of a cultural nature, stemming from a clash between a traditional and a modernizing civilization.[18] In Chechnya a clear distinction is drawn between *adaat* (custom) and *Shari'a* (religious code). Many aspects of Chechen culture, which the Russians perceive as Islamic, and therefore alien, are in fact traditional customs. A good example of this might be Chechen attitudes to women or, indeed, the blood feud. Of course, some aspects did have profoundly political and geopolitical ramifications (not least the imperial ambitions of successive Russian and Soviet regimes and the subsequent expectation, on the part of the Chechens, of the same rights to self-determination as those enjoyed by Estonia, Georgia or Turkmenistan).

Moreover, these factors need to be understood in the context of not only a collapsing empire, but also a disintegrating superpower. The emergence of, and increased emphasis upon, the so-called 'Islamic factor' since the collapse of communist ideology and Soviet patriotism in 1991 needs to be set in the context of all former Soviet peoples, including the Russians and the Chechens, establishing new national and cultural identities with which to fill the ideological vacuum.[19]

That for the ethnic Russians this included the integrity of a Russian Federation, in which they had become a significant majority, inevitably had consequences for all non-Russian citizens.[20] For many Russians, the attractiveness of their new, smaller homeland, alongside the promised benefits of democracy, a free market economy and a law-governed state, was the apparent resolution of the 'Islamic question', which had been perceived as a growing menace to Slavic numerical superiority in the last years of the USSR.[21]

The Russian Federation, although still a multicultural entity, is markedly less so than was the USSR. Despite its Eurasian landmass, the loss of the Central Asian republics made the new Russia a much more Eurocentric country in cultural terms. It promised its citizens (both Russian and non-Russian) a new, prosperous and voluntary commonwealth. To the extent that it failed to deliver, it is not surprising that the discourse of the Russians became more traditional (nationalistic and authoritarian), leaving the disaffected and defiant to find a new discourse of their own. Paradoxically, although in traditionally Muslim cultural areas of the former USSR, Islam predictably became the new discourse, in the Central Asian republics the nationalist and authoritarian successor governments combined these discourses to ensure the pre-eminence of secular over militant Islam in that region.

A similar mix of nationalist, authoritarian and Islamic discourse enabled an accommodation to be reached with Tatarstan and other republics within Russia containing titular nationalities of a nominally Muslim cultural background, including all of Chechnya's neighbours in the North Caucasus. Few would argue that the Chechens were less secular or 'European' than these neighbours or the Tatars. The Russian political commentator, Pavel Fel'genhauer, noted at the outbreak of the first war that: 'Most Chechens drink, eat pork, and don't really know the Koran.'[22] The problem would appear to be the 'unfinished business' of determining the exact relationship between the Chechens and the Russians in the post-Soviet era. Both sides had scores to settle. As an American observer concluded at the end of the first war:

> In the Russian imagination...Chechnya is an obsession, an image of Islamic defiance, an embodiment of the primitive, the devious, the elusive. For more than three centuries, the czars and the general secretaries – and now a democratically elected president – have tried to obliterate the Chechens, first by war on horseback, then by deportation in cattle cars, and now by heavy artillery bombardment and carpet bombing.[23]

For the Russians, Chechnya seemed to provide the 'small, victorious war', which would put right any number of wrongs, from the ignominious defeat in the Afghan War to the loss of the Cold War.[24] For the Chechens, the disintegration of the Soviet Union represented an historic opportunity for the small mountain republic to escape from its perceived structurally repressive relationship with Russia (not least the forced incorporation into the Russian and Soviet empires and the deportations of the Second World War) and to attain an element of political and cultural self-determination, what they would call 'freedom'.[25]

Galtung would recognize this relationship as one of 'structural violence', that is, injustices perceived to stem from the dominant order.[26] According to this concept, insurgency (direct violence) is perceived by the authorities solely as a security issue to be dealt with by 'legitimate' forces of law and order, whereas the insurgents may view direct violence as the only means of liberating their people from a structurally unjust system (apartheid, imperialism, slavery and so on). What such a theory helps us to understand is why nations fight against all odds and utilize all means for self-determination. It is a new and frightening common feature in this struggle – that of a fundamentalist Islamic ideology sanctioning suicide attacks – that allows parallels to be drawn between Chechnya, Palestine and 11 September.[27]

The danger of applying Galtung's theory to explain acts of terrorism is that the 'ends' may be used to justify the most unacceptable of 'means' (for example, the attacks of 11 September and the Moscow theatre siege). The danger of ignoring his theory altogether, however, is that solutions may be sought that address the symptoms rather than the root causes of the conflict.[28]

Prior to the outbreak of hostilities, there is evidence that the majority of both the Chechen and Russian people were opposed to the first war. For example, prior to the first conflict, the International Alert fact-finding commission reported from Chechnya in 1992 that:

> Any conversation of more than 15 minutes with a Chechen touches on the humiliation they suffered at the hands of successive Russian governments, starting with the period of Tsarist expansion into the Chechen lands in the eighteenth century, continuing through the deportation to Central Asia in February 1944, and culminating in failure of the Soviet state to return property to them when they were allowed to return in the late 1950s, or compensation for losses and sufferings during their Central Asian exile. On the other hand, we heard surprisingly few comments that characterized Russians as a people in unreservedly negative terms or berated Russians now living

in Chechnia [sic] for arrogant behaviour. Resentment against what Chechens regard as colonialisation in Tsarist times and Stalinist repression during the Soviet era does not translate into rancour against the current Russian component of the republic's population, who for the most part are seen as victims of the Soviet system, like everyone else who lived under it.[29]

It would appear that the economic, political and military elites of both sides played down the chances for a peaceful resolution and exploited instead the racial, cultural and religious differences between them in order to prosecute the conflict.[30] The late retired Lt. General Aleksandr Lebed, who negotiated with Maskhadov the ceasefire that ended the first war, characterized that conflict as: 'a mafia squabble at state level. The roots are primarily economic, then political, and only after that military.'[31] Certainly, the confrontation between the Russians and the Chechens acquired a symbolic importance for both sides way above that which the situation, objectively, merited.

The brutal and arbitrary conduct by the federal forces in that first war, which left up to 100,000 (mostly Chechen civilians) dead,[32] served to sharpen these differences, as did the role, by August 1996, in defeating the Russian occupying forces by rebel commanders of a more fundamentalist Islamic orientation, such as the Chechens Basayev and Raduyev, and the Arab Khattab. Although the Russian government and its supporters in the media had raised the spectre of terrorism from the outset of the first war, it was only really brought home to the Russian population at large by the actions of such field commanders in the course of that conflict.

Basayev and Raduyev had launched spectacular 'terrorist' attacks (the seizure of hostages in Budennovsk in June 1995 and Kizlyar/ Pervomaiskoye in January 1996), while Khattab pulled off a string of successful attacks on military targets, such as the ambush which culminated in the killing of 76 Russian troops at Yarysh-Mardy in April 1996. That all of these actions occurred when the federal forces were on the brink of rendering ineffective the Chechen armed opposition highlights not only the utility of 'terrorist' acts to shore up sagging morale at home during times of military weakness, but also the manner in which the 'success' of such acts erodes the sympathy for the underdog amongst the adversary's public.

Again, as the events of 11 September have demonstrated graphically, while such acts are employed to dramatize the rebel cause, it tends to be the drama of the situation that attracts media and public attention rather than the cause itself. Thus are the perpetrators of such acts regarded as martyrs for the cause by their supporters and as demonic and dangerous criminals by the public at large who feel threatened by them.[33]

The failure of the Russian forces to distinguish between combatants and civilians (both Russian and Chechen) during this war, the widespread abuse of alcohol and drugs by the Russian troops, and their inability to isolate even the more extremist of the Chechen leaders, made any reconciliation with the Russians dependent on a radical change in Moscow's attitudes to its rebellious southern territory. This change was urged upon Russia by human rights' organizations in both Russia and the West and, to a lesser extent, by certain Western governments. Official Russian responses to such representations were both surly and dismissive, if not outright threatening.

Unfortunately for the Chechens, they failed to gain any international recognition for their cause during the first war. Their subsequent regrettable, albeit understandable, shift towards more overt manifestations of their adherence to Islam was interpreted in the West as a profoundly retrograde step. All that occurred in the period of 'independence' between 1996 and 1999 served to validate this interpretation in the eyes of Western observers.

Chechnya endured in the interlude between the two wars a diplomatic, economic and military blockade, which, significantly, did not extend to high-level contacts of a decidedly criminal nature. This led, perhaps inevitably, to a significant rise in the profile of a more sharply-defined religious orientation, portrayed in the Russian media as one of the most extreme forms of Islamic fundamentalism – 'Wahhabism' – and backed up with open displays in Chechnya of actions perceived in the West as being of either atavistic or fundamentalist character. In three years of de facto independence the Chechen regime, through a series of high-profile kidnappings[34] and gruesome murders[35] of Westerners (and Russians), and a series of public executions under the newly-imposed Shari`a law,[36] had alienated further the West and diluted any romantic notions among Russians as to the rectitude of their cause. Moreover, the presence on Russian soil of foreign Islamic militants, the Wahhabites, could be, and was, portrayed by the Russian media as representing the same threat to Russian democracy as fundamentalists such as Osama bin Laden did to the West.[37]

Rather than encourage the growth of that particularly benign type of secular Islam to which the overwhelming majority of Chechens aspired,[38] there appears to be some evidence that elements in the Russian leadership provoked the 'Wahhabite' incursion into Dagestan in August 1999,[39] if not the apartment house bombs in Moscow and elsewhere.[40]

Clearly, under international law, the Russian authorities were entitled, even obliged, to take action, not only over Dagestan, but also over the lawlessness in Chechnya. The problem was Russian public opinion. Whatever one thinks of the web of conspiracy theories surrounding the bombings in Moscow and Volgodonsk, there is no doubt that they changed fundamentally the Russian population's attitude to dealing with the

Chechen problem once and for all. In this sense the explosions in the capital had an impact in hardening the Russian public's demand for both action and revenge similar to that of the 11 September 2001 attacks on the American popular consciousness and, arguably, the Palestine suicide bombings on Israeli public opinion. Certainly, the events in Chechnya, Dagestan and Moscow were sufficiently linked in the perception of the average Russian citizen as to give an unambiguous green light to a second invasion of Chechnya, ostensibly to root out international terrorism or, as Putin put it in the macho discourse that came to characterize the counter-terrorist operation: 'to kill the terrorists even in the shithouse'.[41]

In the period leading up to the invasion, those members of Russia's nascent 'civic society', such as Grigorii Yavlinskii from the 'Yabloko' party, journalist Anna Politkovskaya and human rights' activists from 'Memorial', who urged restraint and caution or raised doubts about the Chechen policy, were pilloried in the mass media as 'traitors'.[42] A public opinion that proved to be easy to manipulate, in effect, replaced 'civic society' in sanctioning the actions of Russia's policy-makers. The former speaker of the Russian Parliament, Ruslan Khasbulatov, an ethnic Chechen, notes this trend: 'In the absence of civic society its role is played by the population with its "public opinion". This population has been worked over with propaganda and almost everyone supports the war in Chechnya.'[43]

Spurred on by the federal forces' initial success, the Russian generals insisted on chasing the rebel formations into the mountains,[44] using many of the tactics (carpet bombing, thermobaric bombs, sweeps and elite force raids) that the Americans have since employed in Afghanistan. Russian commentators have noted ruefully, however, that the Americans have been much more efficient in their campaign, distinguishing between friend and foe among the Afghan population in a way that Russian forces signally have failed to do.[45] The fact that the Taliban was ousted in little over a month, whereas the Russians have been bogged down in Chechnya for years with still no end in sight while continuing to suffer heavy military losses,[46] would appear to suggest that the situation Russia finds itself in cannot be compared easily to that of the US in Afghanistan.

The Russian leadership, it would seem, is playing the 'Islamic terrorist' card unashamedly in order to crush the rebellious Chechens militarily. The strategy appears to rest upon the assumption that the Chechens would turn to their occupiers for security, if the only local alternative – the 'terrorists' – were taken out of the equation. There seems little prospect of success. Even such a fervent Russian nationalist as Eduard Limonov wrote recently:

> Chechnya is not defeated and we can now state with confidence that it will not be defeated. The fighting spirit of the Chechen people has

turned out to be stronger than the Russian Army. We need to end the war in Chechnya and give Chechnya its independence. Because the war in Chechnya can be won only by exterminating all Chechens. But this is genocide. The two peoples – the Chechens and the Russians – will not have common cause to live together for some time yet. Perhaps they never will. There is too much blood between us.[47]

These views are strikingly similar to those of the Chechen President, Aslan Maskhadov, whose five-year term in office has just come to an end. Even prior to 11 September this former officer in the Soviet Army wrote:

This war has opened our eyes. Even for the ordinary Chechen. The ordinary Chechens have seen what Russian occupation means. Even those, who yesterday were loyal to Russia, have now adopted a different stance. After this war Russia has finally lost Chechnya.[48]

However, since 11 September, few Chechen, let alone Russian, commentators see complete independence as a solution. Those that do, such as Basayev and other field commanders of the more militant 'Islamic' persuasion, have been obliged to rely much more on financial support from Islamic sources and, arguably, need terrorist 'spectaculars' such as the Moscow theatre siege to keep the donations flowing. Thus, even before the October 2002 hostage crisis, the Russian authorities were unwilling to engage seriously in peace talks with any Chechen separatists.

The current Russian-backed Head of Administration in Chechnya, Mufti Akhmed Kadyrov, widely-regarded as a puppet and traitor by Chechens, requests temporary dictatorial powers and a dose of the 1937 purges to bring his rebellious fellow citizens to order.[49] Ruslan Khasbulatov, who is qualified to play a role in Chechnya analogous to that of Eduard Shevardnadze in Georgia, seeks a special status for Chechnya in which the country would be autonomous without destroying the territorial integrity of Russia, with international security guarantees provided by such organs as the Council of Europe and OSCE.[50]

Dzhabrail Gakayev, a respected Chechen academic and public figure, agrees, stating that the Chechens must 'realise their national idea...within the framework of a commonwealth of peoples of Russia'.[51] The shady Chechen 'businessman', Khozh-Ahmed Nukhayev has suggested that Chechnya be divided into two parts. The northern (lowland) Chechnya would remain part of Russia and the mountainous south would become autonomous. He argues that it is the mountain Chechens who 'are the staunchest bearers of the pre-modern national traditions, refuting any form of statehood whatsoever, be it Russian "constitutional order" or a Wahhabi "Islamist state"'. Nonetheless, he warns against kowtowing to the West, urging Russia and Chechnya to join the anti-Western alliance.[52]

A major problem is that, as in other 'terrorist/national liberation' movements, criminal gangs appear to have gained the upper hand and, in Chechnya, have undermined the traditional *teip* (clan) system.[53] There are those who claim that these criminal fraternities are in cahoots with the Russian military commanders and that both sides have a financial interest in prolonging the conflict.[54] Certainly, there is a consensus among all those who seek a peaceful political solution in Chechnya that there is no room for the Chechen field commanders and ideologues of the more militant Islamic orientation, such as Basayev, Yanderbiyev and Udugov. Neither the Russians nor the Chechens appear to be in the mood for all-inclusive amnesties. While Russia insists that certain leaders of the Chechen resistance will be killed or put on trial,[55] the Chechen deputy to the Russian State Duma, Aslembek Aslakhanov, demands that Russian military commanders be brought before a Hague War Crimes Tribunal.[56]

Until the Moscow theatre siege there appeared some prospect of ensuring the participation in determining Chechnya's future of such influential 'pro-Western' Chechens seeking a 'European' (i.e., not militant Islamic) solution, such as Maskhadov, Gelayev and Zakayev. However, the World Chechen Congress in Copenhagen, which coincided with the Moscow hostage crisis and attracted the participation of, among others, Zakayev, Khasbulatov, and former high-ranking Russian and American officials, was bitterly denounced by Putin. His demand that the Danish authorities extradite Maskhadov's envoy, Zakayev, as a terrorist, would seem to have closed off yet another hitherto promising avenue.[57]

CONCLUSION

It has become a truism that the events of 11 September 2001 ushered in a new epoch. Such was the impact of the attacks on New York and Washington that there has been a tendency by the Western alliance to view subsequently all conflicts through the prism of the war on terrorism. Thus, if in Chechnya, Western criticism was confined largely to human rights and other Non-Governmental Organizations (NGOs) prior to 11 September, after the suicide attacks on New York and Washington, Western leaders including Bush and Tony Blair have gone out of their way to draw parallels between the Russian and American experience of combating Islamic terror, utilizing the same formula that the coalition was not against 'Islam' or the 'Chechen people', but against the cancer of international terrorism.[58] This was most notable during Putin's visit to President Bush's ranch in Texas in November 2001.[59]

The problem in Chechnya is that the war against 'Islamic' terrorism in Chechnya overlays other conflicts that have little in common with the targets of the Bush-led coalition. The Russo-Chechen war might equally be perceived as an unresolved war of conquest against a more traditional way of life, as a war of liberation from colonialism, or indeed, as a war against anarchy, crime and lawlessness that, in Russia, threatens to spill over from the periphery to the heartland.

The danger for Russia, the West, and for all those who seek a political solution to the conflict, is that the longer Chechens perceive that these underlying tensions are being ignored, the more they will regard the overlying conflict as one between the West and Islam, leading to an even greater sense of injustice and, effectively, throwing such peoples into the arms of the extremists, the only forces perceived to be capable of opposing such power. To ignore this is to reject the real and understandable desire of such peoples as the Chechens to live according to their Islamic customs and traditions as fully-fledged citizens of their state, albeit attached to Russia as an enclave with a degree of autonomy.

How ironic that, but for Stalin, Chechnya, and perhaps even the 'mountain peoples', might have had a status equivalent to that of Estonia, and now be independent. Ironic, too, that such concepts as Uzbek and Kazakh nationalism, which have helped to create the very secular Islamic states that the US sees as both a base and a bastion against Islamic fundamentalism, stem from that same Stalinist policy on ethnic-territorial divisions.

One is struck between the parallels in Chechnya of the events depicted in Gillo Pontecorvo's classic film, *The Battle of Algiers* (Italy/Algeria, 1965). Although the French crushed the wave of Algerian terrorism, it was accomplished using such means (torture, indiscriminate killings and so on) that the entire Algerian population, not to mention a good proportion of the French, was alienated and, within a few years, Algeria was liberated. One fears that those military commanders and politicians in Russia who are familiar with this film have adopted the short-term military tactics, while forgetting the longer-term political consequences.

George Bernard Shaw complained that we learn nothing from history. History, however, has a tendency to make us pay for the lessons that we do not learn. For Russia, the cost has been much more than just two bloody, unwinnable wars, but arguably, the chance of a normal, democratic and law-governed existence. The more than a million Russian troops who have already served in the chaos that is Chechnya, many of whom have returned home suffering from the 'Chechen syndrome', that is, alienated from normal society by their experiences, violent, addicted to drugs and alcohol, threaten to undermine the very fabric of Russian society at a time when the billions of dollars that the state spends annually on subduing Chechnya are desperately needed by the civilian economy. Perhaps, more importantly, once Russian society, or indeed any other, society, is effectively denied the opportunity to question the 'rightness' of each and every application of 'might', a slide into authoritarianism cannot be ruled out.

NOTES

1. www.amina.com/article/anthem.html.
2. On 2 March 2000, for example, Agence France Presse quoted the Kremlin spokesman on Chechnya – Sergei Yastrzhembskii – as stating that: 'The West does not understand the circumstances of terrorism in Russia. No country in the world has confronted terrorism on such a grand scale.'
3. For the 'arc of Islamic fundamentalism', see Vadim Belotserkovskii, 'Kakaya "duga" ugrozhaet miry?' [Which 'Arc' Threatens the World?], *Novaya Gazeta*, no. 31, 20 July 2000.
4. For an example of these parallels being drawn, see the article by Aleksandr Pikayev of Moscow's Carnegie Institute, 'Islamskii fundamentalism – obshchii vrag Rossii i SshA [Islamic Fundamentalism – the Common Enemy of Russia and the USA]: , 2 Oct. 2001.
5. See, e.g., NATO Secretary-General George Robertson's comment that 'we have come to see the scourge of terrorism in Chechnya with different eyes', *The Guardian*, 29 Nov. 2001.
6. See Eric Margolis, 'The Evil Empire Lives...with U.S. Support', *Toronto Sun*, 10 Oct. 1999.
7. *Le Monde* reported on 6 April 2001 that, for the first time since the launch of the second war in Oct. 1999, the percentage of Russians opposed (46.4%) to Moscow's Chechnya policy exceeded the percentage for (42.8%). The Interfax news agency reported on 1 Feb. 2002 that 51% of Russians favoured peace talks over Chechnya.
8. The All-Russian Centre for the Study of Public Opinion (VTsIOM), claimed support for Putin as President in 2001 rose from 56% in July to 65% in Oct.: www.wciom.ru/vciom/new/public/020325_putin.htm.
9. For the first time since 2000, those favouring a continuation of the war (46%), exceeded those favouring peace talks (44%), see VTsIOM poll on 29 Oct. 2002: www.wciom.ru/vciom/new/press/021029_terror.htm.
10. An impressive account of the Russo-Chechen conflict, published recently in Moscow, devotes an entire chapter to the 'Islamic factor'. See Chap. 3 in Aleksei Malashenko and Dmitrii Trenin, *Vremya Yuga: Rossiya v Chechne, Chechnya v Rossii* [The Time of the South: Russia in Chechnya, Chechnya in Russia], (Moscow: Gendal'f 2002).
11. John Russell, 'Mujahedeen, Mafia, Madmen...: Russian Perceptions of Chechens During the Wars in Chechnya, 1994–1996 and 1999–to date', in *Journal of Communist Studies and Transition Politics* 18/1 (March 2002) pp.73–96.
12. A feature of opinion polls amongst Russians is the relatively high proportion wishing to adopt the toughest measures against Chechens and Chechnya. An opinion poll in May 2002 registered 24% urging a tougher line, including some advocating covering the territory in asphalt, blowing up all Chechens or deporting them to Siberia! See www.fom.ru/virtual/frames/.
13. See George Bush's message to Maskhadov, reported in *Novaya Gazeta*, 15 Oct. 2001.
14. See Lev Lurie, 'The Russian Media Turns', *Institute for War and Peace Reporting: Caucasus* 14 (14 Jan. 2000).
15. Towards the end of the first war, the American journalist James Walsh suggested that: 'Whatever form it ultimately takes, Islam's reawakening across Russia is being shaped by the hammer and fire visited by Moscow on breakaway Chechnya', *Time,* 19 Feb. 1996, p.22.
16. One Russian journalist complained during the second war that the words 'terrorist', 'Caucasian' and 'Muslim' had merged into one demonic figure: Marina Koldobodskaya, *Novoye Vremya* 42, 2000, p.5.
17. Gordon M. Hahn, 'Putin's Muslim Challenge', *The Russia Journal* 5/2 (25–31 Jan. 2002).
18. For a good survey of this clash, see Richard Sakwa, 'Chechnya: the Pre-politics of Partition', London Centre of International Relations, Working Paper 4, 2001.
19. A good Russian interpretation of this may be found in Yurii Mironov 'Osleplenie nenavist'yu' [Blinded by Hate]: http://pravda.ru/hotspots/2001/12/18/34908.html.
20. In an attempt to render the difference in English between 'russkie' (ethnic Russians) and 'rossiyane' (citizens of the Russian Federation), Bill Bowring has suggested that the latter be termed 'Rossians': see his 'Austro-Marxism's Last Laugh?: The Struggle for Recognition of National-Cultural Autonomy for Rossians and Russians', *Europe-Asia Studies* 54/2 (March 2002) pp.22–50.

21. Paradoxically, given the low Russian and high Muslim birth rates, it is estimated that, within 25 years, approximately one in three citizens of the Russian federation will be Muslim. See Andrei Cherkizov, 'Snyatoye obvineniye – islamofobiya ne pomekha' [The Accusation is Withdrawn – Islamophobia is No Obstacle]: http://ntvru.com/chas/15Nov2001/fobia.html.

22. *Segodnya*, 17 Dec. 1994.

23. David Remnick, *Resurrection: The Struggle for a New Russia* (NY: Random House 1997) p.266.

24. Vadim Dubnov, an outspoken critic of the second war in the Russian press, noted that: 'The Chechens are paying, in a sense, for everything, for the Baltics, for the Black Sea fleet, for Georgia trying to get into NATO, for Gorbachev and Shevardnadze', *Novoye Vremya* 52, 2000, p.21.

25. The role of the concept 'freedom' in the Chechen psyche is as central as it is to, for example, the Roma. Chechens, on greeting, say 'Be free!' See Emil Pain and Arkadii Popov, 'Vlast' i obshchestvo na barrikadakh [Power and Society at the Barricades], *Izvestiya*, 10 Feb. 1995.

26. Johann Galtung introduced the concept of 'topdogs versus underdogs'. See his *Peace. Research. Education. Action: Essays in Peace Research*, Vol. 1 (Copenhagen: Christian Ejlers 1975) pp.23–4.

27. Note the symbolic linkage between Russia, Israel and the US of their respective 'Black Septembers'.

28. The Forum on Early Warning and Early Response lists as its first 'dangerous assumption in responses to terrorist attacks': 'The management of the symptoms of terrorism, rather than tackling the root causes of conflict that foster the growth of terrorism, is sufficient to defeat terrorism'. Assumption 9 is: 'Terrorism can be defeated militarily. The lessons from history that military responses strengthen the resolve of terrorist groups and their supporters can be ignored': http://reliefweb.int., 8 Oct. 2001.

29. www.international-alert.org/simple/projects/fsu/chechen2.htm., p.3. Russian popular opposition to the first war has been well documented. See, e.g., Anatol Lieven, *Chechnya: Tombstone of Russian power* (New Haven, CT: Yale UP 1999) pp.196–7.

30. Valerii Tishkov, 'Geopolitika chechenskoi voiny: "natsional'nyi interes" kak sopernichestvo biurokratii i elit' [The Geopolitics of the Chechen War: "National Interest" as Rivalry Between Bureaucracies and Elites], in *Svobodnaya mysl'* 4, 1997, pp.65–74.

31. *Komsomol'skaya pravda*, 19 March 1996.

32. Sergei Kovalev, 'Russia After Chechnya', *The New York Review of Books*, 17 July 1997, p.27.

33. In a thought-provoking address delivered at a *Guardian*/RUSI conference on the 'War against terrorism' in the wake of 11 September, Malise Ruthven made the point that 'every step towards bin Laden's demonization raises his stature among his supporters', *The Guardian*, 30 Oct. 2001.

34. The most publicized was the kidnapping of British aid workers Camilla Carr and John James, who were released with the assistance of Berezovskii and Raduyev in Sept. 1998. See *Sunday Times*, 11 Oct. 1998. It was estimated that kidnappings throughout the region in 1997 earned the Chechen gangs at least $20 million, *Argumenty i fakty* 48, Nov. 1998, p.11.

35. In Dec. 1996, six Red Cross workers were killed. In Dec. 1998, the severed heads of four British telecommunication engineers were found: www.russiatoday.com/rtoday/news/ol.html. 8 Dec. 1998.

36. I witnessed the first of these on ORT on 4 Sept. 1997.

37. *Segodnya*, 14 Sept. 1999.

38. A good account of the Chechen attitude to 'Wahhabism' is that provided by the French journalist Anne Nivat in her *Chienne de Guerre: A Woman Reporter Behind the Lines of the War in Chechnya*, (NY: Public Affairs 2001). See especially Chap. 1, pp.1–30.

39. Boris Berezovskii had been accused by Basayev of financing the invasion of Dagestan in Aug. 1999. See *Izvestiya*, 17 Sept. 1999.

40. On 14 Dec. 2001, Berezovskii claimed that the FSB had organized the apartment house bombs in Moscow and Volgodonsk, as well as the 'training exercise' in Ryazan in Sept. 1999. See 'Berezovskii: vzryvy v Moskve i Volgodonske organizovali rossiiskie spetssluzhby' [The Russian Secret Services Organized the Explosions in Moscow and

Volgodonsk]: www.ntvru.com/russia14Dec2001/bb.html. This claim had been made much earlier by several Western and Russian journalists and was the subject of the Channel 4 *Dispatches* programme, 'Dying for the President', screened on 9 March 2000. As early as July 1998, the journalist Andrei Piontkovskii had predicted that 'a couple of urgently organized terrorist acts in Moscow' might lead to a State of Emergency being declared and 'a second small, victorious war' could be launched, *The Moscow Times*, 16 July 1998.

41. See *Nezavisimaya Gazeta*, 25 Sept. 1999.

42. Yavlinskii, for example, was called 'an enemy of Russia' on the message board of his own Party's website: www.yabloko.spb.su/club/messages/64.html. Despite her best efforts to resolve the Moscow hostage crisis in Oct. 2002, Anna Politkovskaya won the sympathy of only 3% of those polled by VTsIOM, Yavlinskii gaining 6%, Putin 16% and the singer-turned-politician Iosif Kobson 36%. See: www.wciom.ru/vciom/new/press 021101_moscow.htm.

43. 'Voina: ostanovka po trebovaniyu [The War: a Request Stop], *Novaya Gazeta*, 28 Feb. 2002.

44. A strategy questioned by Putin's predecessor as prime minister, Sergei Stepashin, in his article claiming that the attack on Chechnya had been planned in the spring of 1999, *Nezavisimaya Gazeta*, 14 Jan. 2000.

45. Vyacheslav Izmailov, 'Chem bandity v Chechne luchshe talibov?' [In What Way Are the Bandits in Chechnya Better Than the Taliban?], *Novaya Gazeta*, 15 Nov. 2001.

46. For example, the shooting down by Chechen fighters of the Mi-26 helicopter in Aug. 2002 with the loss of 118 Russian lives. See *Izvestiya*, 19 Aug. 2002.

47. In Boris Kagarlitskii, 'Topor proigrannoi voiny' [The Axe of a Lost War], *Novaya Gazeta*, 14 May. 2002.

48. Aslan Maskhadov, 'Posle etoi voiny Rossiya okonchatel'no poteryala Chechnyu' [After This War Russia Has Finally Lost Chechnya] in *Novoye Vremya* 26, 2001, p.8.

49. Interview with Anna Politkovskaya, 'Esli by diktatorom v Chechne byl ya...' [If I Were To Be Dictator in Chechnya...], *Novaya Gazeta*, 21 March 2002.

50. Ruslan Khasbulatov, 'Zachem Rossii nuzhna Chechnya? [Why Does Russia Need Chechnya?], *Novaya Gazeta*, 26 Jan. 2002.

51. See his article 'Chechnya okazalas' na ostrie bor'by raznykh geostrategii' [Chechnya Has Found Itself on the Spike of the Battle of Different Geostrategies], *Yabloko Rossii* 45, 30 Oct. 1999, p.4.

52. From 'Eurasia Insight', 14 Sept. 2001 at: www.reliefweb.int/w/R.

53. Khasbulatov noted the demise in the influence of the *teip*. See 'Gosudarstvo, politika i separtizm' [State, Politics and Separatism], *Nezavisimaya Gazeta*, 14 Dec. 2000. Kovalev regrets the criminalization of the Chechen gangs, in his 'Dve voiny' [Two Wars] in *Novoye Vremya* 47, 1999, pp.12–14.

54. Anna Politkovskaya, 'S kem vesti peregovory v Chechnye' [With Whom We Should Negotiate in Chechnya?], *Novaya Gazeta*, 1 Oct. 2001.

55. Salman Raduyev has since died in prison in Russia, while in March 2002, Khattab was killed in Chechnya by federal forces. According to a pro-Chechen website, he was poisoned by Russian agents. See 'Amir Khattab stal shakhidom' [Emir Khattab Has Become a Martyr]: www.kavkaz.org/rus/article , 28 April 2002.

56. Interview in *Franfurter Allgemeine Zeitung*, 1 Feb. 2002.

57. The emergence of Zakayev, a former actor, as a leading player in the peace talks might have provoked Basayev, who has claimed responsibility for the Moscow hostage crisis and had personally criticized Zakayev's quest for a political solution, to locate his terrorist act in a theatre as a symbolic way of discrediting his erstwhile ally.

58. Blair, for example, drew parallels between the Moscow bombings of 1999 and 11 Sept. when he entertained Putin at Chequers in Dec. 2001. See *The Guardian*, 22 Dec. 2001.

59. For example, the article by Georgii Bovt and Svetlana Babayeva, 'Bush prinyal Putina kak otsa rodnogo' [Bush Greeted Putin Like His Own Father], izvestiya.ru, 15 Nov. 2001.

The Russo-Chechen Information Warfare and 9/11: Al-Qaeda through the South Caucasus Looking Glass?

GRAEME P. HERD

On 11 September 2001, as al-Qaeda terrorists committed atrocities in Washington DC and New York, 46 Russian journalists from eight television channels, news agencies and newspapers received, in the St Catherine's Hall of the Kremlin, the Order of Courage, the Order of Merit, the For Valour Medal or the Medal for Service to the Homeland. Russian President Vladimir Putin noted that the state awards journalists not when the media 'pats the authorities on the back', but when the media demonstrates civil courage and tells 'the truth'. The medal ceremony was also recognition of the media's role in defeating the terrorists in Chechnya both in the military war and in the information war. Putin then rhetorically asked: 'What created the bloody mess which you and I observed during the so-called first Chechen campaign? A lack of understanding of what was happening. We ourselves could not get to grips with what those events meant.'[1]

For the Russian Federation the first Chechen war (1994–96) represented military disaster and national humiliation.[2] This failure has been ascribed to a number of factors. It was generally recognized that the media 'war' was not contested – federal media strategy was non-existent, Russian and international (Western) public support weak or non-existent, and considerations of the relationship between presentation and policy formulation completely uncoordinated. Russia failed to gain and hold an information advantage or 'superiority' over the Chechen fighters.

Russian public opinion was psychologically unprepared for such a conflict, whilst the ethnic Chechen population within Chechnya had been radicalized and politicized under Dzhokhar Dudayev in the years preceding the conflict, and Islamic communities and some official state structures in the Middle East were prepared to support the separatist movement ideologically, economically and militarily, albeit surreptitiously. As the independent media freely reported daily front-line broadcasts of Russian troops in combat, it highlighted the gulf between government information and reality. Media power was all the more effective when juxtaposed, as it was, with the strict censorship and state propaganda which had characterized the sanitized Soviet coverage of the Afghan conflict. Indeed, public opinion, particularly in the electronic media, played a key role in forcing Moscow to abandon its military campaign.

Key television channels, such as NTV, highlighted blatant discrepancies between the government line on Chechnya and live video footage of dead, maimed and captured Russian soldiers and candid interviews from the front; this undermined government credibility. As Igor Malashenko, the director of NTV, sardonically noted of government news reports: 'They don't care how many people are killed. But they do care how many dead bodies are shown on television.'[3] Thus, public opinion, that clearly did not support the first campaign, hindered the government's ability to fight effectively and justify the war in both the domestic and international arenas, so undermining the perception of Russia as a state in transition towards democratic consolidation.

Remarkably, in the short intervening period between the first and second Chechen campaigns, Russia had learned information warfare lessons. It reformed and rationalized its information warfare structure and capability to more effectively wage the second campaign. From the outset of the second Chechen war there was an immediate realization and acknowledgement within the Russian government and military that there were two wars to be fought – the actual military campaign and an 'information war'.

Russian understanding of 'information war' was developed through the 1990s, culminating in the drafting of an Information Security Doctrine in 2000.[4] Information security in Russian eyes had a broader meaning than cyber attacks in information space designed to shut down military command, control, communications and intelligence systems or attempts to exploit vulnerabilities in enemy weapons systems through 'information attacks' and developments in information-based revolution in military affairs.[5] Rather, it aimed to clarify Russian 'politics, the state position on domestic and foreign issues'.[6]

This doctrine has both peacetime and wartime applications.

In peacetime it includes the necessity of gaining predominance in 'information space' within the CIS to sustain Russia's diaspora and its identity within the CIS, through, for example, the broadcasting of Russian language and cultural programming to neighbouring states. This is achieved through the strengthening of the state media and can be understood as 'public diplomacy'.

In warfare its remit is covered by what might be termed 'old-fashioned propaganda'. That is, selecting and presenting information to various publics with the aim of shaping public perception to favour the politico-military (and other) objectives of any given actor. In the context of the second campaign this included the need to legitimize and justify the war to the Russian public, to international – particularly Western – public opinion, and to diminish as much as possible adverse reaction within the Islamic world.[7] Russian government of Vladimir Putin was able, albeit after a bumpy start to its second campaign, to overcome a legacy of mistrust and ham-fisted intervention and, despite doubts, proved extremely effective in building and consolidating a psychological environment within the Russian populace in favour of the campaign.[8]

A key factor in this regard was the way in which growing anti-Chechen sentiment was reinforced by the bombings of in Russian cities (Moscow, Volgodonsk and Buynaksk) in 1999. These had the combined effect of preparing the Russian population to accept the rationale and necessity of conducting a second campaign. Once the campaign had begun, Putin was able to place effective pressure on the media oligarchs in Moscow to shape coverage of the war; continued control was maintained by the government over the information blockade around Chechnya. The 'exile' of Gusinsky and Berezovsky broke the back of independent non-governmental media coverage of the campaign and the harassment of *Novaya Gazeta* journalist Anna Politkovskaya served to highlight the lack of independent reporting from the front.[9]

9/11 AND RUSSIAN STRATEGIC REALIGNMENT?

With the events of 11 September 2001, a new dynamic entered the information war – the potential for Russian realignment with the West and greater integration into the Euro-Atlantic security order. The events of 9/11 have been described variously as a watershed in international relations and a systemic shock to the international system, with Colin Powell stating that it marked, finally, the real end of the Cold War, while Richard Holbrooke attributed to it the ending of the post-Cold War era. A key feature of all interpretations of the significance of 9/11 for World Order paradigms has been its significance in finally and irrevocably integrating Russia into Euro-Atlantic security.[10] This 'war' has been interpreted variously as prompting, providing the pretext or acting as the catalyst for initiating a fundamental strategic realignment of Russian foreign and security policy, anchoring Russia firmly with the West.

For some analysts, such realignment is self-evident as Russia plays a critical role in the 'coalition of the willing' and the joint cooperation in the war against international terrorism, and a warming of Russia-NATO relations, evidenced by NATO enlargement secured by the November 2002 Prague Summit. For others, though, 9/11 has not produced a fundamental realignment, but rather the illusion of such a policy.

Three counter-arguments can be presented.

First, prior to 9/11 it was clear to the Russian president and key advisors that there was no policy alternative to strategic realignment with the West. Domestic critics who attack Putin have yet to project an alternative foreign policy vision after the devaluation of multipolarity as an option.

Second, strategic realignment is a policy driven by systemic drift, in particular Russia's failure to benefit from global economic integration in the 1990s, its inability to reform its disintegrating military and other power structures, and its demographic crisis. Isolation from the Euro-Atlantic security community deepens the impact of these systemic factors, while integration ameliorates the worst effects.

Third, it is a policy of choice – or at least reflects a willingness by key sections of Russia's power elite to make a virtue out of necessity. The three lobby groups traditionally credited with supporting Putin in power – the security group, the St Petersburg economists and the Presidential or 'family' group – all support strategic realignment to the extent that it provides them with space to consolidate their power within Russian domestic power politics.[11]

Thus strategic realignment was already an existing, though underlying, trend in Russian foreign policy prior to 9/11. However, if we accept that strategic realignment has occurred, what are its limits? While accepting strategic realignment, for example, can we make a distinction between levels of global partnership? Is Russia prepared to project and protect a broad Russia-US global partnership, and willing to consider closer integration into the Euro-Atlantic order, but still attempt to preserve its sphere of influence and its regional power status in the South Caucasus?

In the wake of 9/11 the US has published a new US National Security Strategy (15 September 2002), stating its desire to prevent any state or group of states from challenging is pre-eminence and power and its willingness to use a policy of pre-emption to maintain the status quo, so bringing into focus and consolidating trends apparent prior to 9/11. How might Russia reassess its role as strategic partner to a hegemonic US? Might we hypothesize that Russia, in recognition of the weakness of its political-military instruments (its 'hard power'), has reinforced and extended the role of its 'soft power' in maintaining its traditional sphere of influence and regional power status? Further, that it legitimizes the use of threats of pre-emptive strikes by reference to the fulfilment of the overarching US strategic partnership in the global war against terror?

AL-QAEDA/CAUCASUS AND 9/11 INFORMATION BATTLES

Control of information is set to become an even more fundamental element of warfare in the twenty-first century. Information now constitutes states' strategic resource. 'Information warfare' or 'soft war' is driven by inter-related factors, primarily the distribution of power in an information age, the technological revolution in an era of globalization and a reassessment of the nature of sovereignty and intervention.

However, the inadequacy and limitations of traditional military power to combat uncertain, seemingly unpredictable, diffuse, transnational terrorist networks was not apparent until 9/11 and its aftermath. That aftermath included the global war against terror and the collapse of the Taliban/al-Qaeda regime in Afghanistan, the proliferation of these networks into South-East Asia and the Bali bombings of October 2002. Such terrorist networks target civilians and legitimize their actions by using the full range of information dissemination technologies on offer.

Thus, the question remains: to what extent does Russia, as its 'hard power' diminishes, compensate by developing 'soft power' (increasing its reliance upon 'information power') to maintain influence over the foreign and security policies of its near neighbours? An analysis of the role of Russian information warfare in Chechnya and the South Caucasus (Russia's 'soft southern underbelly'), following the events of 9/11 and the Nord-Ost Theatre siege in October 2002, is instructive. It provides examples of three information battles and reflects – however opaquely – Russia's understanding of strategic partnership and the way in which traditional 'hard' objectives are increasingly achieved through the deployment of 'soft' means.

The Battle for 'Good' and 'Bad' Terrorists, 'Double Standards' and Internal Legitimacy

The Russian elite has argued that the anti-terrorist coalition was not winning the information war in Afghanistan in the face of 'information bazaars arranged by the so-called Taliban ambassador in Pakistan'.[12] President Putin observed: 'I think that the United States to some extent are [sic] losing the war [against terrorism] in the information, not military, sphere. How strange it may seem, I think the terrorists are outscoring all of us at the information field. They act more offensively, more aggressively, and they are setting forth their position in a more graphic way. They act more emotionally. They achieve better goals than those combating terrorism.'[13]

At the same time, regular information exchange between Russia and the US concerning the activity of Osama bin Ladin and international terrorist organizations has been increased: 'Contacts between Russian and American special services have never been so strong', according to Russian presidential aide, Sergey Yastrzhembskiy. 'Russia was the first to begin fighting international terrorism on its territory, and Russia has gained experience which the West lacks.' He argued that 9/11 must lead the US to reject double standards and the division of terrorists into 'good and bad'. He noted that 'Russia has ample proof that terrorist acts are financed through Osama bin Laden and his organization Al-Qa'idah.' Indeed, 'Those people who sent kamikazes to New York and Washington had learned to organize terrorist acts in different places, including Chechnya.'[14] By November 2001 Yastrzhembskiy observed that the 9/11 terrorist acts had noticeably changed the American attitude to the Chechen issue:

> The US recognition of this element is very important. We have talked about that all the time, providing numerous evidence about financial flows coming from the Middle East to feed international terrorism in Chechnya. We spoke about mercenaries who had been trained in the Al-Qa'idah camps. Until recently, this information was simply ignored. Now it has been recognized.[15]

However, the Chechen website, Kavkaz-Tsentr, closely associated with the Chechen ideologist Movladi Udugov, had accused Russia of exactly this double standard a month earlier, in October 2001. It argued that Moscow wanted to open talks with the Chechen rebels only because it wished to concentrate on propping up friendly governments in Central Asia possibly taking part in an Afghan campaign. For this reason, according to the website, the Russians have categorized some Chechen rebels as 'bandits' – those who follow rebel President Aslan Maskhadov. 'These are – "good", "responsible" and "decent" people, who, as it turns out, have always been concerned about the fate of the Chechen people'. Then there are the 'terrorists' – 'those who are linked to so-called "international terrorism", that is, bin Laden, the organization al-Qaeda and other fashionable enemies of the 'civilized world'. This tactic, Udugov argued, is designed to reach agreement with the former group headed by Mashkadov: 'It is not difficult to understand that Moscow plans to give the role of the leader of "the good bandit formations" to Maskhadov and the role of the leader of "the bad terrorists" to Shamil Basayev.'[16]

Moreover, Kavkaz-Tsentr then argued that the initiative of Boris Nemtsov, leader of the Russian Duma's Union of Right Forces faction, aimed at holding talks with rebel Chechen President Maskhadov, appeared to be an attempt by Russia to acquire political capital by convincing the world community that it sought to resolve the conflict peacefully. However, talks were also a pretext to deprive Maskhadov of legitimacy, as evidenced by the Southern Federal District head General Viktor Kazantsev himself in front of television cameras in Rostov: 'One could hold talks with militants only with one purpose: to mislead them and then unexpectedly attack them!'

It went on to argue that the current Russian 'elite' believes that the Khasavyurt agreements of 1996 were Russia's political defeat; accordingly, the second Chechen war is revenge. It noted a September 2000 *Nezavisimaya Gazeta* article published by the political research institute director, Sergei Markov (an analyst close to the Presidential administration), which indicated that Russia first had to strip Maskhadov of his legitimacy as a condition for talks with him. This would undermine the spirit of the Chechen people and their aspiration to freedom: 'The Russian elite should understand that methods to establish constitutional order in Chechnya are not only Russia's internal affair because they are connected with the killing of civilians. Moscow should justify itself in the eyes of the international community and there is nothing shameful in this – it is a reality of modern life.' Indeed, 'The talks should become the key method for Moscow to win the information war against Wahhabism, to win morally and to gain support from the population of Chechnya and world public opinion.'[17]

It is clear that both Russia and Chechen factions have perceived 9/11 to be an information weapon that could damage the opposing side and provide virtual victories in the information war. Prior to 9/11, Moscow had attempted, largely unsuccessfully, to argue that Chechen fighters were not freedom fighters who at worst could be labelled 'separatists' but rather were 'terrorists'. The events of 9/11 have radically realigned the West's psychological environment, creating the necessary preconditions for an acceptance of the latter definition.

Within Chechnya itself, a split had occurred prior to 9/11 between President Maskhadov and Movladi Udugov, with Maskhadov publicly stating that Udugov's 'people and structures' were hostile to, and opposed to, the 'president and the government' of Chechnya.[18]

This split in Chechen ranks was partly fuelled by the introduction of Islamic fundamentalist support into the Chechen conflict and partly reflected an ongoing tension of clash within Islam itself, between a fundamentalist or radical variant of Islam and liberal Islam. Liberal Islam argued that 'Islamicization should be a cultural process within civil society.'[19] By contrast, Al-Qaeda represented the extreme of the radical wing – an extra-national or even anti-national organization whose leader argued that Islam was not compatible with national identity. To fight for independence and Chechen freedom was therefore to fight the wrong fight – rather the Chechens ought to fight for the independence of the whole Arab world in a global jihad to reconstruct the world as Islam demands. The first Chechen campaign had fought for Chechen independence – the second began with Chechen incursions into Dagestan to 'Wahhabitise' the whole of the North Caucasus.[20]

Thus, to claim, as Udugov does, that Russia has attempted to utilize 9/11 to divide and rule Chechnya is to be economical with the truth. It does not acknowledge the reality of splits within the Chechen politico-military elite;

for Maskhadov, Udugov is clearly a 'bad' Chechen. Nevertheless, 9/11 did provide Russia with a tool for dividing the rebel opposition in Chechnya into 'good' and 'bad' terrorists. As Putin himself stated: 'Political means will be used to finally resolve the problems with the Chechen people, while international terrorists will be brought to trial and destroyed.'[21]

Al-Qaeda/Chechen Collaboration and the Battle for External Legitimacy

Russian attempts to demonstrate a link between al-Qaeda terrorists and Chechen separatists have been a constant feature of the information warfare in the second campaign. In July 2000, for example, President Putin observed: 'We are witnessing today the formation of a fundamentalist *internationale*, which is sowing instability from the Philippines to Kosovo', adding that the 'international Islamic front, headed by number one terrorist Osama bin Laden, has set before itself the task of establishing an Islamic Caliphate'.[22]

Chechnya had recognized the importance of Afghanistan's decision to open mutual interstate relations, and the de facto recognition of their sovereignty and territorial integrity – and therefore independence on 16 January 2000 – marked an important victory in its information war campaign. Zelimkhan Yandarbiyev, Maskhadov's representative on foreign relations, reported to have travelled widely throughout the Middle East, including 'ambassadorial' visits to Saudi Arabia, Qatar, Abu Dhabi, Pakistan and Afghanistan. This propaganda coup had been exploited in the information war: 'In this connection, all [Russian Federal] comment that Afghanistan itself has not been recognized by "the world community" sounds unconvincing. It is sufficient to recall that the nuclear power Pakistan [as well as Saudi Arabia and UAE] has direct diplomatic relations with Afghanistan.'[23]

In October 2001, however, the Kavkaz-Tsentr website denied the US-Russian claims that Arabs from the organization were fighting in Chechnya. The 'military amir of the Supreme Majlis-ul Shura of the mojahedin, Khattab', for example, has reasoned that such links made little military sense and can be attributed to Russian anti-Chechen information warfare tactics.[24] Sergey Yastrzhembskiy, the head of the Russia's Federal Media Management office, was quick to utilize the Chechen refusal to admit a history of al-Qaeda collaboration to attack and undermine the legitimacy of Maskhadov and his representative Akhmed Zakayev. Both were: 'trying to present wishful thinking as reality'. Yastrzhembskiy's office stated that it proceeds from the assumption that one: 'cannot successfully fight Al-Qa'idah in Afghanistan and at the same time to all intents and purposes encourage its actions in Chechnya by calling for talks with those who deny the link between Chechen rebel gunmen and this organization'. In this sense, relations with al-Qaeda were promoted as a kind of 'litmus test, a test of maturity. It is clear that

Maskhadov and his 'protégé Zakayev have not passed this test', the presidential aide's office concluded.[25]

This tactic was partially successful in that Russia has not initiated overt peace talks with the Chechen leader, but failed to completely halt US and Council of Europe contacts with Maskhadov. The Russian Foreign Ministry reported that: 'this contradicts the spirit of cooperation and partnership between the countries and our close cooperation in the struggle against international terrorism'. Furthermore: 'It is surprising that the US administration, which speaks of the need for a relentless struggle against all manifestations of terrorism throughout the world, should, effectively, be encouraging Chechen extremists, for whose direct ties with Osama bin-Ladin and Al-Qa'idah there is ever more irrefutable evidence.'[26] The resolution adopted by the Parliamentary Assembly of the Council of Europe on 25 January 2002 recommended the involvement of Chechen President Maskhadov in negotiations on a political settlement to the conflict. The Kavkaz-Tsentr website responded by declaring that the honeymoon is over for Russian-US cooperation on 'terrorism', and further cited US State Department spokesman Richard Boucher who had criticized human rights abuses and the use of force against civilians in Chechnya. The commentary also highlighted remarks by another State Department official on the distinction between 'Chechens and Arab mojahedin'.[26]

Whereas, prior to 9/11, Yanderbiyev, Udugov, Khattab and others within the fragmented Chechen politico-military leadership perceived Taliban recognition as an important first stepping stone to outright independence, post-9/11 such recognition had the reverse effect. First, it is widely recognized that the Taliban regime was dependent for its survival on the al-Qaeda organization. Second, al-Qaeda had demonstrably exported terror and was supported by a network of 'rogue states'. Russia's aim was to demonstrate that the Chechens and Taliban/al-Qaeda links were operational before and after 9/11. Thus, this information attack on the Chechen separatists should have been particularly effective in removing the necessity of Russo-Chechen political contacts and providing the Russians with carte blanche to adopt massive bombing campaigns against Chechen separatists, along the 'coalition of the willing' Afghan model (Tora Bora).

However, the US and the Council of Europe does accept the distinction between Chechen separatists and al-Qaeda terrorists. This distinction was reinforced by the Russia-EU Brussels Summit of November 2002, with the EU side arguing that Russo-Chechen political negotiations should be resumed.

Al-Qaeda and Russia's South Caucasus Policy

Throughout the 1990s both Georgia and Azerbaijan consistently resisted

Russia's hegemony in the South Caucasus, while Armenia proved to be a traditional Russian ally. In the early 1990s Azerbaijan and Armenia fought a bitter war of control over the Armenian exclave of Nagorno-Karabakh. This war ended in an exhausted stalemate, with Armenia still in control of the exclave. Georgia and Azerbaijan are linked by their antipathy to Moscow's hegemony and by geo-economic commonalties, in particular hydrocarbon transport corridors that link Baku with Tbilisi, and the destabilizing levers of influence over domestic politics offered by separatist regions on their territory.

During the second Chechen campaign they further shared an extensive network of Chechen information centres with 'official representatives' of the 'Chechen Republic of Ichkeria' (CRI) located in Georgia and Azerbaijan. These Chechen missions tend to have a multiple role. They act as official representation, organizing and coordinating visits of Chechen officials to their host country, and providing the base for a fledgling press service and electronic information banks, which disseminate a Chechen interpretation that feeds into local media broadcasts and publications. The use of 'official representation and information centres' by Chechen Minister of Information Movladi Udugov has proved effective, but difficult to characterize. The question of their status is ambiguous and this is reflected in the attitude of host countries where unofficial tolerance has sat uneasily with official silence on the subject of their status. For example, on 1 February 2000 the Georgian Foreign Minister Irakli Menaghavishili stated that Khizri Aldamov – 'a representative of Ichkeria' – was a citizen of Georgia acting on his own initiative, effectively closing the Chechen Tbilisi mission.[28]

An Information Analytical Centre was established in Baku by President Mashkadov's representative on foreign relations, Zelimkhan Yandarbiyev, in late 1999. According to its director, Ali Ulkhayev, it aims to: 'inform the international community of the issues often neglected by some countries and international organizations (genocide, utter devastation of towns and villages, violence applied to women and children and so on)'.[29]

The events of 9/11 have added a new dynamic to Russia's asymmetric policy towards the South Caucasus. They have promoted both closer US-Georgian and US-Azerbaijani military cooperation in the 'war against global terror' and Russian fears that a US presence is undermining Russian hegemony over its traditional and historical 'sphere of influence'. Georgia, for example, though not previously included in the area of responsibility of the US Central Command, has been incorporated into the responsibility of NATO's Supreme Allied Command, Europe. The Commander-in-Chief of the US Central Command, General Tommy Franks, has registered Pentagon concern over the situation in Georgia's Pankisi gorge. He noted that the US was rendering substantial assistance and support to Georgia in the creation of anti-terrorist forces and the strengthening of the national army. However, General Franks was evasive when asked about the possible use by Georgia of its US-trained army in the forcible reintegration of Abkhazia and South Ossetia, stating only: 'I know that very competent people in the USA are working on this situation, and I believe they will take the right decision.'[30]

Russia has reacted by attempting to shore up its sphere of influence and has, according to Georgian and Azerbaijani analysts, adopted information warfare tactics to achieve this end. On 26 December 2001, the Russian State Duma unanimously ratified a bilateral agreement between Russia and Armenia on jurisdiction and mutual legal assistance on issues related to the deployment of a Russian military base on the territory of Armenia.[31] Azerbaijani analysts argued that Russian information warfare strategists have applied the worst traditions of the Cold War geopolitics to the 'frozen' Armenian–Azerbaijani conflict. Russia was attempting, they argued, to 'warn' Azerbaijan and Georgia against establishing close military cooperation with the US. In accordance with this strategy, Moscow demonstrates its friendship with Armenia, while stirring up an anti-Turkish, anti-Azerbaijani and now anti-Georgian mood in Yerevan, particularly by persistent efforts made to provoke a conflict in Georgia's Armenian-populated Javakheti region.[32]

Georgia has also accused the Russian mass media, State Duma and Kremlin of acting in concert to exploit anti-terrorist sentiments to intimidate Georgia and undertake anti-terrorist operations in the Pankisi gorge in north-eastern Georgia and the Kodori gorge in north-western Georgia. On 20 September 2001, the Russian *Utro* newspaper and Interfax news agency alleged that 400 Chechen militants, headed by Chechen field commander Ruslan Gelayev, were moved from the Pankisi gorge to the town of Tsalenjikha on board lorries belonging to the Georgian internal troops. The Russian media has also claimed that a training base has been opened for Chechen militants in the Pankisi gorge. Kakha Sikharulidze, the director of the Public Relations and Information Department of the Georgian Ministry of Foreign Affairs, responded by stating: 'Any possibility of any kind of terrorist training camp existing in Georgia is ruled out.'[33]

Russia has also argued that Georgia is implicated in supporting the Chechens, highlighting the links between Gelayev and President Eduard Shevardnadze. Shevernadze has denied such links, noting that in 2001 several thousand refugees from Chechnya, most of them women, children and the elderly, found shelter in Georgia's Akhmeta District, where ethnic Chechen-Kisten have lived for over a century. At the same time Shevardnadze acknowledged that several dozen people who had taken part in the fighting in Chechnya and been wounded there had arrived, infiltrated that district along with the refugees, but added that he had never met or spoken to Gelayev.[34]

However, the US chargé d'affaires in Georgia, Philip Remler, stated in January 2002 that numerous al-Qaeda and Taliban fighters have taken refuge throughout the whole Caucasus. A representative of a Chechen law-enforcement agency reinforced this statement by arguing that al-Qaeda and the Muslim Brotherhood: 'are trying to turn Georgia and Azerbaijan into a stronghold for preserving the combat and ideological potential of international terrorism'. Georgia was being used as the main training and trans-shipment centre. 'Territories are being seized and Wahhabite enclaves are being created in Georgia. The same was observed in Dagestan's Kadar zone in 1997–99.'

Citing Saykhan Khamzatov, (a rebel close to Chechen field commander Khattab) who was captured in February 2002, Remler argued that 'a Chechen autonomous district, with its centre in the village of Dunisi in the Pankisi gorge' may be proclaimed in Georgia's Akhmeta District, where rebels led by Gelayev and foreign mercenaries are based. He alleged that the demand to establish a Chechen autonomous district in Georgia is being voiced at rallies of Chechen refugees organized by rebels in the Pankisi gorge. Among the organizers are Uvays Akhmadov and Khizir Alkhazurov, both associates of Khattab. The rallies are being financed by the Muslim Brotherhood.

According to the same source, at the end of January, the Supreme Military Majlis ul-Shura, operating in Chechnya and led by terrorists Khattab and Shamil Basayev, made a decision to open a 'Chechen human rights centre' in Baku. Officially this centre has been set up 'to facilitate the resumption of the International Tribunal for Chechnya and to gather information about Russia's military crimes in Chechnya'. Documents that belonged to 'Brigadier-General' Khizir Khachukayev, who was killed in Staryye Atagi on 16 February 2002, suggest, according to the pro-Moscow Chechen representative, that the Chechen human rights centre in Azerbaijan will be a front organization for transferring mercenaries and money to the Chechen rebels.[35]

Clearly, the Russian allegation that not only were Chechen separatists in direct contact with al-Qaeda prior to 9/11, but that remnants of the al-Qaeda network have fled from Afghanistan and have taken refuge in Georgia and Azerbaijan, places these states on the defensive in the information war. Russia's main lever of pressure is to allege that Chechen separatists and al-Qaeda elements are taking refuge in Georgia's Pankisi gorge. Thus, Russian information warfare tactics are not confined to winning the campaign in Chechnya itself, but have a wider purpose. Russia attempts to utilize the al-Qaeda/Chechen nexus to illustrate the weakness and fundamental instability of Georgia and Azerbaijan and so to promote them as states incapable of full sovereignty and unreliable as Western partners. Ironically, US support for the Russian allegations – a rare strategic realignment within the information war – has provided Georgia with a means of combating increased Russian pressure – by providing the *raison d'être* for increased US military deployment to Georgia.

Armenian, Azerbaijani and Georgian Instrumental Use of al-Qaeda

Throughout 2002 both Georgian and Azerbaijaini security services have had to respond to Russian and US allegations that Chechen-al-Qaeda fighters are based on their territories by addressing the issue directly. The allegation now threatened the existence of the twin pillars of Georgian statehood – its territorial integrity and sovereignty. As Charles Blandy has noted: 'Restoring law and order in the Pankisi is one matter in which the Georgian government must take the lead, if it is going to survive as an independent state.'[36]

Georgian Minister of State Security Valeri Khaburdzania and his deputy Lasha Natsvlishvili admitted that they did not rule out the possibility of mujahidin who have fled Afghanistan infiltrating north-eastern Georgia and hiding among refugees from Chechnya. Commenting on Russia's claims that Georgia was harbouring the Chechen warlord Gelayev, or Chechen field commanders Khattab and Shamil Basayev, they noted that if Russia, with its extensive security infrastructure and capability, could not capture these warlords, it should not shift the blame to Georgia. The Georgian ambassador to Russia, Zurab Abashidze, stated that all criminals detained in Georgia, including members of al-Qaeda, will be handed over to those countries whose citizenship they hold. He described the situation in the Pankisi gorge as 'complicated', because, in his words, there are 'various criminal elements, rebels and foreigners' there.[37] The Georgian security services argued that Russia continues its information war with Georgia.[38] Zurab Zhvania, the former parliament speaker of Georgia, reinforced this perception:

> Many Russian politicians have been trying to turn the issue of Pankisi into an instrument of exerting pressure on Georgia in order to undermine Georgia's international reputation. I have said at many meetings here that current propaganda is aimed at creating the impression that it is Pankisi that has caused the Chechen conflict, rather than the other way round. The Americans see this issue in this way: first, Georgia must make sure that it does not become a haven for fighters and terrorists of Chechen or any other nationality; second, this issue cannot be turned into an instrument of blackmailing Georgia; third, the resolution of this issue is essential for more active steps to be taken to create a more stable situation in our region. That is their approach.[39]

Azerbaijan responded to the Russian Foreign Minister Ivanov's refusal to rule out that the al-Qaeda leader, Osama bin Laden, could be in either Georgia's Pankisi gorge, or Nagorno-Karabakh. The head of the Azerbaijain Foreign Ministry press service, Martin Mirza, suggested that as Azerbaijan's border regime is permeable and fails to filter out smugglers, it is possible, that bin Laden was hiding on the uncontrolled Nagorno-Karabakh territory. 'Anything can take place on this territory which is under Armenian occupation: from the cultivation of narcotic substances to the burial of atomic waste. Everyone knows that Nagornyy Karabakh [*sic*] has turned into a nest of Armenian terrorists and mercenaries. Azerbaijan is unable to control this territory because the conflict remains unsettled. That is why Azerbaijan is not responsible for crimes committed on the occupied territories.'[40]

A retired colonel of the Azerbaijani Security Ministry, Ilham Ismayilov, reinforced this highly partisan interpretation by stating that Azerbaijan, far from harbouring al-Qaeda, was itself a target for their terrorist activities:

> Terrorism is possible everywhere. We wonder whether there are any bin Laden cells in Azerbaijan? This cannot be ruled out completely. This issue should be examined to find out what the bin Laden organization could get out of it. Then, Azerbaijan's enemies have a hand in it. We are talking about alleged terrorist acts against the Western companies in Azerbaijan. The aim of this is to instigate hatred against Azerbaijan in the West. However, it is not ruled out that the pro-Armenian forces have a hand in spreading such information.[41]

However, such allegations have not been received unanswered; Armenian media and political sources have in turn accused the political authorities in Azerbaijan of close links with al-Qaeda. The Armenian newspaper *Azg,* for example, reported cooperative links between senior officials from the International Muslim Brotherhood, the National Islamic Front and several branches of Islamic Jihad as well as Osama bin Ladin and the authorities in Azerbaijan. It alleged that this cooperation was based on a 1997 agreement which outlined the dynamics of the relationship. Bin Laden's organization would not threaten President Heydar Aliyev's rule in exchange for the free movement of men, weapons and supplies through Azerbaijan to Chechnya. The paper alleged that funds from Saudi Arabia via Beirut 'totalling tens of millions of dollars' were also channelled through organizations operating in Azerbaijan and that the bombings of the US embassies in Kenya and Tanzania were directed from Baku. The Azerbaijan-based infrastructure was aimed at directing mujahidin to frontline training and al-Qaeda operational bases in Chechnya, as well as launching operations against Russia and Armenia (including Nagorno-Karabakh).[42]

Armenia has also questioned the increased military cooperation between Turkey and Georgia following 9/11. A Turkish military delegation visited

Georgia on 7 March 2002 to meet representatives of the Georgian authorities in Akhalkalaki, a part of Georgia with a large ethnic Armenian population, with the aim of stationing Turkish troops on the Georgian–Turkish border. The Turkish authorities are particularly concerned about the populist actions of Armenian separatists, who, according to the State Security Ministry of Georgia, threatened the security of several pipelines and the Kars–Tbilisi railway. Although Georgia has assured Armenia that Turkish–Georgian cooperation is not directed against Armenian interests, Armenia has noted the 'hysteria' of the Georgian press and authorities that 'nationalist' and 'separatist' tendencies are allegedly visible in Akhalkalaki. A Georgian official has also announced that Russians sell weaponry from their military base in Akhalkalaki to local Armenians. Georgian State Security Minister Valeri Khaburdzania also alleged that there may be members of the al-Qaeda terrorist organization in Abkhazia: 'The hint is obvious: US President George Bush swore to punish terrorists no matter where they hide. So, following the same logic, can one assume that one day Tbilisi may declare that there are al-Qaeda terrorists or Taliban in Akhalkalaki?'[43]

Finally, Georgia has been equally adept at utilizing the issue of al-Qaeda for its own ends, accusing the breakaway republics of Abkhazia and South Ossetia of providing safe-havens for al-Qaeda fighters in order to undermine stability within these de facto republics.[44] The failed attempt by a mixed detachment of Gelayev's Chechen separatists and Arab mercenaries to cross the Kodori gorge into Russia in October 2001 was critical in this respect. They were allegedly forced to retreat to the Pankisi gorge, and relocated to Abkhazia. The head of the security service of Abkhazia, Zurab Agumava, argued that such allegations served a dual purpose: to establish a US Special Forces-supported bridgehead in the Kodori gorge (to create the pre-conditions for the invasion of Abkhazia) and to discredit Abkhazia 'in the eyes of the international community'.[45]

An Abkhaz Ministry of Foreign Affairs statement reinforced this interpretation: 'The operation might be launched from the direction of Kodori gorge, or it might start with an amphibious landing to break through the Georgia-Abkhazia border in the region of the Inguri river. The Georgian side is currently spreading disinformation to create an excuse for the military operation.'[46]

One solution – proposed by the pro-independence Chechen Prime Minister, Akhmed Zakayev – may be to consider the creation of a Georgian-Chechen confederation on the basis of a voluntary association of the two independent states, in return for Abkhazia and South Ossetia establishing closer ties with Moscow, including membership of the Russian Federation.[47]

CONCLUSIONS

In the second Chechen campaign the goal of Russia's information warfare strategy has been:

- to isolate Chechnya from re-supplies of both practical aid – men and military materiel – and moral and ideological support from the West and the Islamic world;
- to de-legitimize and divide internal Chechen opposition to the war (this was mirrored in the 'Chechenization' of the military conflict); and
- to ensure that the Russian public gave strong support to the campaign's conduct and objectives.

Notwithstanding the ridiculing by Sergeiy Kovalev – a human rights activist and MP – of accusations in August 2002 by the command of the Joint Troops in the North Caucasus that international human rights organizations finance Chechen separatists,[48] and the November 2002 EU Brussels Summit criticisms of human rights violations in Chechnya, Russia has succeeded in this endeavour far beyond that which the disasters of the first campaign might have suggested.

The events of 9/11 and the spectre of Islamic fundamentalism provided ideal conditions for the internationalization of Russia's war against Chechnya, the framework within which Russia's prosecution of that war can be interpreted as part of a larger strategic realignment westwards. As Russian Defence Minister Sergei Ivanov noted on 24 September 2001, in a meeting with US National Security Advisor Condoleezza Rice: 'Chechnya and Afghanistan are branches of the same tree.' Russian Foreign Minister Igor Ivanov added: 'We have our own bin Ladens in Chechnya.'[49]

The instrumental use of the al-Qaeda/Chechen nexus by all states and clients in the region does partly reflect an existing reality, but it also delimits the nature of conflicts within this volatile region. To take an example – the supposed infiltration of Abkhazia by al-Qaeda in October 2001 – one analyst has provided a far more prosaic explanation for the presence of this 'phantom menace':

> Every autumn in the wild walnut collection season close to the Kodorskoye gorge a minor Abkhaz–Georgian war begins... During the period of nut collection a golden time arises for different partisan groups, such as Georgians fighting for the 'liberation' of Abkhazia and unemployed Chechen fighters who provide 'protection.' Russia is simply lucky that in the Caucasus mountains cocaine does not grow and the nut collection does not provide 'cover': The Caucasus fighters could take control of a considerably greater narco-business, like their brother partisans in Colombia.[50]

Since 9/11 the issue of al-Qaeda within information warfare battles has been made dominant. However, the potency of this information weapon reflects not only Russia's increased capabilities in information warfare, but also the weaknesses of its information targets. The inability of Georgian power structures to agree on a united response to Russian accusations of a 'Georgian trail' in the 9/11 attacks and repeated denials of infiltration of 'Al-Qaeda fighters/Arabs' into Chechnya from Georgian territory through 2002, as well as the question of their arrest and deportation to Russia, undermined the coherence of Georgia's position in the war against terror and increased the effectiveness of Russian 'information attacks'.

Information warfare sheds light on the limitations and nature of strategic realignment. It reveals that Russia is willing to broadly cooperate in the 'global war against terror', but only to the extent that its strategic interests are enhanced or maintained, rather than diminished. The Nord-Ost Theatre siege of October 2002 in Moscow to an extent represented a culmination of all these information warfare tactics, not least because the siege was presented as a new episode in the global war against terror. The Chechen hostage-takers were branded international terrorists in the al-Qaeda mould. Russian responses in storming the theatre were entirely justified,[51] and the event itself described as 'Russia's 9/11'; the fallout exacerbated divisions in both Chechnya and the South Caucasus.

The Chechen President, Maskhadov, denied links between his fighters and the al-Qaeda network, arguing that in trying to:

> ...convince the world that the whole Chechen people are defective, Russian propaganda discovered thousands of Chechens in Afghanistan, Kashmir, Kosovo, Israel, Abkhazia, that is, in all the famous hot-spots. One could get the impression that we are going to compete with the USA, Russia and China. To boost this impression they are discovering the same number of foreigners (Arabs, Chinese, Kashmiris etc.) in Chechnya.[52]

But the October 2002 siege in Moscow undermined such an interpretation. Instead, it reinforced support for Russia's contention that the link was clear and dangerous and increased the need to elaborate a draft national security blueprint that enshrines the military's right to launch pre-emptive strikes in order to root out terrorists taking refuge in 'training and sabotage camps' and 'ideological or financial sponsors of terrorism', specifically in Georgia.[53] Such pre-emption is justified as a Russian response to its own 9/11 and in keeping with US stated strategy – as Sergey Ivanov stated, Russia's Pankisi ultimatum is against rebels, not Georgian leaders, and if the Shevarnadze regime is unwilling or unable to take action then Russia would act in accordance with Article 51 of the UN Charter (the right of self-defence).[54]

The events of late autumn 2002 have also exacerbated pre-existing tensions in the South Caucasus, within and between the three states of this turbulent region. Georgia's opposition leader, Igor Giorgadze, for example, suggested that drugs and arms trafficking yields about $200 million per year and corrupts key power ministries – including the Ministry of Internal Affairs, Ministry of State Security, the customs service and the border protection department – and so the state is unable to respond effectively.[55] Armenia reinforced its determination to ensure its security and protect its borders following the hostage crisis, particularly as 'Armenia continues to remain in a state of war with Azerbaijan, which for many years has sheltered international terrorists'.[56]

As well as demonstrating the use of 'soft power' in Chechnya and the South Caucasus, the instrumental use of al-Qaeda in this region also delineates the limits of Russia's strategic partnership with the US and vice versa. The US appears determined not to countenance an 'Iraq for Georgia deal'[57] (that is, Russian support for a US attack on Iraq in return for US support for Russian pre-emptive strikes inside Georgian territory), while Russia resists US attempts to promote an al-Qaeda/Iraq nexus to help legitimize a US-led ground invasion and forcible regime change in Iraq.

This analysis of the trends and patterns which characterize the practice of information warfare in the North Caucasus has moved more visibly into the South Caucasus following the events of 9/11. Those events and the 'global war against terror' have provided the context for the emergence of a dominant leitmotif that increasingly characterizes information warfare in this region – the omnipresent spectre of al-Qaeda – and which has proved a highly effective information weapon. It is utilized by Russia, Chechnya, the three South Caucasian states and various separatist provinces that litter the region to legitimize pre-existing policies and objectives, and it has exacerbated latent stresses, cleavages and tensions that thread through this turbulent zone.

NOTES

The views expressed here are those of the author and do not necessarily reflect the official policy or position of the George C. Marshall European Center for Security Studies, the US Department of Defense, the German Ministry of Defence, or the US and German governments. I would like to express my sincere thanks to Rick Fawn for encouraging me to write on this topic by his invitation to present at the conferences he has organized so well, and Charles Blandy, Michael Mihalka, Sergei Medvedev and the internal referee for reading and commenting on earlier drafts. All errors of fact and weaknesses of interpretation are mine alone.

1. Radio Mayak, Moscow, 11 Sept. 2001. All news reports, unless otherwise stated, are derived from the BBC Summary of World Broadcasts (Part 1, Former Soviet Union) on-line service. <http://warhol.monitor.bbc.co.uk/>.

2. For earlier assessments of information warfare and the second Chechen campaign, see: Timothy L. Thomas, 'Manipulating Mass Consciousness: Russian and Chechen "Information War" Tactics in the Second Chechen-Russian Conflict', in A.C. Aldis (ed.), *The Second Chechen War* (Camberley: CSRC, RMA Sandhurst, June 2000) p.31, pp.112–29; and Graeme P. Herd, 'The "Counter-Terrorist Operation" in Chechnya: "Information Warfare" Aspects', *The Journal of Slavic Military Studies* 13/4 (Dec. 2000) pp.77–83.
3. Genine Babakian, 'Propaganda Struggles to Survive Onslaught', *The Moscow Times*, 5 Jan. 1996, p.3.
4. Timothy L. Thomas, 'Russia's Information Warfare Structure: Understanding the Roles of the Security Council, FAPSI, the State Technical Commission and the Military', *European Security* 7/1 (Spring 1998) pp.156–72.
5. Roger C. Molander, Andrew S. Riddile and Peter A. Wilson, 'Strategic Information Warfare: A New Face of War', RAND Corporation, MR-661, 1996 at <www.rand.org/publications/MR/MR661/>. See also Zalmay Khalizad, John P. White and Andrew W. Marshall, 'Strategic Appraisal: The Changing Role of Information Warfare', RAND Corporation, MR-1016-AF, 1999: at <www.rand.org/publications/ MR/MR1016/>.
6. This was approved by the National Security Council, 23 June 2000; endorsed by Putin, 12 Sept. 2000. For full text (in Russian), see <www.rg.ru/oficial/doc/min and vcdom/mim bezop/doctr.shtm>. See also Gordon Bennett, 'Vladimir Putin and Russia's Special Services', *CSRC Papers*, C108, Aug. 2002, p.21.
7. For an analysis of the growing strategic importance of 'soft power', see Robert O. Keohane and Joseph S. Nye Jr, 'Power and Interdependence in the Information Age', *Foreign Affairs* 77/5 (Sept./Oct. 1998) pp.81–94; and Joseph S. Nye Jr, 'Redefining NATO's Mission in the Information Age', *NATO Review*, No. 4 (Winter 1999) pp.12–15.
8. Meredith L. Roman, 'Making Caucasians Black: Moscow Since the Fall of Communism and the Radicalization of Non-Russians', *Journal of Communist Studies and Transition Politics* 18/ 2 (June 2002) pp.1–27.
9. Anna Politkovskaya, *A Dirty War: A Russian Reporter in Chechnya*, trans. from the Russian and edited by John Crowfoot with an Introduction by Thomas de Waal (London: The Harvill Press 2001).
10. For a discussion of the significance of 9/11, see 'Viewpoints', *Security Dialogue* 32/4 (Dec. 2001) pp.499–509; and Therese Delpech, 'Four Views of 9/11', *Transatlantic Internationale Politik* (2/2002) pp.3–24.
11. These arguments are elaborated in Graeme P. Herd and Ella Akerman, 'Russian Strategic Realignment and the Post-Post Cold War Era?', *Security Dialogue* 33/3 (Sept. 2002) pp.357–72.
12. The deputy head of the Committee on International Affairs of the Russian Federation Council, Mikhail Margelov, as cited by Ekho Moskvy News Agency, Moscow, 8 Nov. 2001.
13. NTV, Moscow, in Russian, 8 Nov. 2001.
14. Interfax News Agency, Moscow, 2 Oct. 2001. See also Michael Doran, 'The Pragmatic Fanaticism of al-Qaeda: An Anatomy of Extremism in Middle Eastern Politics', *Political Science Quarterly* 117/2 (2002) pp.177–90. For US–Russian intelligence cooperation post-9/11, see M.E. Herman, '11 September: Legitimizing Intelligence?', *International Relations* 16/2 (Aug. 2002) pp.227–41.
15. ITAR-TASS News Agency, Moscow, 2 Nov. 2001.
16. Bilal Eski, 'The Kremlin Has Divided Chechens Into "Bandit Formations" and "Terrorists"', Kavkaz-Tsentr News Agency website in Russian, 3 Oct. 2001; Theodore P. Gerber and Sarah E. Mendelson, 'How Russians Think about Chechnya', PONARS Policy Memo No. 243 at <www.csis.org/vuseura/ponars/policymemos/ pm0243pdf>; Theodore P. Gerber and Sarah E. Mendelson, 'The Disconnect in How Russians Think About Human Rights and Chechnya: A Consequence of Media Manipulation', PONARS Policy Memo No. 244 at <www.ibid ... 0244pdf>; Fiona Hill, '"Extremists" and "Bandits": How Russia Views the War Against Terrorism', PONARS Policy Memo, No. 246 at <www.ibid. ... 0246pdf>.
17. Kavkaz-Tsentr news agency website, 20 Nov. 2001. For an analysis of Russo-Chechen

'peace-talks', see Aude Merlin, 'Negotiations and Peace Deals in Chechnya – misleading initiatives?', *Insight* 2/5 (2001) pp.1–2.

18. www.dwellew.de/ (in Russian), 11 April 2000.
19. Emmanuel Sivan, 'The Clash Within Islam', *Survival* 45/1 (Spring 2003) p.42.
20. Sharon LaFraniere, 'How Jihad Made its Way ot Chechnya', *The Washington Post Foreign Service*, 26 April 2003, p.10. See also: Khaled Abou El Fadl, 'Islam and the Theology of Power', *Middle East Report* 221 (Winter 2001) pp.28–33.
21. BBC Monitoring Research, 7 Sept. 2002.
22. ITAR-TASS news agency, Moscow, 6 July 2000.
23. Kavkaz-Tsentr website, 18 Jan. 2000.
24. 'The Chechens themselves can teach whoever you like to fight and they won't need to go to Afghanistan. This all the Russians' propaganda, in order to show that they are with America.' Kavkaz-Tsentr news agency website, 7 Oct. 2001.
25. Interfax news agency, Moscow, 22 Jan. 2002; Dmitriy Kosarev, 'Forgotten Video Tape – Irrefutable Evidence of Chechen terrorists' Ties to Bin-Laden found', *Rossiyskaya Gazeta*, Moscow, in Russian, 23 Jan. 2002, p.7.
26. Interfax news agency, Moscow, in Russian, 25 Jan. 2002.
27. Kavkaz-Tsentr news agency website, in Russian, 25 Jan. 2002.
28. Prime-News news agency, Tiblisi, 28 Jan. 2000; 'There is Only One Representative of Russia – the Russian Embassy in Georgia', *Svobodnaya Gruzia*, No. 27, 1 Feb. 2000, p.2.
29. Gorkhmaz Hasanli, 'Pro-Chechen Information Centre Set up in Baku', *Azer-News*, No. 11 (141), 15–22 March 2000.
30. ITAR-TASS news agency, Moscow, 20 March 2002.
31. This was signed in Moscow on 29 Aug. 1997.
32. N. Nurani and N. Aliyev, 'Documents on Russian-Armenian Military Co-operation Approved', *Ekho*, Baku, in Russian, 27 Dec. 2001, p.4.
33. Georgian Television, Tbilisi, in Georgian, 21 Sept. 2001.
34. Ekho Moskvy radio, Moscow, in Russian, 8 Nov. 2001.
35. Interfax news agency, Moscow, in English, 24 Feb. 2002.
36. C.W. Blandy, 'Pankisskoye Gorge: Residents, Refugees and Fighters', Conflict Studies Research Centre Occasional Papers C.37, March 2002, p.19.
37. ITAR-TASS news agency, Moscow, in Russian, 1 March 2002.
38. *Dilis Gazeti*, Tbilisi, in Georgian, 13 Feb. 2002.
39. Rustavi-2 TV, Tbilisi, in Georgian, 18 Feb. 2002.
40. Esmira Namiqqizi, ANS TV, Baku, in Azeri, 16 Feb. 2002.
41. Sabina Avazqizi, 'Is Terrorism Plotted Against Western Companies in Azerbaijan?', *Yeni Musavat*, Baku, 27 March 2002, p.2
42. Ara Martirosyan, 'Terrorist No 1 Co-operating With Azerbaijan', *Azg*, Yerevan, in Armenian, 22 Sept. 2001, p.3. See also 'Al-Qa'idah and Other Terrorist Groups are Operating in Azerbaijan', *Azg*, Yerevan, 30 July 2002, p.5.
43. Tatul Akopyan, 'Will Turkish Military Bases be Deployed in Georgia, in Particular in Samtskhe-Javakheti?', *Azg*, Yerevan, 8 March 2002, p.1
44. For an excellent analysis of Abkhaz security politics, see Rick Fawn and Sally N. Cummings, 'Interests Over Norms in Western Policy towards the Caucasus: How Abkhazia is No One's Kosovo', *European Security* 10/3 (Autumn 2001) pp.84–108.
45. Kavkasia-Press news agency, Tbilisi, in Georgian, 1 March 2002. Ajaria's head, Aslan Abashidze, who is the Georgian president's personal representative on Abkhazia, added: 'Unfortunately, I am sure that the US instructors will train the Georgian military not to combat terrorists but to "establish order" in other regions of Georgia'. *Kommersant*, Moscow, 27 March 2002.
46. Artem Vernidub, 'They Will Look for Bin-Ladin in Abkhazia', *Gazeta.ru* website, 12 March 2002. According to the Abkhaz authorities, Georgia's strategy will be first, to 'cleanse' the Pankisi gorge of rebels; second, to overthrow the separatist regime in Sukhumi; third, the rebel fighters will make their way into Russia, into Kabarda-Balkaria or Krasnodar Territory

(into Sochi, for example).

47. Kavkaz-Tsentr news agency website, in Russian, 2 March 2002.
48. 'All this talk aims to bring back military censorship. These tactics are tried and tested and used by the federal side in the information war', Ekho Moskovy news agency, Moscow, 17 Aug. 2002.
49. BBC Monitoring Research, 7 Sept. 2002.
50. Pavel Felgengauer, 'Malen'kaya gryaznaya voyna v Abkhazii', *Moskovskiye Novosti*, No. 42, 16 Oct. 2001, p.13, as cited by Blandy, 'Pankisskoye Gorge' (note 36) p.2.
51. Sergei Medvedev argues that the hostage crisis has contributed to Russia's hardening: 'de-humanizing' of Russia in the late 1990s was reflected in a greater willingness to accept losses and the securitization of public consciousness (Alexey Balabanov's films: *Brother-1*, *Brother-2*, *War*; *Spetsnaz* serial; *Lube* hits: *Kombat, Let's drink to...*). Sergei Medvedev, 'Russia's 9/11', Faculty Presentation, George C. Marshall European Center for Security Studies, Garmisch-Partenkirchen, 5 Nov. 2002.
52. Chechenpress website, Tbilisi, 23 Oct. 2002.
53. *Rossiyskaya Gazeta*, Moscow, 6 Nov. 2002; Simon Saradzhyan, 'Military Gets OK to Strike Abroad', *Moscow Times*, 6 Nov. 2002.
54. *Kommersant-Vlast*, Moscow, 16 Sept. 2002.
55. *Rossiskaya Gazeta*, Moscow, 14 Sept. 2002. As the Georgian opposition leader Mikheil Saakashvili (National Movement faction leader) noted, post-9/11, Georgian authorities damaged the country's image by not cracking down hard enough on suspected terrorists and corruption in the consular services, so allowing Russian pressure on Georgia to escalate, *Dilis Gazeti*, Tbilisi, 11 Sept. 2002.
56. Mediamax news agency, Yerevan, 28 Oct. 2002.
57. PAP news agency, Warsaw, 25 Sept. 2002; Kavkaz-Tsentr news agency website, 1 Oct. 2002.

Russia's Reluctant Retreat from the Caucasus: Abkhazia, Georgia and the US after 11 September 2001

RICK FAWN

Russia's strategic interests in the Caucasus have both benefited from and been fundamentally challenged by the terrorist attacks of 11 September 2001. While far removed from the World Trade Center and the Pentagon, Russia succeeded in rhetorically linking the actions of Chechen insurgents to al-Qaeda, and thereby forging commonality with the US in fighting a shared international 'Islamic' foe. Wrote an American account: 'No longer are 85,000 Russian troops and police officers simply engaged in crushing a battle for independence; instead, Chechnya has become Russia's war on terror.'[1] The Moscow hostage crisis of October 2002, when some 50 bomb-laden Chechens seized a crowded theatre, further served to illustrate this apparent commonality. The potential gains to Russia from a realignment with the US are great. As other contributions in this collection explain, President Vladimir Putin will not achieve all his foreign policy objectives, but he nevertheless has qualitatively changed the US-Russian relationship to that of being partners. In more practical terms, the increased criticism by Western governments of Russian military actions in Chechnya, which even extended to the suspension of Russian participation in the Parliamentary Assembly of the Council of Europe, has since abated.

After 11 September, the arguments that the Yeltsin and Putin administrations had advanced about the Chechen insurgents being part of an international Muslim network gained new significance and acceptance in the West. President Bush's statements of 26 September 2001 demonstrated his administration's willingness to treat Russian perceptions of that conflict more positively by affirming the American belief that connections existed between the Chechens and al-Qaeda. He even declared that 'We do believe there's some Al-Qaeda folks' in the breakaway republic.[2]

But unlike in Chechnya, where Western recognition of a common Islamic foe should free Russia's hand, Russia's position in Georgia has weakened considerably since 11 September. Russia has retained an interest in Georgia for various reasons.

Among them are strategic advantage and the material potential that Abkhazia offers, and that will be discussed presently. It may also be that

Russian involvement in Georgia generally and in the Abkhaz conflict in particular has been motivated by 'hardliners' who have sought to punish Georgian President Eduard Shevardnadze for 'losing' Eastern Europe when he was Soviet foreign minister. Shevardnadze resigned that post in December 1990, claiming he was forced out by such hardliners and warning of an impeding coup. From December 1992 Shevardnadze charged members of the Russian military of backing the Abkhaz to impair Georgian independence, and he even referred to 'those [Russian] bastards who did everything they could to raise Abkhaz separatism to the level of fascism'.[3] Such motivations remain under-explored and deserve attention, although the emphasis here is more on foreign policy outcomes than inputs.

Russian interests in Georgia, particularly over the armed stalemate in Abkhazia, were changing before 11 September. This was the result both of Russian reassessment of the relationship between Russian interests and abilities in that conflict and also the changing status of Georgia. But the American global war on terrorism has hastened both processes. The deployment of American military forces – even in their official role as trainers only – has altered the balance of power on each of the three sides of the triangle in the Abkhaz conflict: between the Abkhaz and the Georgians; between the Georgians and the Russians; and between the Russians and the Abkhaz.

The term 'terrorism' has been applied by the Georgian and the Abkhaz sides against each other since the onset of the conflict in 1992. The Georgians used the term to describe Abkhaz military actions as well as its leadership; the Abkhaz have accused the Georgian government and Georgian individuals of engaging in terrorism to undermine the Abkhaz's hold on power. In the context of a global war on terror, those who are successfully branded as terrorists by world opinion risk isolation and elimination.

Rather than giving a historical narrative, which contains emotive and subjective features in any case, this study will explain features of this conflict as relevant to these dimensions. It will consider how Russian interests in the Abkhaz–Georgian conflict have changed and particularly how, with American responses to 11 September, Russian influence in Georgia has been further reduced. As access to the disputed area of Abkhazia is extremely difficult, foreign reporting is limited and major features of the conflict are disputed, much of the arguments to be drawn about this conflict must necessarily rest on perceptions.

This essay thus seeks to mobilize a range of open sources which can be cross-referenced. With such caveats in mind, it proceeds first to offer a brief summary of the strategic significance of this conflict to each of the key parties: the Georgians, the Abkhaz and the Russians. It then considers how US military involvement in Georgia after 11 September potentially changes the dynamic between the Abkhaz and the Georgians, and how that relationship affects Russian interests. It concludes that, very reluctantly but with spurts of defiant military action, Russian influence in Georgia is waning.

STRATEGIC SIGNIFICANCES OF THE ABKHAZ–GEORGIAN CONFLICT

The origins, atrocities and outcomes of the Abkhaz–Georgian conflict are disputed. The dates, sadly, are not always correctly recorded either. The otherwise august magazine *The Economist* referred to it as having been in 1991.[4] At least most sources agree, origins aside, that in August 1992 fighting broke out between ethnic Abkhaz and Georgian troops in Abkhazia, the north-western part of Georgia.[5]

By August 1993, the Abkhaz, with the assistance of various volunteer forces from across the Caucasus and with the selective military support of Russian forces, expelled the Georgian soldiers from the Abkhaz capital, Sukhum. Those troops, retreating eastwards towards the rest of Georgia, sparked a flight of the settled Georgian population. About 250,000 Georgians were said to have fled across the Inguri River that formed the internal demarcation of the Abkhaz republic within Georgia. Since 1993 the de facto Abkhaz government[6] has held all the territory of Abkhazia, save for part of the Kodori Gorge in its easternmost flank.

What does this loss of Abkhazia represent for Georgia? In strategic terms, Abkhazia constitutes about nine per cent of Georgia's total territory and nearly half of its Black Sea coast. Abkhazia also rests against the Russian border and could potentially have influenced the direction of Caucasian oil pipelines. Abkhazia was also relatively wealthy; nicknamed the Soviet Riviera, it was home to dachas for many of the Soviet hierarchy (including Stalin and Beria), and provided holiday resorts for the military elite. Its produce included citrus fruit, tobacco and lumber. Its location today could be important to Caucasian oil pipelines, with a line now planned across Georgia to its Black Sea port of Supsa. Some have suggested that the pipeline would be at risk, particularly from 'terrorist' attacks, if the Abkhaz–Georgian situation were aggravated.[7] Indeed, American military initiatives towards Georgia since 1999 have arguably been undertaken precisely to secure new pipelines across the country.

More importantly, the loss of control over Abkhazia compounded the impression that post-Soviet Georgia was disintegrating. South Ossetia, in the northern-central part of the country, broke from central rule and sought unification with North Ossetia in the Russian Federation. Only Russian engagement and an eventual peacekeeping deployment prevented further conflict (if Russian intervention had not arguably provoked or aided the conflict in the first place).[8] Adjaria, an autonomous region in south-western Georgia, has avoided war with the centre but also runs its affairs separately. Thus, the territorial erosion of Georgia seemed underway.

A psychological attachment to Abkhazia could be said to exist in Georgian official and popular circles. While Georgians can no longer simply enter Abkhazia as they could before 1992 because of the armed stand-off – the state currency and advertisements depict Georgia as territorially integral. Highway signs still give distances to the Abkhaz capital, Sukhum, although a Georgian motorist would almost certainly be shot long before reaching it.

Furthermore, those displaced from Abkhazia in 1993 have formed powerful political lobbies and hold disproportional influence over the Shevardnadze government. The exiles number between 250,000 and 300,000, a considerable constituency in a country whose total population is just over five million. In Georgia 27 September is now marked as the 'Day of Memories and Hopes' in mourning of the Abkhaz seizure of Sukhumi on 27 September 1993. The displaced Georgians have held rallies in front of the Georgian parliament, and others have seized and barricaded themselves in facilities in Tbilisi in protest at inaction or the lack of a place to live. Some reside in conspicuous buildings in Tbilisi, including on the capital's main thoroughfare. These images have also been transmitted to the West. The title of an April 2002 article in *The New York Times* ran: 'In a Sad Hotel, Caucasus War Refugees Make Do', and names them as refugees from Abkhazia.[9]

In criticizing the Georgian government's handling of the Abkhaz stand-off, some exiled leaders have called for the withdrawal of peacekeeping forces,[10] which would almost certainly lead to greater conflict. As the BBC reported in October 2001, 'the 250,000 Georgian refugees…are demanding a full-scale mobilization and the withdrawal of Russian peace-keeping troops from Abkhazia'.[11] Leaders of the Abkhaz government-in-exile, the body representing the displaced Georgians, have claimed that international terrorist bases have been operating inside Abkhazia. Their leader, Tamaz Nadareishvili, has even openly called for guerrilla operations in Abkhazia against the ethnic Abkhaz rulers, a demand Georgian President Shevardnadze has criticized.[12] So counter-productively influential is the government-in-exile on Georgian politics and Abkhaz–Georgian relations that Shevardnadze's special envoy for Abkhazia, Aslan Abashidze, Chairman of the Supreme Council of Adjaria, even suggested disbanding it.[13] This is a well-organized, vocal group that seeks, and could potentially incite, war in Abkhazia. Thus, regaining actual control over Abkhazia is a major issue in Georgian political life.

For the Abkhaz leadership, retaining the republic's de facto independent status is central to its existence. Despite Western and Georgian arguments to the contrary, Abkhaz officials emphatically maintain that they never were 'secessionist' and never declared 'independence' from Georgia, either before or after the war in 1992–93.[14] Only thereafter, maintain Abkhaz officials, did they become secessionist, and 'independence' was written only into the new Abkhaz Constitution of 1994. Regardless of how these terms may be defined and these assertions proven, the Abkhaz leadership stands by the position that Abkhaz autonomy must be maintained and cannot be relinquished to Georgia.

The legal re-affirmation of this status (specifics notwithstanding) has been a precondition for the Abkhaz government to enter into negotiations with Tbilisi. Paul Henze has argued that the Abkhaz leadership, led by historian Vladislav Ardzinba, is an old-style communist group whose political purpose rests solely on this position, one that isolates itself from the majority of the Abkhaz population. Similarly, in May 2002 *The Economist* reported: 'Old attitudes still affect relations with the Caucasus, where the Kremlin's client regimes in forgotten places like Abkhazia and South Ossetia maintain their miserable misrule.'[15] This argument means that de facto Abkhaz independence is the only policy option, except for some form of formal alliance with, or even integration into, the Russian Federation, proposals that have actually been raised by the Abkhaz during the 1990s.

The Abkhaz state is, however, too weak on its own to maintain its de facto independence without Russian assistance. The Abkhaz number only 95,000 people and their region has been devastated by war and continues to be riddled with unexploded landmines. They have also been subjected to a blockade by the Commonwealth of Independent States (CIS) which has largely ensured that its population cannot travel and its goods cannot reach foreign markets. Unemployment is estimated at 90 per cent and those earning have wages of about US $5 per month.

The weakness of the Abkhaz state and Russian support of it has given Russia – whether Moscow sought such from the outset or not – tremendous leverage over Georgia. And herein lie Russian interests in the Abkhaz–Georgian conflict. Soviet Georgia was, along with the Baltic states, probably the most independence-minded of the Soviet republics . With the break-up of the USSR in December 1991, newly independent Georgia, like the Baltic republics, sought distance from Soviet successor bodies. Thus it was alone among the non-Baltic Soviet successor states in refusing to join the CIS. Georgia also housed four Soviet-era military bases, which became Russian bases after 1991 (with two of them located in Abkhazia). The independent Georgian government wanted these Russian forces withdrawn and the bases either closed or given over to the Georgian armed forces. Instead, the Abkhaz defeat of Georgian forces in 1993, combined with an uprising in Western Georgia, 'posed a deadly threat to the weakened

Shevardnadze regime. He had no option but to appeal to Russia for help'.[16]

In return for Russian assistance in containing the secessionist conflicts in Georgia and for the deployment of a Russian-led CIS peacekeeping force between the Abkhaz and the Georgians, Shevardnadze reversed both policies: Georgia entered the CIS and delayed its policy on the removal of Russian forces and the closure of the military bases. Abkhazia, therefore, gave Moscow a physical military presence in Georgia that the Georgian government would not have otherwise wanted or allowed. When Shevardnadze announced Georgia's entry into the CIS on 8 October 1993 the Russian press reported him as saying that the move was 'the last chance' to spare Georgia from collapse. This was done, according to Western reporting, despite fury among Georgians. Russia's ITAR-TASS reported that the agreement on military facilities gave Russia joint use of all Georgian ports and airfields and Russian Chief of Staff Colonel General Mikhail Kolesnikov said the treaty provided no date for the withdrawal of Russian military personnel from Georgia.[17]

Thus, the disintegration of Georgia in the early 1990s, particularly with the war in Abkhazia and the resulting loss of Georgian control over it, gave Russia immense advantage over the beleaguered post-Soviet republic. Russian diplomacy was also a regular feature in conflict negotiations, the Russian Foreign Ministry making numerous peace proposals and hosting several levels of talks both in the Black Sea Russian city of Novorossisk and in Moscow. Russia was also included in UN discussions and negotiations brokered by that organization. As a 1997 assessment concluded, 'any stable political arrangement for…Abkhazia would weaken Russia's position, reduce its influence on future developments and call into question the rational for its military presence'.[18] American support for the Georgian central government after 11 September would present a significant challenge to Russia's influence on the Abkhaz–Georgian conflict.

THE IMPACT OF 11 SEPTEMBER 2001

While the dynamics in the triangular relationship between Abkhazia, Georgia and Russia have had their own momentum in the decade since war began, US military involvement in Georgia following 11 September has added a new, and potentially potent, element. As will be discussed, the *perception* of that American involvement may be more important than its objective contribution to the stand-off. But perceptions of course matter, as much, and sometimes more in the realm of conflict analysis, than objective facts.

This section begins with the implication of American involvement in Georgia on the Abkhaz–Georgian situation, then considers Abkhaz reactions to, and perceptions of, this American involvement, how Georgian factions and outside observers have cast the Abkhaz, particularly in light of the vocabulary of 'terrorism' after 11 September and, lastly, the implications of these developments for Russia's position in Georgia.

The US Impact

The US government announced on 26 February 2002 that American forces were to be sent to Georgia, arriving there a month later, to aid in the training of special Georgian forces to combat 'terrorism'. The Georgia 'Train and Equip' program (officially abbreviated to GTEP) was set to run for 20 months at a cost of US$ 64 million, and was expected to involve about 150 and no more than 200 US military personnel. The operation was also said to be a model for future American training efforts in up to 20 other countries.[19] American officials said the measure was in response to a request from Shevardnadze to combat terrorism in his country. Thus, GTEP stems from the belief – largely agreed by Georgian, Russian and American officials – that Muslim terrorists have entered the Pankisi Gorge in north-eastern Georgia, a geographically sensitive area adjacent to Chechnya in difficult terrain which makes monitoring difficult. The deployments come also from a recognition – both Georgian and American – that the Georgian armed forces are generally under-trained and under-resourced, especially in dealing with low-intensity conflict and particularly with terrorism. In a sense, the American training effort comes in the wake of other initiatives during the 1990s, including the training of bodyguards following assassination attempts against Shevardnadze. In 1999 the US government began a three-stage military assistance programme to Georgia, of which GTEP was later redefined to be a final part.[20]

But GTEP is qualitatively different, both to anything previous in Georgia and in the Bush administration's multi-pronged war on terrorism. Even though the American deployment numbered only about 200, the objective of the training was to generate long-term, self-sustaining improvements in the training and operation of the Georgian armed forces. One of the conditions of the American military aid was that the individual Georgian personnel receiving the training would be obliged to remain in the Georgian armed forces for at least a further three years.

The significance of the US operation is considerable for the future of the Georgian armed forces, considering how weak, even non-existent, they were as an established, integrated force. The Georgian army after 1991 has routinely been seen as weak and unreliable. Indeed, the post-Soviet experience of the country up until the mid-1990s was one of lawlessness and roaming armed bands. Georgian officials also accused the Russian government of having stripped Georgia of military hardware or of denying it a rightful share in the post-Soviet division of armaments. As one

American journalist commented recently: 'By any measure, Georgia's Army is underfunded, poorly disciplined, and disorganized – and Georgians themselves complain of low morale and little respect for higher-ranking officers.'[21] Similarly, an American academic study in 2001 wrote that the Georgian army's 'foundations are recent and fragile' and that it 'served successive outside political interests, with the officer corps changing with each turn of the political wheel'.[22]

Thus GTEP is an initiative the benefits of which are meant to accrue over the long term. It involves training Georgian military personnel from throughout the ranks – from the highest commanding officers to a selection of foot soldiers, and across all the military and security services of the Georgian government. Those trained by American troops are expected to train other Georgian personnel.

Considering the relative weakness of the Georgian armed forces – including that the numerically inferior Abkhaz could defeat the Georgians in 1993 – GTEP would seem to change the Georgian military ability, especially in a conflict like one against Abkhazia which would be classified as low intensity. It is almost certainly in this light that American and Georgian officials have reiterated that US forces would not themselves be used in combat. US Army Colonel Scott Thein said in Tbilisi on 2 May 2002: 'It is not the intention of my government, nor do I know of any plans for US forces to be involved at all in the internal security issues of Georgia.'[23] Georgian officials also sought to reassure Russian officials about the presence of an American military force in so sensitive an area. Therefore, the practice behind GTEP generally has officially been one of transparency. As Colonel Giorgi Giorgobiani, Deputy Chief of the Georgian General Staff said: 'The leadership of Georgian Armed Forces believes that the process should be as open as possible in order to avoid inaccurate information and rumours.'[24]

US officials were impressed with the potential of Georgian forces. An American military instructor predicted to Georgian journalists that the country's army could be fully ready within two years. Shevardnadze reiterated that the US forces threaten neither Russia nor other neighbours.[25] The better the American project of GTEP succeeds, the more – potentially – that both Russia and Abkhazia have to fear. To be sure, US officials have taken very clear steps to reassure Russia; indeed, the operation has been given a relatively high degree of publicity and transparency as reassurance. US Secretary of Defense Donald Rumsfeld phoned his Russian counterpart, Sergei Ivanov, on 1 March 2002 to inform him of the American military programme in Georgia. Even with public reassurances about the limitations of the American initiative, commentators and officials in the region still assert that the US training could have a life of its own.

While reassuring to most, the statements could be interpreted as reinforcing the territorial integrity and stability of Georgia. A US Department of Defense news release said GTEP would 'increase stability in the Caucasus' and concludes 'Georgia and the United States remain solid partners dedicated to the promotion of peace and stability in the Caucasus region'.[26] This is a generally positive aim that supports the status quo, but which contradicts both Russian and Abkhaz interpretations of what is just and in their interests. Any reference to the 'stablity' of Georgia or the maintenance of its territorial integrity in the context of the Abkhaz–Georgian conflict can be construed as measures against Abkhazia. A shift in Abkhazia's status is then also a threat to Russian influence in Georgia, an influence which has already diminished in the last year with Russian military withdrawals. Each of these interpretations and their consequences will be considered in turn.

Abkhaz Perceptions

The Abkhaz leadership has always feared either Georgian insurgency or a full-scale attack since the flight of the Georgian population in the summer of 1993. Despite the failure of substantial negotiations between the Abkhaz and the Georgians, a few thousand Georgian expellees have resettled in the eastern part of Abkhazia. The region has also been subject to what the Abkhaz government has called 'terrorist' activities by Georgians who take cover among the resettled farmers. Paramilitary groups such as the 'White Legion' or the 'Forest Brothers' are said to operate, and evidence from the effectively impartial UN observer force indicates that some military activity has occurred, including the laying of new mines and some attacks on Abkhaz militiamen. More intense fighting erupted in 1998.

Throughout these incidents the Abkhaz leadership has maintained that the operations are assisted, even coordinated, from Tbilisi. An Abkhaz press statement of 12 March 2002 declared: 'Georgia actively uses terrorists against Abkhazia and peacekeepers over the past eight years, and this fact was recognized, including [by] the U.N. Security Council.'[27] Abkhaz Vice-Prime Minister Raul Khadzhimba charged Georgia with deploying terrorists in Abkhazia, whom he said were also responsible for the abduction of four Russian peacekeepers in March 2002. He blamed Shevardnadze directly, declaring 'this practically means that the head of state covers the activities of bandits' and regretted the lack of international condemnation of Georgia, which explained 'why Georgian terrorists are continuing to act in Abkhazia, and this time Russian peacekeepers became their victims'.[28]

The Abkhaz Foreign Ministry also charged Georgia with hypocrisy in claiming to fight terrorism internationally while sponsoring it locally. An Abkhaz Foreign Ministry statement of 27 March 2002 pronounced 'The leadership of Georgia, while declaring its active participation in the anti-terrorist coalition, is basically carrying out the policy of state terrorism.' It further warned 'Georgian authorities are making preparations for large-scale actions against Abkhazia, one of the stages of which is terrorist acts aimed at destabilizing the situation in Abkhazia and creating an atmosphere of fear' and called on the UN, Russia and others involved in the peace process 'to take decisive measures with regard to Georgia in order to stop terrorism and prevent an escalation of the conflict'.[29]

The immediate impact on Abkhazia of the GTEP has been the fear that either the US soldiers themselves, or at least their reorganized, re-armed Georgian protégés would attack Abkhazia. Already the language of the international war on terrorism alarmed the Abkhaz authorities for fear of how it could be appropriated by the Georgian government. The Foreign Ministry of Abkhazia press statement of 12 March 2002 declared that Georgian references to international terrorist bases in Abkhazia 'will create a pretext for launching combat operations and involving US anti-terrorist groups in the Abkhazian territory'.[30]

Western media also reported Abkhaz fears that a strong Georgian army could be diverted from fighting 'terrorism' and turned against Abkhazia.[31] One American journalist even reported that following the American military arrival, 'top Georgian generals are "exuberant", speaking of a lightning strike that will have them in Sukhumi, the capital, within 24 hours'.[32] Another quoted Georgian Special Forces Captain Shalvab Badzhelidze, who was participating in GTEP, as declaring: 'Pankisi is a minuscule problem. Regular troops and police can handle that.' Instead, he said, 'We are doing something much more serious. We are training for an operation in Abkhazia.'[33]

Popular Georgian support for both a war against Abkhazia and American participation in it was observed by David Filipov of *The Boston Globe*. In late March 2002 he wrote: 'Many Georgians want to reclaim large chunks of territory lost to Russian-backed secessionists', namely Abkhazia, and that 'they would like the United States to get involved' in this process.[34] Western reports recounted the Abkhaz view that war was imminent because of the American military presence in Georgia. Wrote *Time* magazine: 'If that [the threat of another war with Georgia] happens, Abkhaz officials say, blame the US military advisers.'[35]

These concerns have been reiterated in Abkhaz statements. Abkhazia's Chief of General Staff General Vladimir Arshba warned that the Georgians would undertake 'a full-scale attempt to solve the Abkhaz problem by force before the onset of autumn' and said they were already conducting 'semi-covert mobilization' and threatening exercises. He added that should an attack occur 'I do not exclude the participation of US advisers.'[36]

Any reassurance to the Abkhaz was probably limited when a Georgian official answered questions about whether the four battalions of US-trained Georgian troops would be assigned near or along the Abkhaz frontier. While he first said the Georgian government was committed to a peaceful settlement, he also said no suitable facilities were near Abkhazia in which the battalions could be stationed.[37]

Abkhaz fears of Western military action against the region might also have been heightened by unprecedented NATO military exercises that were held in Georgia in late June 2002, which included troops from the US, Turkey and Canada, along with those of six non-NATO members of Partnership for Peace. This has potential significance because the Georgian government has invoked charges of ethnic cleansing against the Abkhaz and perhaps hoped for a Kosovo-style NATO intervention to aid Georgia in ending the stand-off. Georgia's closer dealings with NATO make that possibility at least seem more likely. This also gives Abkhazia cause to think that the Georgian government would be successful in invoking a call for international (NATO) military intervention.[38]

Members of the Abkhaz government-in-exile have also sought to associate the Abkhaz with the supply of materials for weapons of mass destruction to al-Qaeda. The expellee group claimed in July 2002 that a former scientist at the Sukhumi Institute of Physics could have sold fissile materials, including weapons-grade uranium to Iran, Iraq or terrorists. This was recorded by media sources as appearing as 'a new attempt' by the government-in-exile to 'discredit' the de facto Abkhaz government. The Director of the Institute then denied the charge, declaring that weapons-grade uranium was never held in Abkhazia and inviting the International Atomic Energy Agency to inspect.[39]

The international community has not been swayed by arguments that the Abkhaz are terrorists. The UN mission (which is separate from that mandated by the CIS, but with which it retains relations) suffered the loss of four military observers and five local staff when a UN helicopter was shot down on 8 October 2001. In his report of 24 October on Abkhazia, following the shooting, UN Secretary-General Kofi Annan declared that the attack 'marked a low point in the situation', which had already 'been deteriorating' in the previous six months, but accorded no blame.[40] Generally UN officials have been careful not to assign blame or submit to rhetorical accusations by either side. Instead, the UN Secretary General's special representative for Abkhazia, Dieter Boder, said in late September 2001: 'It is hard to say what their [insurgents'] exact whereabouts are because the Georgian and Abkhaz sides come up with conflicting reports... I cannot say whether that group [of armed people] is in the [Georgian-controlled] Kodori gorge or [the Abkhaz-controlled] Tqvarcheli because I do not have accurate information.'[41]

Thus, while little evidence exists to suggest Western governments have accepted such charges, the association of being 'Muslim', and having apparently declared independence illegitimately from a Western ally, could naturally place Abkhazia in a profoundly undesirable position following the 11 September war on terrorism.

Being labelled as Muslim or terrorist, or worst of all, both together, was never ideal but is destructive to any group's standing in the international environment after 11 September. Thus, the frequent misconception in the West of the Abkhaz as a predominantly Muslim people has particular significance in this context. One commentator noted that 'The claim that the Abkhaz are Muslim is now alleged to have been a deliberate Georgian misrepresentation.'[42] More recent media reports have indicated the ambiguity over the Abkhaz Muslim identity – a United Press article, written as a mock brief to the US President, explicitly stated: 'Abkhazians feel like they're "brothers" with the Chechens, Ossetians and Ingushetians, but they are not Muslim. Only 10 percent are Muslim.'[43]

In addition, collapsed states, such as Afghanistan, or areas of states that appear to have escaped from central control, are seen as breeding grounds for terrorism. Abkhazia falls into this rhetorical category when it is referred to as a 'breakaway province'. Georgia may garner automatic sympathy from the association of Abkhazia with this conventional wisdom, and some Georgian officials have unabashedly made such assertions. Said Georgian parliamentary speaker Nino Burdzhanadze: 'Any territory controlled by separatists and not controlled by central authorities is good ground for any terrorism.'[44]

The application of American military force against such 'failed' regions or countries seems at the heart of the Bush administration's war on terrorism and the new direction of American military planning. As an American military strategist wrote in 2002, 'the combination of failed states, elite casualty phobia, and unfolding aerial precision strike and associated technologies is profoundly altering the locus and style of future US military interventions overseas. The United States is beginning to practice a new way of warfare in parts of the world peripheral to traditional American security interests.'[45]

Abkhazia's existing international isolation, and the potential for more, makes the Abkhaz government even more reliant on Russia as its only ally, even if an inconsistent one. Russia has at times gone against the interests of Abkhazia, such as agreeing to the Georgian request for the CIS to impose a blockade on the republic. Russia, while militarily supporting Abkhazia, even accused it of widespread ethnic cleansing in October 1993, a term the Abkhaz have energetically sought to avoid being used against it by international organizations. (The Russian government made this accusation after Georgia consented to enter the CIS and to continue the Russian military presence in Georgia.)[46]

The Abkhaz leadership still relies on Russia for protection and the maintenance of the tenuous status quo. Despite Russian measures that have harmed Abkhaz interests, the Abkhaz government requires the Russian-led CIS peacekeeping force to remain in place. As it is renewed on a half-yearly basis, the deployment could in practice be ended easily. Ardzinba said he wanted the duration of the deployment renewed and the mandate enlarged to allow deployments throughout the Gali district in eastern Abkhazia in which much of the fighting between Abkhaz and Georgians has occurred.[47] The Abkhaz leadership has also sought the deployment of Russian forces in the Georgian-held Kodori region of north-eastern Abkhazia.

By contrast, Georgian authorities regard the Russian peacekeeping presence as an impediment to a permanent solution to the conflict; Shevardnadze's government has favoured greater multilateral, rather than Russian, involvement. The Georgian interpretation, from rounds of nominal negotiations, also suggests that for them an acceptable outcome means the reincorporation of Abkhazia into Georgia (even if with some autonomy) and the return of all the displaced to Abkhazia. Even if the Abkhaz leadership accepts the former, the latter condition signals to them that they will be outnumbered by non-Abkhaz and after any post-settlement election would therefore lose whatever political control they might retain after reincorporation in Georgia.

Yet, Russia's interest and ability to act in and for Abkhazia fell throughout the 1990s, partly because of Russia's own weakness, and is hastened by American involvement in Georgia through GTEP. It was arguably neo-imperialists in Moscow, those seeking to re-establish Russian pre-eminence, if not direct rule, in parts of the former Soviet Union, that supported the Abkhaz;[48] their sway in Moscow waned in the later years of the Yeltsin government and continues to do so under Putin's government.

It is therefore potentially more beneficial to Russia to achieve a modus vivendi with Georgia – especially a Georgia that is now a more stable, functioning state. The Georgia of the mid-1990s was already different from that of the early 1990s, where lawlessness and economic breakdown were the norm. While still weak, by 1996 Georgia had nevertheless achieved one of the highest economic growth rates in the world.

While Russia had secured some strategic advantages in the early 1990s, these seem to be evaporating now. This includes Russian agreement at the OSCE Istanbul Summit in November 1999, under heavy pressure from the Clinton administration, to withdraw some of its forces from Georgia (as opposed to those in the CIS peacekeeping force), and to close one Russian base inside Abkhazia and a second near Tbilisi (where American GTEP forces were initially stationed). Russian resistance to these agreements in practice is evidenced by the refusal to abandon the base at Gudauta in Abkhazia. Thus, the physical Russian presence was decreasing already. But Russian officials were not only weary of, but even hostile towards, the arrival of American military forces.

Russian Reactions to the US Military Presence

The initial Russian stand was perhaps one of wishful thinking. Russian Foreign Minister Igor Ivanov suggested that Washington might cancel sending personnel to Georgia in part because the Russians 'have become more articulate in our concern over international security issues'.[49] The next view was more instrumental, interpreting American statements and actions as an acknowledgement of Russian views on Islamic terrorism in the Caucasus generally. Russian presidential aide Sergey Yastrzhemskiy told Interfax that the White House's statement calling on the Chechens to end links with bin Laden showed 'understanding in the USA, albeit still with reservations, of the fact that a normalization of the situation in Chechnya is closely linked with the struggle against international terrorism'. He continued, 'this statement effectively confirms something that Moscow has repeatedly indicated – the close links existing between international terrorist groups, including bin Laden's organization, and the irreconcilable leaders of the Chechen leaders'.[50]

That is not to say that Russian foreign and security officials want to relinquish interests in Georgia entirely, or to suggest that their forces can and will operate on Georgian territory in certain circumstance. Russian special forces were deployed in the Kodori valley in April 2002 without Georgian knowledge or consent, ostensibly to search for Muslim terrorists. The troops withdrew after Georgian protests at this 'attempt at aggression', marked by Shevardnadze's flight to the region.[51] That Moscow deployed them may have been a result of a genuine threat perception; the size of the deployment (about 80 soldiers) and the willingness with which they were then removed suggests otherwise. If their surprise deployment was meant as a signal to Georgia that this could be done, then again the Russian consent to end the mission would surely weaken the value of such a message.

Nevertheless, the Georgian government has also kept Russia at bay with its refusal to conduct joint military operations with Russia in the Pankisi gorge against suspected terrorists.[52] Georgian officials wanted confirmation that an 'attack' by Russia would not occur. Returning from Moscow, Georgian Chief of Staff Joni Pirtskhalaishvili said, 'I will tell you straightforwardly that there is no danger of any kind.'[53] The Governor of Russia's Ulyanovsk region, Vladimir Shamanov, said on Russian national television on 29 September 2001 that 'We should insist on air strikes against terrorist bases that mostly accommodate mercenaries from other countries', referring to Georgia.[54] As late as 29 July 2002 Russian Defence Minister Ivanov categorically insisted on the stationing of Russian soldiers in the Pankisi gorge, declaring 'the Pankisi problem will not be solved without involvement of Russian special purpose forces. Georgia is not capable of dealing with this issue independently.'[55] Georgian government accusations that Russian aircraft had bombed Pankisi at least six times in 2002 indicated Georgian perceptions and fears of Russian intervention in Georgian space.

While Russia continues to test its influence in Georgia, Putin's fundamental interests rest on good relations with the West, especially after 11 September. Putin has called Russia a 'reliable ally' for the West.[56] Further Russian involvement, particularly military engagement, for the sake of Abkhazia does little to present Russia as a reliable ally. Considering the reliance of the Abkhaz government on Russia, the future of the Abkhaz leadership's present policies looks even bleaker after 11 September.

The Georgian state, and especially its armed forces, will be stronger after GTEP. The need to concede to Abkhaz demands for formal autonomy (which is also an Abkhaz precondition for any negotiations) will thus be even less likely to be recognized by the Georgian side. The October 2002 vote by the Georgian parliament that Abkhazia should be a republic within Georgia suggested that the Georgian position is being made firm. While Shevardnadze and other senior Georgian officials have made numerous statements that force will not be used in settling the Abkhaz question, the possibility of a military strike, and a more successful one, must loom more credibly in the minds of the Abkhaz leadership. Indeed, statements by the Abkhaz government indicate that to be the official view.

Georgian efforts to gain NATO membership further suggest that Tbilisi will not moderate its opposition on Abkhaz independence. At the Euro-Atlantic Partnership Council meeting in Prague on 22 November 2002 Shevardnadze announced that Georgia would apply for Alliance membership, and a day later indicated that resolution of the Abkhaz conflict was a prerequisite.[57] Practical assistance for the application was promptly offered by France and the three Baltic republics. US Joint Chief of Staff General Richard Myers, visiting Georgia in later November 2002, called GTEP a good foundation for the country's entry into NATO.[58]

In these circumstances of improved military capability and even the prospect of NATO membership, the likelihood of Russian forces shoring up beleaguered Abkhazia in any conflict with Georgia seems increasingly remote. Such an engagement would be very different from 1993 when the ill-trained Georgian forces disintegrated in the face of concerted opposition. Diplomatically, such Russian military action would also undermine the improved US-Russian relations after 11 September, the Iraq war notwithstanding, that are so fundamental to Putin's overall foreign policy.

Russia is also extremely unlikely to consent to border changes, including ones that would bring Abkhazia into the Russian Federation, as much as some Abkhaz leaders have advocated the idea. The five countries overseeing UN negotiations between Georgia and Abkhazia, including Russia, had agreed another draft proposal in December 2001 making Abkhazia 'a sovereign entity with the rule of law within the state of Georgia', a measure seen as signalling a change in the Russian position on Abkhazia's de facto independence.[59] Apart from the indications of Russian intentions in such an international diplomatic statement, redrawing Caucasian frontiers would put the question of Chechnya on the diplomatic drawing table. The Chairman of the Russian Federation's Security and Defense Committee, Viktor Ozerov, put this Russian view clearly during a trip to NATO in February 2002. Not only did he reiterate Russian interest in a peaceful solution to the conflict but also that 'Abkhazia's separation from Georgia and recognition of its independence is unlikely to benefit our interests'. Furthermore, he warned: 'If we start talking about independence for Abkhazia, our opponents may bring up the question of independence for Chechnya.'[60]

Short of territorial changes, Russian diplomacy in late 2002 still advocated Abkhaz interests, including the insistence that Abkhazia be represented at discussion at the UN Security Council; the Georgian government condemned this as 'a demonstration of Russia's non-constructive approach to settling the Abkhaz conflict'.[61]

The events of 11 September have increased the potential importance of the Abkhaz–Georgian conflict for all parties. This has resulted in a tactical trilateral anti-terrorism alliance among Washington, Moscow and Tbilisi, where the latter two, despite obvious differences, have now agreed that Muslim 'terrorists' do operate in Georgia's Pankisi region.[62] Sensitive to the tension between Russia and Georgia that might affect American relations with each, President Bush at once pledged to Shevardnadze that 'the US consistently supports the sovereignty, independence, and territorial integrity of Georgia', but also asked for close Georgian-Russian cooperation to resolve both Pankisi and Abkhazia.[63]

While no concrete evidence seems to exist of Abkhazia's participation in terrorism or its current harbouring of terrorists, the encircled de facto republic may well be the overall loser in this realignment of power politics in the Caucasus. The US GTEP is small, and is not meant to be permanent. But it is nevertheless unprecedented and changes the situation for the parties in the Abkhaz–Georgian conflict. This comes on the back of fearful Russian assessments throughout the 1990s of deliberate American meddling in the Caucasus and a disrespect for Russia's perceived rights and interests in the region.[64] In relation to this, Russia seems unable to maintain security along all of its post-Soviet borders and therefore feels remarkably vulnerable.[65]

CONCLUSION

Igor Torbakov has argued that Russian acquiescence to the American military presence in Georgia, along with personnel and the use and enlargement of air bases in Central Asia, denotes the end of a post-Soviet Russian sphere of influence. His distillation of the Russian press suggests a move in strategic vocabulary away from the use of adjectives such as 'post-Soviet' and an end to the concept of 'Eurasian'.[66]

Russian interests in the Caucasus have been challenged following developments related to 11 September, but must also be seen in the totality of the strategic transformation after the terrorist attacks. Russia stands to gain much from its realignment with the US; Russia initially appeared to risk a great deal with an American military presence in Georgia. But the Abkhaz stand-off has not been altered yet. Indeed, the fact that attempts by some Georgians to associate Abkhazia with al-Qaeda have so far failed and that clear statements have been made that US-trained Georgian troops would not be used against Abkhazia means that the status quo may actually continue. The status quo means some continued Russian influence on Georgia through Abkhazia. Such influence will be even more important to Russia if the American deployment in Georgia, along with those in Central Asia, signals the end of hopes for a Russian-dominated post-Soviet space. Ultimately, however, the ability of Russia, both militarily and diplomatically, to retain influence in Georgia, especially through the Abkhaz conflict, is likely to ebb. That process is hastening an undesired retreat that was underway already.

NOTES

1. Steven Lee Myers, 'Russia Recasts Bog in Caucasus as War on Terror', *The New York Times*, 5 Oct. 2002.
2. Office of the Press Secretary, 'President Meets with Muslim Leaders: Remarks by the President in Meeting with Muslim Community Leaders', 26 Sept. 2002: www.whitehouse.gov/news/releases/2001/09/20010926-8.html.
3. *Die Press*, 16 Dec. 1992, and ARTE, 8 Oct. 1993, cited in Liz Fuller, 'Eduard Shevardnadze's Via Dolorosa', *RFE/RL Research Report*, 2/43, 29 Oct. 1993, pp.21 and 23.
4. 'Strange Bangs: Trouble is Brewing in the Caucasus as Chechen Fighters Head West', *The Economist*, 11 Oct. 2001. The article twice referred to the war as having been in 1991.
5. Among accounts of the war are, Edward W. Walker, *No Peace, No War in the Caucasus: Secessionist Conflicts in Chechnya, Abkhazia and Nagorno-Karabkh* (Cambridge, MA: Strengthening Democratic Institutions Project, Harvard University, Feb. 1998); and Svante E. Cornell, *Small Nations and Great Powers: A Study of Ethnopolitical Conflict in the Caucasus* (London: Curzon Press 2001) esp. pp.163–74. Contributions from both sides are included in Jonathan Cohen (ed.), *A Question of Sovereignty: The Georgia-Abkhazia Peace Process* (London: Conciliation Resources, Accord No. 7 1999). A collection on the Abkhaz, including chapters relevant to the war, is George Hewitt (ed.), *The Abkhazians: A Handbook* (London: Curzon Press 1999).
6. Since Abkhazia lacks international recognition, this essay will adopt the language used in

UN documents dealing with the conflict, such as the 'de facto Abkhaz government'.

7. See Robert M. Cutler, 'U.S. Interests and "Cooperative Security" in Abkhazia and Karabakh: Engagement Versus Commitment', in Mehmet Tütüncü (ed.), *Caucasus: War and Peace: The New World Disorder and Caucasia* (Haarlem, Netherlands: SOTA 1998) p.135.
8. For an overview of some of the contradictions in Russian peacekeeping in the Near Abroad, see Dov Lynch, *Russian Peacekeeping Strategies in the CIS: The Cases of Moldova, Georgia and Tajikistan* (London: Macmillan with the Royal Inst. of Int. Affairs 2000); and more specifically in Abkhazia, *The Conflict in Abkhazia: Dilemmas in Russian 'Peacekeeping'* (London: RIIA 1998).

    Svante E. Cornell writes that at the time of the war 'The close relations between Abkhaz leaders and Russian military forces in the North Caucasus are fairly well known, so it is likely that the heavy military equipment supplied to the Abkhaz was in keeping with existing agreements'. Cornell, 'Autonomy as a Source of Conflict: Caucasian Conflicts in Theoretical Perspective', *World Politics* 54/2 (2002) p.265
9. Michael Wines, 'In a Sad Hotel, Caucasus War Refugees Make Do', *The New York Times*, 16 April 2002, p.A8.
10. ITAR-TASS, 27 Sept. 2001.
11. 'Abkhaz Planes "Bomb Georgian Forces"', 11 Oct. 2001: http://news.bbc.co.uk/hi/english/world/europe/newsid_1593000/1593716.stm.
12. Reported, for example, by Civil Georgia, 'Shevardnadze Criticizes Calls For Guerrilla Movement in Abkhazia': www.civil.ge on 7 Aug. 2002.
13. RFE/RL Newsline, 6/ 124, Part I, 3 July 2002. This report also noted that Abashidze stated the Georgian government would be unlikely to offend the displaced by disbanding their organization. Considering the apparent strength and consolidated views of the displaced, the dissolution of their government-in-exile would likely provoke a very hostile reaction.
14. This was consistently and firmly stated by Abkhaz officials in interviews in Sept. 1999.
15. 'What Russia Wants: Vladimir Putin's Long, Hard Haul', *The Economist*, 16 May 2002.
16. Pavel Baev, *Russia's Policies in the Caucasus* (London: Royal Inst. of Int. Affairs 1997) p.47.
17. Liz Fuller, 'Georgia Joins CIS', and 'Russian-Georgian Troop Agreement Signed', RFE-RL News Briefs, 2/42, 11–15 Oct. 1993, p.7.
18. Baev, *Russia's Policies* (note 16) p.58.
19. John Diedrich, 'This Week Green Berets Began Trying to Turn Georgia's Soldiers into Professionals', *The Christian Science Monitor*, 30 May 2002.
20. For a Georgian account of the evolution of US military assistance to Georgia, see Salome Jashi, 'The Format of U.S. Military Assistance to Georgia Changed', http://www.civil.ge, posted 5 March 2002.
21. Diedrich, 'This Week Green Berets ...' (note 19).
22. Charles Fairbanks, C. Richard Nelson, S. Frederick Starr and Kenneth Weisbrode, *Strategic Assessment of Central Eurasia* (Washington, DC: The Atlantic Council of the United States, Central Asia-Caucasus Institute, Jan. 2001) p.65.
23. Caucasus Press, reported in *Central Asia Caucasus Analyst*, 8 May 2002, p.13.
24. 'Briefing on Georgia Train and Equip Program at Georgian Ministry of Defense', 2 May 2002: http://web.sanet.ge/usembassy/mindef.htm.
25. RFE/RL Newsline 6/82, Part I, 2 May 2002.
26. 'Georgia "Train and Equip" Program Begins (News Release of the US Department of Defense)', 17 May 2002: http://web.sanet.ge/usembassy/gtep.htm.
27. As reported by ITAR/TASS, 12 March 2002. The statement also declared the Abkhaz government's desire to cooperate with the CIS and the UN in fighting terrorism.
28. ITAR-TASS, 20 March 2002.
29. 'Abkhazia Blames Terror Acts on Georgian Terrorists', ITAR-TASS, 27 March 2002.
30. As reported by ITAR/TASS, 12 March 2002.
31. See, e.g., Patrick E. Tyler, 'A Nation Challenged: Separatists in Georgia Seek "Association" with Russia,' *The New York Times*, 1 March 2002, p.A13.

32. Paul Quinn-Judge, 'Down But Not Out: The Breakaway Republic of Abkhazia Braces for Another Attack from Georgia', *Time* International, 20 May 2002.
33. Anna Badkhen, 'Georgia Has Its Own Agenda: US Trainers Seen as Allies Against Secessionists', *San Fransisco Chronicle*, 21 March 2002.
34. David Filipov, 'US Aid Bolsters Georgia's Militancy', *The Boston Globe*, 31 March 2002.
35. Quinn-Judge (note 32).
36. Ibid.
37. 'Media availability with Secretary of Defense Donald Rumsfeld and Georgian Defense Minister General Lieutenant David Tevzadze', 7 May 2002: www.defenselink.mil/news/May2002/t05072002_t0507ma.html.
38. These fears were stated frequently by various Abkhaz, both in government and the wider population, during a visit to Abkhazia three months after the Kosovan war. For interpretations of Kosovo and possible international military intervention in the conflict, see Rick Fawn and Sally N. Cummings, 'Interests over Norms in Western Policy Towards the Caucasus: Why Abkhazia is No One's Kosovo', *European Security* 10/3 (Autumn 2001) pp.84–108.
39. RFE/RL Newsline, 6/122, Part I, 1 July 2002, also citing Caucasus Press and Interfax. The report also cited doubts to the contrary by Georgia's National Security Minister. See RFE/RL Newsline, Vol. 6, No. 123, Part I, 2 July 2002.
40. 'Report of the Secretary-General Concerning the Situation in Abkhazia, Georgia', presented to the Security Council, 24 Oct. 2001.
41. Kavkasia-Press, 27 Sept. 2001.
42. Paul B. Henze, 'Abkhazia Diary – 1997', in Mehmet Tütüncü (ed.), *Caucasus: War and Peace: The New World Disorder and Caucasia* (Haarlem, Netherlands: SOTA 1998) p.101.
43. 'Joe Bob's America: What's an Abkhazia?', United Press International', 22 April 2002.
44. ITAR-TASS, 25 March 2002.
45. Jeffrey Record, 'Collapsed Countries, Casualty Dead, and the New American Way of War', *Parameters: US Army College Quarterly* XXXII/2 (Summer 2002) p.4.
46. ITAR-TASS, 14 Oct. 1993.
47. RFE/RL Newsline, Vol. 6, No. 124, Part I, 3 July 2002.
48. Henze (note 42).
49. ITAR-TASS, 28 March 2002.
50. Interfax, 26 Sept. 2001.
51. Alice Lagnado, 'Russians Withdraw After Stand-Off', *Financial Times*, 15 April 2002.
52. Interfax, 27 Sept. 2001.
53. Georgian TV1, 27 Sept. 2001, in FBIS, 27 Sept. 2001.
54. See Jaba Devdariani, 'Georgia Fears Russia's Anti-Terrorism Drive': ww.eurasianet.org posted 10 Oct. 2001.
55. Cited in Giorgi Sepashvili, 'Still Far From Stability in Pankisi': www.civil.ge, posted on 31 July 2002.
56. See, e.g., during Putin's state visit to Germany on 27 Sept. 2002. ITAR-TASS, 27 Sept. 2001.
57. RFE/RL Newsline, 6/221, Part I, 25 Nov. 2002.
58. RFE/RL Newsline, 6/222, Part I, 26 Nov. 2002.
59. For foreign commentary, see Andrew Jack, 'Russian Change May Lead to Breathrough on Abkhazia', *Financial Times*, 11 Dec. 2001.
60. Reported by ITAR-TASS, 28 Feb. 2002.
61. *The Moscow Times*, 13 Nov. 2002, cited in RFE/RL Newsline, 6/214, 14 Nov. 2002.
62. Sepashvili (note 55) wrote: 'The Georgian government had to admit that there are armed Chechen and Arab fighters in Pankisi together with some 3,700 Chechen refugees. Sephashvili, 'Still Far From Stability in Pankisi'.
63. Cited in RFE/RL Newsline, 6/179, Part I, 23 Sept. 2002.
64. For a strong argument outlining this Russian position, see Sergo A. Mikoyan, 'Russia, the US and Regional Conflict in Eurasia', *Survival* 40/3 (Autumn 1998) pp.112–26.
65. E.g., Sherman W. Garnett wrote in 1997 'Russia cannot be uniformly strong along its entire

border, yet, judging from the statements and writings of the Russians themselves, security challenges of one kind or another are emerging along the perimeter of Russia'. 'Russia and its Borderlands: A Geography of Violence', *Parameters: US Army College Quarterly* XXVII/ 1 (Spring 1997) p.19.

66. Igor Torbakov, 'Does Moscow's Reaction to Developments in Georgia Herald the End of Eurasia?': www.eurasianet.org/departments/insight/articles/eav030502.shtml, posted on 5 March 2002.

Abstracts

Post-Soviet Russian Foreign Policy: Between Doctrine and Pragmatism
Ludmilla Selezneva

The contribution examines post-Soviet Russian foreign policy in terms of what will be called a doctrinaire and a pragmatic approach. I argue that four periods in this framework can be distinguished: 1991–96 was dominated by the ideological approach, as had been the case in the Soviet era, but with the important difference that now the ideology was anti-communist and anti-Soviet. The years 1996–99 were the time of Primakov's 'alternative' policy, when the ideology of 'Great Russia' started to capture the imagination of the Russian political establishment. In 2000–01 this ideology was confirmed as official governmental policy, but it arose as the most pragmatic and balanced foreign policy to date, even if relations with the West were still only lukewarm. Finally, after 11 September 2001, official Russian policy has come to regard the West, NATO and the US more closely than it has done in the past. Because of a powerful culture of doctrine in Russia, however, a large section of the Russian political class does not subscribe to the president's advanced view. It forms a quiet, passive opposition.

Russian Foreign Policy and Its Critics
Mary Buckley

Relations between the Russian Federation and the US, like US-Soviet relations before them, have endured periods of hostility, argument, warming, cooperation and subsequent enmity. Periods of good relations have also simultaneously borne tensions and strains. This essay argues that, although the events of 11 September 2001 facilitated improvements in US-Russian relations, particularly after the antagonisms concerning NATO intervention in Kosovo, the Bush leadership is unlikely to grant Russia all the benefits that Putin would like to reap. At home, many in Russia are critical of what they perceive as Putin's concessions to the US. After the Moscow hostage crisis of 23–26 October 2002, some Russian human rights groups also accused Putin of imitating Bush's anti-terrorist platform as a justification for renewed campaigns in Chechnya.

NATO Enlargement and Eastern Opinion
Ian McAllister and Stephen White

The evidence of representative surveys conducted in Belarus, Moldova, Russia and Ukraine in 2000 and 2001 is that relatively few believe there is a serious and immediate threat to their security. Of potential threats, however, the US remains the most important, followed by Iran, Iraq and China. Attitudes towards NATO, in particular, are more polarized, with more concern in Russia and Belarus about the alliance's enlargement than in Moldova and Ukraine. People who are older, female and who regard themselves as on the political left are more likely to oppose NATO enlargement and the possibility of their own country's membership, although the statistical effects are generally modest. Attitudes of this kind are of limited importance in short-term decisions within the region, but are likely to impose limits upon a more definitive reorientation towards the West in the aftermath of 11 September.

A Bumpy Road to An Unknown Destination? NATO-Russia Relations, 1991–2002
Martin A. Smith

Relations between NATO and Russia have evolved through six distinct phases since December 1991. An initial 'honeymoon' in 1991–93 was followed by deterioration. This was temporarily arrested in 1996–97 by NATO upgrading its institutional links with Russia. The relationship was severely tested during the Kosovo crisis in early 1999. Relations were not severed, however, and a gradual rebuilding occurred from the summer of 1999. The impact of 11 September 2001, finally, has been limited. Since 1991, the development of NATO-Russia relations has been uneven. Overall objectives have not been identified by either side. Nevertheless, an underlying stability has become apparent in the relationship.

Strategic or Pragmatic Partnership? The European Union's Policy Towards Russia Since the End of the Cold War
Graham Timmins

This essay evaluates the development of EU-Russian relations since the end of the Cold War and considers the motivating factors influencing the evolution of EU policy. Both the EU Common Strategy on Russia and the Russian Medium-Term Strategy for Development of Relations with the

European Union, published in 1999, highlight the concept of strategic partnership. It is, however, argued here that, although the EU and Russia have mutual interests, they are far from sharing a common agenda and that pragmatic rather than strategic partnership is more relevant to our understanding of the relationship between the EU and Russia.

Exploitation of the 'Islamic Factor' in the Russo-Chechen Conflict Before and After 11 September 2001
John Russell

The bombings in Moscow in September 1999, attributed to Islamic terrorists, brought about the same damascene conversion of public opinion towards a hard line in combating terrorism as occurred in the US after 11 September 2001. Did Putin's exploitation of the 'Islamic factor' merely intensify after the attacks on New York and Washington in order to keep open for Russia the prospect of a military solution to the war in Chechnya? How critical to the Russo-Chechen conflict were the changes in Western perceptions post-11 September? Most significantly, perhaps, as we assess the implications of the Moscow theatre siege of October 2002, what options did the Chechen separatists consider were left open to them after Russia had joined the international coalition against terror?

The Russo-Chechen Information Warfare and 9/11: Al-Qaeda through the South Caucasus Looking Glass?
Graeme P. Herd

This study focuses on the information warfare aspects of the second Russo-Chechen campaign (1999–) before and after the events of 11 September 2001. Since 11 September the Russian state has attempted to 'internationalize' the conflict, to argue that the objectives of the state and the conduct of its security services are legitimized by the wider threat posed by the links and collaboration between Chechen separatists, al-Qaeda fighters and the war in the context of the 'global war against terror'. Russia is now fighting information battles in the South Caucasus and the Chechen–al-Qaeda nexus has been utilized instrumentally by all states in the region.

Russia's Reluctant Retreat from the Caucasus:
Abkhazia, Georgia and the US after 11 September 2001
Rick Fawn

This contribution considers how Russian interests in the Abkhaz–Georgian conflict have changed and particularly how, with American responses to 11 September, Russian influence in Georgia has been further reduced. It first provides a brief summation of the strategic significance of this conflict to each of the key parties: the Georgians, the Abkhaz and the Russians. It then considers how US military involvement in Georgia after 11 September potentially alters the dynamic between the Abkhaz and the Georgians, and how that relationship affects Russian interests. It concludes that, very reluctantly but with spurts of defiant military action, Russian influence in Georgia is waning.

About the Contributors

Rick Fawn is Senior Lecturer in International Relations, University of St Andrews, Scotland. He is editor of *Global Responses to Terrorism: 9/11, The War in Afghanistan and Beyond* (Routledge 2003); co-editor (with Stephen White) of *Russia after Communism* (Frank Cass 2002); co-editor of *The Changing Geopolitics of Eastern Europe* (Frank Cass 2001); author of *The Czech Republic: A Nation of Velvet* (Routledge 2000) and co-editor of *International Society After the Cold War: Anarchy and Order Reconsidered* (Palgrave 1996).

Ludmilla Selezneva holds PhDs in History from Rostov-on-Don State University and from the Russian State University for the Humanities, Moscow, and is currently at the State University of Television and Broadcasting in Moscow. Among her many books are *Zapadnaya demokratiya glazamy rossiyskih liberalov nachala XX veka* (Rostov-on-Don State University 1995); and, as chief editor and co-author, *Dialogue. Compromises. Consensus* (Russian State University for the Humanities-UNESCO 1998) and *Orbits of a Civic Society* (Russian State University for the Humanities-UNESCO, 2000, published in Russian and English).

Mary Buckley taught for 17 years in the Politics Department at Edinburgh University and briefly at Royal Holloway, University of London. She is author of *Women and Ideology in the Soviet Union* (Harvester/Wheatsheaf 1989), *Redefining Russian Society and Polity* (Westview 1993), editor of *Post-Soviet Women: from the Baltic to Central Asia* (CUP 1992) and co-editor of *Kosovo: Perceptions of War and its Aftermath* (Continuum 2002).

Ian McAllister is Director of the Research School of Social Sciences at the Australian National University, Canberra, and Adjunct Professor at the Institute of Governance, Public Policy and Social Research at Queen's University, Belfast. A specialist in comparative electoral behaviour and survey analysis, he is co-author of *How Russia Votes* (Seven Bridges Press 1996); and co-editor of *New Developments in Australian Politics* (Palgrave 1997) and *The Cambridge Handbook of Social Sciences in Australia* (CUP 2003).

Stephen White is Professor of International Politics at the University of Glasgow, and a Senior Research Associate of its Institute of Central and East European Studies. A specialist in the comparative politics of Russia and the former communist countries, his recent books include *Russia's New*

Politics (Cambridge 2000), *The Soviet Elite from Lenin to Gorbachev,* with Evan Mawdsley, (Oxford 2000) and a forthcoming co-edited volume on post-communist Belarus.

Martin A. Smith is Senior Lecturer in Defence and International Affairs at the Royal Military Academy, Sandhurst. His main research interests are in the fields of international and European security, with a particular focus on NATO's post-Cold War evolution. Recent books include *NATO in the First Decade after the Cold War* (Kluwer 2000) and, co-edited with Graham Timmins, *Uncertain Europe: Building a New European Security Order?* (Routledge 2001). He has also recently published articles in *World Affairs, Geopolitics* and the *Journal of Strategic Studies.* His current work includes book projects on the EU, NATO and Russia and an introduction to European security theory and practice.

Graham Timmins is Jean Monnet Professor in European Integration Studies and Head of Politics at the University of Stirling. His research specialties cover European and German politics and recent publications include *Building a Bigger Europe: EU and NATO Enlargement in Comparative Perspective* (Ashgate 2000) and *Uncertain Europe: Building a New European Security Order?* (Routledge 2001) which were co-authored with Martin A.Smith.

Graeme P. Herd is a Professor of Civil-Military Relations at the George C. Marshall European Center for Security Studies, Garmisch-Partenkirchen, Germany; prior to that he was Deputy Director of the Scottish Centre for International Security (SCIS) and Lecturer in International Relations at the University of Aberdeen (1997–2002). He holds an MA and PhD from the University of Aberdeen and has published extensively on aspects of post-Soviet security politics in the *Journal of Peace Research, Security Dialogue, Journal of Slavic Military Studies, Co-operation and Conflict, Mediterranean Politics* and *The World Today.* His latest book, of which he is editor, is *Russia and the Regions: Strength through Weakness* (RoutledgeCurzon 2003).

John Russell is Head of the Department of Languages and European Studies at the University of Bradford. The author of articles and chapters on the Russo-Chechen conflict, he is also a specialist in interpreting, co-authoring with Svetlana Carsten *Glasnost: An Advanced Russian Interpreting Course* (University of Bradford 1993).

Index

Other Titles in the Series

The Changing Geopolitics of Eastern Europe

Andrew H Dawson and Rick Fawn,
University of St Andrews (Eds)

This work covers the uncertain geopolitical situation of some
countries of Central and Eastern Europe, including some of those
which are hoping to enter the European Union in the near future,
some for which entry is far off, and some which may never seek or
be eligible for membership. Attention is given to the problems
arising out of economic restructuring and problems of defence. Yet,
all the issues are ultimately founded in those geographic essentials
that have dogged so much of Europe's modern history: the tension
arising from marked differences in the standard of living between
the north-west of the continent and the south and east; the way in
which past migration has created significant ethnic minorities in
many countries; and by the manner in which larger countries have
bullied or courted their smaller neighbours.

184 pages 2002
0 7146 5242 3 cloth
0 7146 8224 1 paper

FRANK CASS PUBLISHERS
Crown House, 47 Chase Side, Southgate, London N14 5BP
Tel: +44 (0)20 8920 2100 Fax: +44 (0)20 8447 8548 E-mail: info@frankcass.com
NORTH AMERICA
920 NE 58th Avenue Suite 300, Portland, OR 97213-3786 USA
Tel: 800 944 6190 Fax: 503 280 8832 E-mail: cass@isbs.com
Website: www.frankcass.com

Russia Between East and West

Russian Foreign Policy on the Twenty-First Century

Gabriel Gorodetsky, *Tel Aviv University* (Ed)

The fall of the Berlin Wall, the lifting of the 'Iron Curtain' and the withering away of Communist ideology evoked tremendous hopes for a unified Europe – a region which now also encompassed the East, including a democratic and economically reformed Russia.

This volume of essays dwells on the challenge facing Russia in establishing its new identity which will have a direct bearing on the course its foreign policy is likely to steer in the future. The book unravels President Putin's efforts to re-establish Russia's position as a major power, attempting to reconcile Russia's traditional national interests with the newly emerging social and political entity taking shape at home. The book's analysis of Russia's role in various conflict regions – the Balkans, Chechnya, the Middle East and China – demonstrates how this process is being affected by which contradictory forces, such as globalization, regionalism and US unilateralism, seem to reign supreme, especially after the events of 11 September 2001.

220 pages 2003
0 7146 5329 2 cloth
0 7146 8393 0 paper

FRANK CASS PUBLISHERS
Crown House, 47 Chase Side, Southgate, London N14 5BP
Tel: +44 (0)20 8920 2100 Fax: +44 (0)20 8447 8548 E-mail: info@frankcass.com
NORTH AMERICA
920 NE 58th Avenue Suite 300, Portland, OR 97213-3786 USA
Tel: 800 944 6190 Fax: 503 280 8832 E-mail: cass@isbs.com
Website: www.frankcass.com

The Caspian Region

Moshe Gammer, *Tel Aviv University*

In the 1990s, following the dissolution of the Soviet Union, new states, most of them Muslim, emerged in Central Asia and the Caucasus. Furthermore, these new states of the southern belt of the ex-USSR soon proved to be both oil-rich and a central part in a strip of conflict and instability stretching from Central Europe to the Far East. A need has thus arisen for information on the new area.

This collection of articles, draws attention to issues neglected so far by both scholarly and popular publications. It thus deals with the water problem and negotiations in Central Asia, and with little-known, possible potential conflicts, such as the issues of 'Southern Azerbaijan', Ajaria and Javakheti and the various problems of multi-ethnic Daghestan. It also examines two attempts at unity in the Northern Caucasus.

Other issues dealt with are the validity of the term 'Caspian Region' and the question of who should be included in this new region and the collection questions the general belief that the Caspian region will be 'a geopolitical centre of the 21st century'.

Volume I 256 pages 2003
0 7146 5247 4 cloth
Volume II 256 pages 2003
0 7146 5248 2 cloth

FRANK CASS PUBLISHERS
Crown House, 47 Chase Side, Southgate, London N14 5BP
Tel: +44 (0)20 8920 2100 Fax: +44 (0)20 8447 8548 E-mail: info@frankcass.com
NORTH AMERICA
920 NE 58th Avenue Suite 300, Portland, OR 97213-3786 USA
Tel: 800 944 6190 Fax: 503 280 8832 E-mail: cass@isbs.com
Website: www.frankcass.com